# SPLIT SECOND

# SPLIT
# SECOND

### Redefining My
### American Dream

# KELLI J. MILLER

**Split Second: Redefining My American Dream**
Published by White Cup Press
Tiffin, OH

Library of Congress Control Number: 2016951589

Miller, Kelli J., Author
**Split Second: Redefining My American Dream**
Kelli J. Miller

ISBN: 978-0-9978817-07

Personal Memoirs

Personal Growth / Happiness

Cover photography by Michaela J. Miller

QUANTITY PURCHASES: Schools, companies, professional groups, clubs, and other organizations may qualify for special terms when ordering quantities of this title. For information, email info@WhiteCupPress.com.

For Tim,
who encouraged me ...
"Just start writing and see where it goes."

and

dedicated to my dad, James D. Adelsperger,
who in life and in death taught me how to live.

"It is not the mountains we conquer, but ourselves."
Sir Edmund Hillary

# CONTENTS

*⋇*

## Chapter 1

# The Perfect Storm

"The trouble is, you think you have time."
Buddha

Outside my bedroom window, the lush green forest glistened in the June sun. It was a rare sunny day in Seattle, for blue skies and sunshine typically wait to settle in after the July 4$^{th}$ holiday. I welcomed the sun, for today was a special day–today our son was graduating.

Cody was dressed and ready to leave for the school where he'd board a bus to Safeco Field–home of the Mariners. His class of 459 would graduate in the baseball stadium since his school did not have a facility large enough to hold the graduating students and their immediate family.

My husband, Denny, called up to me from the bottom of the stairs. "Kel, are you ready?"

He knew better.

I didn't want to acknowledge I wasn't dressed and ready to go. After a moment of silence, Denny continued.

"I'm going to take Cody to school. Your Mom and Dad are ready. You and the girls need to be ready when I get back."

I had wanted everything about our children's graduation days to be perfect. I had envisioned a large gathering of our extended family and friends celebrating Cody's accomplishments, lifting him up and launching him onward to his next phase of life—a vision buried in my subconscious. I wasn't even aware of my ideals until the day began to unfold.

I wasn't ready yet. Rather, I was standing at the window, gazing out at the evergreens that towered up to the flawless blue sky. I shook it off and seconds later found myself staring into the mirror in the bathroom, thinking of my graduation ceremony. That event twenty-eight years prior certainly shaped my expectations for this day.

I had graduated from a small rural high school in northwestern Ohio. I knew most of the forty-two kids in my graduating class and their families from birth. On graduation day, grandparents, aunts, uncles, cousins, friends, and my parent's friends surrounded me. My Mom and Dad were well known and well liked. They were an integral part of my school and our community and were financially secure through their successful farming business. They had a beautiful new and well-appointed home, a swimming pool, and luxury cars. It wasn't uncommon for the house, pool, and yard to be full of family and friends—we hosted parties often. I was the consummate good student, held in good regard by my teachers, classmates, and my classmate's parents. I was the class speaker for my graduation ceremony. These were my marks of success.

Back in Seattle, there would be only six of us in the stands to cheer for our son Cody: my Mom and Dad, Denny, our daughters Michaela and Morgan, and me. The rest of our family was 2,500 miles away in Ohio. We had lived in Seattle only two years—barely enough time for Cody to make friends. After a tough junior year, Cody eventually made friends, but we didn't know them. Denny and I were not an integral part of the school or the community. In fact, we didn't know many people at all. I had what many friends and colleagues deemed an incredible job and career, but the financial security my parents enjoyed eluded us, and my Dad didn't approve. Though I had accomplished a lot, I felt like a failure in his eyes. We never talked to our family and friends about our financial situation, but I was certain those close to us knew something was awry. Even more concerning, Cody had strong grades throughout high school, but he scraped by his last semester of classes. We had recently received a school letter warning us Cody was failing two required classes and that he could not graduate if he did not raise these scores to at least a "D."

Cody recovered those grades, and he was set to graduate, but still my hopes and my reality were incongruent. Tears began rolling down my face as I started wondering if I had failed myself and my son. However, it was a short-lived sign of weakness—I was a strong woman. I wiped the tears away as soon as they came. I moved on to the closet. If the vision I saw in the mirror didn't fully satisfy me, perhaps I'd find an outfit that would dress me for my part. I desperately combed the closet for clothes as I wondered where had life gone off track.

I had, in many ways, created life on my terms starting when I was just eleven years old. At that time, my brother, my only sibling, died of cancer. My mother sank into a deep depression, and my father buried himself in work. In that dark, empty place, I chose to live. I learned to take care of myself and eventually learned to live by my own accord. After graduating high school,

I was expected to honor my parents and my parents' parents by becoming a farmer's wife. Instead, I went off to college to study the emerging field of computer technology. With a college degree in hand, I left my Ohio roots, landed a job in one of the best companies in the world, and built a wonderful life on the East Coast. When Denny and I had our first child, Cody, I was expected to give up my career and be a good mom. We surprised everyone when my husband became a stay-at-home father, and I became the sole wage earner for our family. I was fortunate: my love of learning and growth led me to a wide variety of roles and leadership experiences. When my coworkers (predominately male) expected me to be a curt, swift, and stern leader, I led on my terms; developing people, building collaborative teams, and enabling employees to do their best work.

In many people's eyes, I was a success. I was the breadwinner for my family, earned a rather handsome salary, bonuses, and stock options, and had some of the biggest and best companies on my resume. I was doing a wonderful (yet non-traditional) job of being a mother to three incredibly strong-willed, confident, and beautiful children who were rich in both character and life experiences. I had diverse friends in all corners of the U.S. I had seen the Great Wall of China and the red-light district of Amsterdam, drunk grappa in Italy, watched tiny Fairy Penguins come ashore on Phillip Island, Australia, swum naked in the Atlantic Ocean, and run barefoot through the cornfields of Northwest Ohio. Somewhere along the way, however, the joy of creating a wonderful career and experiencing what the world had to offer yielded to burden, for there were kids to raise, bills to pay, competitions to win, and (admittedly) my ego to feed. I contributed nicely to the American economy; I got caught up in the "Bigger, Better, More" mentality of our culture and became a slave to corporate America. Instead of choosing roles to learn and grow in, I was choosing roles that satisfied my appetite for liquidity. In a world of downsizings, acquisitions, divestitures, and stack ranking performance management systems, I started showing up as an uptight woman hell-bent on my dollar-driven mission instead of choosing to be the best person I could be.

I changed. Under the pressure of growing debt and the fiercely competitive work environment, my marriage turned bitter, my relationship with my parents became strained, I gained weight, and I was spiritually broken.

Now, as my son prepared to graduate, I had just finished a long, six-month, grueling fight to fix software problems. It was an experience that exacerbated a growing discontent with organizations that had a 'win at all costs' focus on the bottom line. At the same time, I needed those companies for the income they provided—a conflict I longed to reconcile. I felt stuck in a lifestyle that continuously demanded me to be smarter, stronger, faster, and more efficient than I was the day before. I felt drained. Nothing about my life was feeding my soul. Nothing was replenishing my energy. Nothing was inspiring me to keep giving away more insight, physical effort, or spirit to my job; I had little to nothing left to give to the people and things I loved. Even a pilgrimage to the ocean shore could not fix whatever had broken in me.

Quitting, however, was not an option. I simply kept carrying on, not seeing a way out of the circumstances I had built over time.

Denny returned to the house and found me in the bathroom.

Denny and I had been together for a long, long time. In my baby book, my mother noted that he was the first boy outside the family to kiss me when I was just three months old. We drifted apart as children, but we were destined to come together again.

We met each other in our late teens, and we were both hooked. There was an undeniable innate love for each other—we both felt we were supposed to be together. After all these years, he was still the same patient, practical, and easygoing man I had married twenty-three years prior. He was extraordinarily kind, quietly supporting our family and me every day, never complaining about the work and the sacrifices he made for us. However, as kind as he was, he couldn't stop himself from pushing the point.

"Come on, Kel, get dressed!"

I changed the subject.

"The lei—did you pick up the lei we ordered?" It was a Seattle area tradition to give boys and girls alike a lei of flowers after the graduation ceremony. I looked forward to placing this lei around Cody's neck—something special to mark the day.

Denny stared back at me bewildered. At that moment, all he cared about was getting to the event on time. He couldn't fathom why a lei had to be important right now. "Yes, I picked up the lei. I gave it to Cody, so he has it with him on the bus."

I exploded. "I'm supposed to have the lei! I can't get the lei now!" Then I accused him of being insensitive.

Of course, it wasn't about the lei—my issues were bigger than the lei and this graduation.

Yelling gave way to crying, and I melted into Denny's arms. Still sobbing, I cried aloud, "It wasn't supposed to be like this!"

Denny longed to fix whatever was broken in me, but I couldn't explain what was wrong, and Denny had no idea how to fix what neither of us could understand.

I collected myself, got dressed, and we all piled into our SUV to make our way to the ball field.

Michaela sat in the far back, in a seat that wasn't quite appropriate for her height. She was finishing her freshman year of high school, but she looked old enough to buy a drink without a bartender questioning her age. She had Denny's family's freckles and my bluish, hazel eyes that changed hues pending her mood and the color of her clothes. Her hair was long, blonde, and wavy. She was five nine at the age of fifteen—three inches taller than me. Cody called her "toothpick" because she was so tall and thin for her age. From my perspective, "toothpick" did not fit Michaela, and the nickname wouldn't stick. Michaela's strong will and ambition would be the features that stood out well beyond her thin physical profile. I was proud to say she got her strong will and ambition from me, for I saw these traits as assets that would carry Michaela to her dreams. Denny, on the other hand, held reservations, for these traits might just leave Michaela vulnerable to pain and despair, or cause harm if not balanced with self-discipline. Denny never let me forget that Michaela inherited these precarious attributes from me as well.

Morgan sat far in the back too. Morgan was thriving. She was nine years old and finishing third grade. She had my mom's brown eyes, but aside from that, she looked just like me—thick brown hair, soft cheeks, and thick full lips that melted into a wide smile. Morgan had Denny's long, lean torso—she was going to be tall too. She already stood nearly a head taller than most kids in her class. She kept Denny and me young with her childlike sense of innocence—always seeing the beauty in everyone around her and always guiding situations for the best of the whole. Hers was the bubbly and dramatic personality that brought people together. She was the peacekeeper who kept them together, too.

Mom sat beside me in the middle of our SUV. She was dressed in bright, sassy colors and took it upon herself to lift the mood in the car through engaging conversation. Mom never questioned taking the 2,500-mile trip from her home in Ohio—she was close to all of us and was determined to be a part of Cody's graduation ceremony. Despite their divorce ten years prior, Mom was kind enough to travel with Dad too. Dad had experienced eighteen years of declining health, but he boarded the plane without help and made the trip to share in the special occasion.

The ceremony was surreal. Gone were the clouds and the familiar Seattle drizzle. The sun shined brightly, so the Safeco field's retractable roof was open. Coming onto the field in alphabetical order, Cody emerged in his green cap and gown in the middle of the procession.

He stood six foot four and had his dad's brown eyes, beaming with love. He was conservative and always played by the rules, but also had a wonderful sense of humor. Like his father, he loved to cook, which was unusual for a boy, but something that made him proud. Although he was burned out from the drama and hype of youth sports and no longer participated in competitive teams, he still loved sports. He had a brilliant mind—he could rattle off sports statistics and stories like no other. More often than not, Cody listened to those around him. However, on those rare moments when he was comfortable and felt so moved, he could fill the air with uncanny humor and hold a sports debate with the most knowledgeable of adults. I loved to listen to him in those moments. Surely Cody loved the fact he was graduating in a major-league ballpark!

Mom, Dad, Morgan, Michaela, Denny, and I all cheered as loudly as we could when Cody received his diploma. After the ceremony, we smothered Cody with hugs and joked about the lei, then made our way to the Space Needle for dinner. From atop the Needle, we saw the city glimmer and Mount Rainier glow in the orange, pink, lavender, and dusty blue sky. We recounted stories from all the stand-out family moments we'd shared—we laughed, we celebrated, and we cried—and I realized I had not failed my son. Denny and I had given him a life full of adventure and had built strong family bonds through our experiences and challenges. Cody had grown into a wonderful young man. It was indeed, a grand time.

It was also a call to get the rest of my life in order.

The day following the ceremony, the kids had celebrated enough and were content to sleep in and spend the day being lazy. I, on the other hand, felt a duty to make the most out of the time we had with Mom and Dad.

"Come on, kids, you never know if we will get another opportunity to be together like this," I said prophetically. We piled into the car again and made our way to Mount Rainier National Park.

Mount Rainier was, in my eyes, majestic. The first time I saw Rainier was from a plane—the peak jutting above the clouds with strength and grace. Now, living in Seattle, we could see this 14,114-foot glacier-covered mountain nearly a hundred miles away (when the infamous Seattle area clouds aren't blocking the view). The first expedition Denny and I took in the Seattle area was a visit to Mount Rainier National Park. The deep sense of peace we experienced each time we visited kept us going back. In the hundreds of acres of parkland, Denny and I found amazing natural beauty. There were national forests untouched by man, waterfalls, gorges, placid lakes, rocky rivers with crisp, clean waters, mountain goats, birds, wildflower fields, and stunning vista after stunning vista of the gigantic mountain—all foreign to our Midwestern eyes. On some visits, binoculars allowed us to see brave human beings scaling the glaciers. Mountain climbing was not a sport I understood—I marveled over the physical condition, knowledge, and determination it must take to climb this mountain.

At the park lodge, I admired the men and women returning from their climb. I longed to be like them—unrestrained, strong, adventurous, and courageous. However, I was not fit enough to hike even a short trail. I had to be content observing as a tourist. I was excited to share this wonderful place with my Mom and Dad. We visited Mount Rainer with a picnic and ate in a scenic viewing area, enjoying the mountain.

Mom and Dad's trip also included time relaxing in a rental house along the Puget Sound, visits to the local casino for Dad, and plenty of dinners out. Soon, they returned to Ohio.

.

A few weeks later, at the beginning of July, our family made the cross-country trip to be in Ohio for rest, relaxation, and many gatherings with friends and family. We celebrated Fourth of July, my mom and her twin sister's seventieth birthday, our nieces' baptism, and Cody's graduation. Although we didn't have anything planned, I hoped to spend more time with Dad. He'd seemed distracted during his visit to Seattle, and he coughed a lot. I hoped spending time with Dad in his environment would allow him to uncover his concerns.

First, though, was Cody's graduation party. I kept my focus on Cody.

The celebration was at the golf course my father owned with his partners. Denny, the kids, and I arrived two hours before the event to decorate and set up the food that our family had prepared. Dad provided the space, bought the drinks, and had a friend roast a pig for the main course. Organizing, decorating, and displays of memorabilia were my responsibilities for the day.

On our arrival, I felt my Dad's energy from afar. He was cleaning the folding chairs, and he was agitated, perhaps angry.

I was uncomfortable—even from across the room, I could feel it. It was the same energy that he'd carried into the house when I was a kid, as he spouted expletives and complained about work. It was the same that he'd held when he had been in a hospital bed instead of being in the fields, commanding and controlling farm work. I knew he had a lot of wrath bottled up inside, and my approaching him would unleash it. I knew I had wrath inside me, too.

Dad and I had long needed to have it out with each other, but we avoided it. Living 2,500 miles apart made it easy to keep our fury inside. We spent time together for holidays, weddings, and funerals—events that required us to keep our emotions in check. Spending time together otherwise was a risk we could not take, for one of us might just let anger loose, and create even more distance between us. I didn't want this day to be that day, but Dad was clearly angry, and I knew I had to cautiously reach out and open a door we preferred to keep closed.

As he wiped down a beat-up metal chair, placed it perfectly at a table, and moved on to the next, I said, "Hi Dad, what's wrong?"

Dad grumbled, "Well, someone has to do all this work." I'd thought the golf course employees did this sort of thing—cleaning and arranging tables. I knew that the owners could use the room, but I didn't know the owners were expected to prepare the room too. Dad was out of breath and sweating, not from heat but from simple exertion. Clearly, he was not in shape to be doing this work, so I said just that and suggested Denny and the kids help him.

That only perturbed him further.

Work was a love and a burden Dad carried with him most of his life. He thrived when working. In recent years, when he could no longer carry the emotions that came with work, he looked to me to carry them for him. His emotions often fueled his rage—a state of mind he hid from most people. On that day, he didn't want Denny and the kids to wipe down chairs because he didn't dare risk exposing the rage he kept hidden inside. They hadn't seen this part of him, and he wanted to keep it that way. Bearing the weight of his emotions was a rare sign that Dad believed in me and trusted me, but I couldn't see it at the time. What I could see was that he wanted me to "do all this work" and we both knew it wasn't about cleaning beaten-up metal chairs, but neither of us said as much. I wanted to go to the computer and prepare my slide show. Mom wanted me to help with a picture display. The kids wanted me to give minute-by-minute direction on what to do. Nonetheless, I did what Dad asked me to do: I stayed by his side, cleaning chairs, saying nothing, and waiting for Dad to say what was on his mind.

Finally, his frustration dissipated and Dad calmly surfaced the news he was holding underneath. "I have a lesion in my lung the size of a golf ball."

I think the brain recognizes things that can damage the heart and soul. I think it can sometimes withhold ideas, concepts, and information until the heart is ready to process them. I did not deny what Dad had just said. Somewhere in the depth of my being, I knew the significance of the words. However, nothing told me how to feel. Instead, I stayed quiet and focused on the fact that a hundred or so guests would soon be arriving and this day needed to be a joyous occasion for my son. A piece of me stayed with my dad throughout the evening, as I fluttered about the room, greeting guests, engaging in conversations with friends and family I rarely see, and hopefully making Cody feel special and feel loved.

Dad quietly left the party early. Someone said it was okay—he was tired, and he needed rest. Everyone knew that my father's health was poor and accepted that he simply needed more time to rest than most. However, they didn't know what I knew. The tired look Dad shared with us that day was not simply fatigue. It was despair.

As our time in Ohio continued, my brain began to let in the cancerous information. I processed it slowly and began to fill with sadness and fear. We celebrated several birthdays that week: my mom and her sister's, Denny's stepfather's, and mine. I made a point to include Dad as much as I could.

As our trip drew closer to a close in mid-July, I took Dad to the hospital for an MRI and PET scan, then to the doctor to hear the results. In the doctor's opinion, this lesion was most likely cancer, but we'd not know for sure until he had a biopsy. I asked to see the pictures. The doctor graciously agreed to my request, taking us outside the examination room, behind the front desk, and into a nook where a computer set. Clearly, the office design did not include technology as an integral part of the doctor's work, but it was worth the jaunt. The picture on the computer made Dad's situation clear. Seeing the dense gray mass relative to the size of the whole lung made an impact on me.

The doctor's next moves seemed rather scripted and strategic. He threw massive amounts of information at me. Repeatedly, he used the clinical name. "Most likely Squamous Cell Carcinoma." The only portion of the name that I retained was the word *carcinoma,* and I heard the word over and over again. He described the clinical studies that defined the course of treatment. He described treatment options and the treatment plan he would suggest if it truly were Squamous Cell Carcinoma and his course of action if it was not. He talked about the next step—a biopsy. He described the doctor who would do the biopsy, how and where they would do it, what Dad could eat and drink before the biopsy, the risks, and what Dad could and couldn't do after the procedure.

He described the medications Dad was currently on and how he would adjust them. As the time available for Dad's appointment ended, he asked, "Do you have all that?" Deep inside I screamed, "*No, of course not! How could anyone digest all that information? All I have is 10,000 reasons to be afraid and sad!*" At the surface, my brain was chewing on the most basic information, and I wanted to ask, "Can I deduce that carcinoma means cancer?" However, stuck in the effort to process everything I was learning, I went on autopilot. I shook my head and solemnly said, "Yes, I have all that."

After leaving the doctor's office, Dad and I focused our conversation on tactics. Who could help him after I leave? Who would go with him to get the biopsy? When could and should I come back?

I was soon busy packing up my family and flying to Washington. Once in Seattle, the effort to reestablish myself into an exasperating job consumed me, and I was busy with Cody's college preparations. The doctors didn't feel Dad's situation was urgent, so there was some time before the next step—the biopsy—took place.

I carried on with life while we waited.

In mid-August, Michaela went off to soccer camp while Denny, Morgan and I moved Cody into his dorm room on the Washington State campus on the eastern side of the state, four-and-a-half hours away from our home in Seattle. Cody was ready to be away from home, and I was ready for him to have this experience. Nonetheless, it was an emotional time. After setting up his small room and ensuring he had ample supplies, we stood on the grassy rise outside his dorm, taking pictures and talking, not quite ready to end our day together. It was there I received a call from my dad. The biopsy results were in: Dad had lung cancer.

I took the news like a champ. I treated it as I would business, for I couldn't dare to layer my emotional reaction to my father's news on top of the emotional reaction of leaving a child at college for the first time. Instead of feeling, I reassured my father and promised to be with him soon. I was encouraging to my son and promised to be with him soon, too. We hugged. Then Denny, Morgan, and I set off back through the golden wheat fields of Eastern Washington, across the Columbia River, through the Cascade Mountains, and back home to Seattle.

I cried. As Denny drove, I stared out the window and cried. The enormity of the news, the changes I wanted and needed to make to love my work and to give to those I loved, the fear I felt for my dad, the inevitable growing pains I saw ahead for my son . . . It all welled up, and I cried. As Denny gently touched my hand, I broke out of my thoughts and looked at him, and he smiled. Life doesn't move him as deeply as it moves me. I pass homeless people on the street and feel their anguish. I hold a conversation with a coworker about her dying grandmother that she cannot see half-way around the world in South Korea and I'm moved to find a way to get her out of work and off to her home country. Not Denny. He observes and understands, but doesn't internalize the kinetic forces in the mind, body, and soul as deeply as I do. With his smile, I knew he was there for me. I knew he would support me and be strong for me. Still, I also knew that I would be the one doing the work. I would feel my dad's pain and be moved to give him exactly what he needed. I would see my son's apprehension, and I would be moved to coax him on. I would hear other's judgments, opinions, sarcasm, and self-doubt cast upon my father and my son, and I would shield them, allowing both to walk the path they chose with the support they needed.

I heard sniffles coming from the back seat of our SUV and turned my attention to my nine-year-old daughter sitting alone. Morgan was very tall for her age and quite mature, especially under the influence of an eighteen-year-old brother and a fifteen-year-old sister. It was easy for me to believe she had the maturity to handle her brother's move to college and her grandpa's news, but her sniffles reminded me this was all hard for her, too. She declined the immediate help I offered, but I was now attuned to her needs and my desire to give to her as well.

The longer we drove, the closer we got to home, and the closer I was to returning to work. I had routinely given my employer 50-60 hours a week, and for the last six months, had given them 70-80 hours a week. I gave them every ounce of energy and passion I had. With Cody leaving for school and my father's cancer fresh on my mind, I felt another emotion welling up—resentment toward my employer for taking much and leaving little. I felt no desire to bulldoze through organizational structure, policy, technology, or business process issues; to do inhumane scopes of work just to be rewarded with a little more money and the opportunity to do it longer. None of it made sense. I'd bought into the game, I played the game, I benefited from the game, but now none of it made sense. All of it seemed terribly distracting for what mattered most in life—love. Love of self, love of family, love of humanity.

Dad's cancer prompted me to consider further the questions that arose on Cody's graduation day, and I was beginning to give my heart an opportunity to be heard. I was beginning to allow the notion of love to be stronger than the intellect. I was beginning to find my true self.

We reached home, and our lives faded into the schedules we had known before we stood on the grassy hillside. Morgan and Michaela had two more weeks to enjoy before school started, and only soccer practices to consume their time. Denny attended to his stay-at-home Dad work—our personal finances, housework, and shuttling our daughters to friends and activities. I returned to work. I kept checking in with Dad over the phone. Soon I learned he had a slow-growing type of cancer, but one that didn't have a history of responding to chemotherapy and radiation. Because of this, he needed an operation to remove the tumor and a portion of his lung. Dad scheduled this operation for September 9th. I trusted that the doctors knew what they were doing, and I made my plans to be there. I would see Michaela and Morgan start school, deliver performance reviews at work; then I would be off to Ohio to be with Dad for surgery.

Before my travel plans were complete, a job opportunity came up in Chicago. It made good sense to try to get closer to Dad to help him through his cancer treatments. I could live in Chicago and be at his side with only a four-and-a-half-hour drive. Plus, there was a good chance I could find an employer with more realistic expectations. I agreed to an interview and made plans to visit the company in Chicago on my way home to Ohio.

Shortly before Labor Day, I received an unexpected call from my dad. He was home at his kitchen table with his brother Mike and Mike's wife, Darlene. Dad said hello, then asked a wide-open question: "What are you going to do about this?"

I was a bit perplexed. We had talked at length about the cancer diagnosis, and we had a plan for me to be with Dad during the upcoming surgery. I didn't understand what his question meant. "What do you mean, Dad?" I replied. Dad had a hard time formulating his thoughts. If Mike and Darlene hadn't been there, he might have yelled out of frustration. Today, though, he simply talked to me in story form: "I'm having a hard time paying the bills. I have bills on the table but cannot pay them." I searched my head for answers . . . What did that mean? Alzheimer's? Was he also forgetting how to do simple tasks? Dad continued, "Mike and Darlene stopped by. Darlene is writing the checks, and I am signing them."

That news touched a nerve. Dad had never let me write his checks, even though I was on the signature card of his corporation. Dad was the master of his business and the master of his money. He didn't entrust either to me. He'd also had some experiences during which he'd come to believe that Mike had taken advantage of him. He had even cautioned me not to trust him. Here he was, though, allowing Mike and Darlene, but not me, to do financial work.

Now I was the one who couldn't articulate. I snapped. "Dad, what are you doing? You taught me not to trust Mike! Why are you doing this?" My words rang out like they'd come from a hurt, spoiled child that didn't get their way. I realized my words were sharp, and that quite possibly Mike and Darlene heard them. I retreated long enough for Dad to explain. His words stunned me.

"I can't see, Kel. I can't see."

Dad couldn't see the bills, he couldn't see checks, and he couldn't see to write the checks. "Mike and Darlene are helping me, but they thought you should know. I probably shouldn't drive either."

This news was heavy. It wasn't a problem I could handle over the phone. I promised to be there soon and got off the phone to contemplate what I had just heard. Was Dad going blind from diabetes? Was Dad having trouble with medication? Nothing made sense.

Dad had never said anything about his eyesight to me before. On this bright, sunny, and flawless day in late August,

Dad revealed he had been to his eye doctor a month prior, and the doctor couldn't explain why Dad was having problems—and couldn't do anything to help him. Today, Mike persisted and eventually persuaded Dad to get a second opinion. This time, the eye doctor got him in right away. He must have seen something significant because he sent Dad for an immediate head MRI on the Friday before Labor Day.

While we waited for the results, I enjoyed Cody's three-day holiday weekend visit home from college. As the holiday weekend ended, Cody went back to school as Morgan started fourth grade and Michaela started tenth. I went to work and delivered performance reviews that were, by corporate policy, designed to make a select few feel gifted and special, the majority feel average and ordinary, and some feel inadequate and unworthy of continued employment. It was a policy that encouraged emotions I had long accepted, but after a year of excruciating efforts to solve software problems and with cancer invading my life, I now saw it as unhealthy and unwarranted. I didn't have the mettle to fight it. I did what my job required me to do; then I was on the plane to Chicago to go to the interview for a potential new job, intending to fly on to Ohio afterward.

It was noon when I got off the plane in Chicago and headed to the baggage claim. I was on time, but the schedule was tight; I had to be efficient. I was wearing a newly acquired black business suit and new heels—I had transformed from the jean-clad hip executive (something the business world back East didn't understand) to a conservative executive with flair (the kind of thing that was repellant to Seattle's business elite). I felt strong—I was dealing with the harsh realities of my job, my father's lung cancer diagnosis, Cody's transition to college, and an interview. I felt powerful—as if nothing could break me.

While rushing to baggage claim, I pulled out my phone and saw a text message from Denny: "Call me as soon as you land." Still walking—being terribly efficient and determined to stay focused on the interview at hand—I called him back. His voice sounded normal, and I had no reason to believe he had anything but a typical day's challenge to share. I expected to hear something mundane like "We've overdrawn our checking account," or "Michaela had a summer assignment that she forgot to do." Instead what I heard changed my life.

"Kel, I don't know how to tell you this, so I am just going to tell you. Your dad has five brain tumors too."

What did he say? How could that be true? How did he know this? I lost the grip on my roller bag; it fell to the floor, and I stopped. In the middle of the O'Hare concourse packed with business travelers rushing about on schedules just as tight as my own, I just stopped. Denny continued.

"Your dad called me this morning to tell me, but you were already on your flight. I didn't know if I should tell you. I asked friends for advice—they told me to simply tell you that your dad has five brain tumors too."

I stood still—Stunned—Dumbfounded in disbelief.

Suddenly, I remembered my interview. Of all the things running through my head, the thought of the interview was the only one I could keep straight, so I jumped on it. I looked at my watch—I had thirty minutes to show up as a cool, calm, professional capable of handling anything with the ease and grace necessary to get the job. I picked up my bag and pressed on. Like a good soldier, I wouldn't allow myself to feel anything; I had business to attend to and a life that depended on that business. I had kids and a husband depending on me—I had to hold myself together.

My reply to Denny was automatic, a flat monotone: "I can't do this, Denny. I can't tend to this now. I have an interview."

Denny said nothing. The void on the other end of the phone made me halt again. I stood in silence in one of the noisiest corridors in the world. I stood alone in a hallway packed with people—a cold, rigid, shell surrounded by cold, unfeeling strangers clad in business suits, all rushing through life unable and unwilling to feel the moment.

My life thus far had culminated in this point. With each previous moment that had presented pain, I had built armor around myself, acquiring it piece by piece to protect myself from future harm. In high school, hurt by teenagers poking fun at me, I had learned to avoid self-expression. Scolded by an adult who turned me down for a job because she felt that I'd been given a childhood of wealth and ease and didn't need a job in college, I learned to work extra hard, so I'd never again had to hear that I was spoiled. Jaded by a coworker belittling me so she could look better than me, I learned to maneuver to appear smarter and more valuable than those around me. Jolted in an interview, passed over by a boss, I hardened myself against disappointments and failures. Piece by piece, I added to my outer shell, protecting myself from professional, financial, and personal hardship. I learned from those around me too. When a co-worker was quietly put on the sidelines, or a friend was downsized, a boss was let go, or a consultant didn't make partner, I learned what not to do, and I armored up. At this most critical moment of my life, and now, after everything I experienced, I could feel nothing. For the sake of business, for the sake of success, for the sake of financial well-being, I was unable to feel.

Then, unbidden and unannounced, my truest self had arrived and taken over. Standing that day in the corridor of O'Hare, the hardened outer shell broke open, and the pieces fell away as the news finally soaked in: my father was dying.

My luggage dropped out of my hand and onto the floor. It came over me like a tidal wave—from the tip of my head to the tip of my toes, I felt it. In a split second, everything changed. In a split second, every cell of my body knew life had changed.

I knew that I was going to be with my dad and give him whatever he needed to live a good life during whatever time he had left. I knew I would walk away from my job and my twenty-five-year career. In a split second, I knew everything had to change.

*I knew I would finally break free.*

## Chapter 2

# A Call to Serve

"The best way to find yourself is to lose yourself
in the service of others."
Mahatma Gandhi

I never went to the interview.
    I gathered myself at the United Airlines customer service
desk, rearranged flights to get to Dad as quickly as possible,
then went through airport security to find my gate. I meandered
through Terminal 1, making my way towards Terminal 2. It would
be a long five hours before my flight. I felt lost, alone, and nearly
numb. In the corridor that connected Terminal 1 to Terminal 2,
I stopped to eat, finding comfort in French fries, a burger, and a
coke. I situated myself on a bar stool facing the corridor. I watched
people passing by—some drifting, others rushing, some enjoying
the company of others, and many alone. I stared at the people
passing by and wondered, "*What's their story?*" Were they flying
off for a business meeting? Were they flying to meet someone in

person for the first time after connecting with them online? Had they lost their job and thus seeking a new opportunity in a new town? Were they returning home to a lover or friend? Was anyone like me? Were they traveling home to a loved one in need?

I thought of the many trips I had taken in the previous 18 years to get to Dad's side. Dad had called me many times for his medical issues, and I always heeded his call. The first had come when I was living in Wilmington, Delaware. I was twenty-seven years old and had just returned to work after Cody was born. In the still of the night, Dad had called at 3:30 a.m. "Kel, I think I'm having a heart attack."

That call was unexpected. There had been no discussions of health concerns or growing symptoms leading up to that moment. The call was quite a shock. Subconsciously, though, I was prepared for it, thanks to the stories Dad had told about my grandfather, Cecil, and the predictions Dad had made for himself.

Cecil had been a farmer. From his legacy of accomplishments and family stories, I knew he took risks to be more than just good—he became both a remarkable farmer and a leader in the community. He led the way, growing tomatoes in an environment that traditionally had preferred grain, and he was aggressive considering the number of acres he farmed. He dedicated long hours to his trade, rarely taking time away from the farm. Parents today strive to attend their children's every sporting event and school activity. Not Cecil. Like other farmers of his generation, it was a rare occasion when he left the fields to be sitting in the stands and watch his children's basketball or baseball games. He was a tough father who worked hard and expected his children to do the same, instilling in them his Prussian-style work ethic. He even called his sons out of baseball practice to tend to important planting duties. Also, Cecil was a community leader, having been elected to serve as a township trustee. What he stood for—hard work, discipline, determination, and leadership—gave him a big presence. His physique gave him a big presence too. He was a big man, carrying an abundance of extra weight in his belly. I found this perplexing. He worked very hard, physically laboring to repair equipment, building a fence for the cattle, and harvesting crops, all in an era that predated mechanical harvesters and when physical labor prevailed. I often wondered how an active man could carry so much weight. In most family photos, his body appears puffy and stressed. He probably had high cholesterol and diabetes, but I can only surmise. Health care was not something tough men of the 1960s spoke of or took the time to learn about. If he went to the doctor, he would not have shared any diagnosis with his family—health was just not understood like it is today and it certainly was not openly discussed. Cecil suffered a stroke at the age of fifty-one. He fell into a coma, and he never recovered. He died a few weeks later, just after he planted the crops in June.

As I grew up, Dad took pride in predicting he would be just like his dad. Without words to say as much, I knew Dad was saying he wanted to be a successful farmer, a well-regarded community leader, and a tough father just like Cecil. I also knew he was predicting he would suffer the same physical ailments and live a mere fifty-one years, just like Cecil. It was a notion that was easy to write off as Dad's quirky self-defeating banter until I got that call. At that moment, I realized that Dad had grown to physically look just like Cecil—overweight, puffy, and stressed. Worse, he'd smoked for fifteen or more years and chewed tobacco too. He had managed to replicate his father's life a little too precisely—much of his prophecy had come true. How could I not know that he would suffer from a cardiovascular ailment? How could I not know I would receive this call?

Still, the call was strange.

Why would Dad defy common sense and call me instead of waking up Mom and calling 911? Additionally, Dad liked to believe I couldn't handle big responsibilities—he liked to believe only he could handle trouble. So why, in a potentially life-threatening situation, did he suddenly believe I was the one who could get him help from over 600 miles away? And why would Dad pull me in close after years of pushing me away?

The call stirred the emotions we had both kept at bay. His call also scared me, but my sense of responsibility was stronger than my fears. I did what I had to do. I made my way from Wilmington, Delaware, to Ohio with my six-month-old son to see Dad in a Toledo hospital where specialists and technology were available to handle his needs. Thankfully, he hadn't had a heart attack. The doctors explained that he did have two blockages in his heart. They told Dad, Mom, and me why they did not recommend open heart surgery (the only vessel-blockage treatment I knew of at this point) and why they recommended angioplasty. Dad didn't ask questions—he'd grown up in an era when doctors assumed their diagnosis and treatments would not be understood and patients avoided questions for fear of appearing foolish. To my surprise, he looked to me for my opinion. I was coldly unconscious of and unconcerned about the fact that Dad skipped past Mom and looked to me—I assumed Mom wasn't up to handling medical emergencies after the traumatic experience of Kraig's death, and I was eager for the opportunity to earn Dad's approval and trust. I stepped in and asked the questions I felt he should have asked, then gave Dad my consent for the angioplasty.

I stayed with him through the procedure. When the moment was right, I sat Cody on his hospital bed and said, "See your grandson there, Dad? You want to see him graduate, right?"

Listening and cooperating were not Dad's strong suits—he was much more comfortable being in charge. But on this day, in the face of crisis, he listened and cooperated with me. He suddenly valued me—he trusted me and allowed me to lead, which he had never done before. I continued, "You're going to have to make lifestyle changes to be there for Cody's graduation." Up until this point, Dad was enjoying the attention he was receiving in the hospital. Now he found the attention and the discussion grim. Maybe it was the weight of the responsibility to be alive and well in eighteen years to see Cody graduate. Maybe it was the realization that he could escape the fate that afflicted his father, or maybe, just maybe, for the first time in his life the thought of living to enjoy things like watching his grandson grow and graduate was more important than being just like his father. Maybe for once, he wanted to live well past the age of fifty-one.

The angioplasty made Dad feel like a new man. Just two days later, he returned home and immersed himself in spring planting. He also returned to his detached, self-determined, autocratic ways, pushing me back to my home and my life in Wilmington. "You have to get back to work, Kel. You can't jeopardize your job." I left Ohio bewildered and wondering why Dad would not engage in a close relationship with me. I'd tried to involve him in my life and get involved in his, but once again, he held little value for that. I wound up keeping my distance out of frustration and accepted that we'd maintain our emotional detachment—until he needed me again.


Just ten months later, he called once more in the middle of the night, but this time from a vacation in Florida. This time Denny, Cody, and I flew to Naples to be by Dad's side. Again, he had blockages, and again he looked to me for direction. Again, he had angioplasty, and again he felt like a new man in just hours. When he was once again healthy and well, he went on with his life, and he pushed me back into mine.

We were like repelling magnets. Each time Dad called, emotions would stir, begging us to acknowledge and resolve a wealth of issues neither of us could name and neither of us could reconcile. Each time a force drew us together—a force I could only explain as love—and each time we were pushed apart by the enormity of emotions that we could not tame.

Mom and Dad had grown apart too. After Kraig had died, they had healed separately. Dad consumed himself with work to divert his attention away from the pain. He healed by working more hours. Mom, on the other hand, went into a long, deep depression. When she finally came out of it, she clung to me—my friends were her friends, my activities were her activities. After some time, Mom and Dad would come together on my behalf, attending my school activities together and providing a home with fun activities like a pool party for my friends and me. Soon they were coming together on each other's behalf too, hosting parties for extended family, friends, and the organizations they belonged to. They even worked together to help plan our village sesquicentennial celebration. Mom seemed content to let Dad take the lead in these endeavors, always playing a supporting role.

However, after I graduated from college and moved to Wilmington, their interests diverged. Mom was interested in exploring the world and having fun. She was more and more unsatisfied playing the support role and increasingly found the will to take a stand for her interests. When Dad would not participate with her, she traveled with friends to new places, doing things like taking wave runners out in Lake Erie, riding in a hot air balloon in Albuquerque, New Mexico, and exploring Europe. Sometimes she managed to talk Dad into traveling with her—the trip to Florida was undoubtedly her doing—but more often than not, she went on adventures with friends. She also wanted to spend time with Denny and me and our budding family. Dad, on the other hand, enjoyed travel only when it was for gambling or hunting with other men. He could justify these trips, as this was something many men in our community did. All other trips were luxuries he believed he could not afford. He instead wanted to continue to dedicate his time and attention to cultivating a successful farming business in an era when farmers were losing their land and their way of life. He also wanted to diversify his business. With little regard for Mom's opinion, Dad entered a partnership with three other men to purchase and operate a golf course. He proceeded to pour his time outside the farm into reviving that business. Neither Mom nor Dad was right, and neither was wrong—they were simply handling their hurts differently, pursuing different interests, and struggling to find common ground. They were both unhappy and searched for something to fill that void. Eventually, Dad got emotionally close to another woman, and Mom left him. She found a house and lived on her own roughly ten miles from Dad for a year or so. They went to counseling and tried to resolve their differences, but they never did. On the Friday following Thanksgiving, while Dad was away on a hunting trip with the men, Mom went back into the house she had built and shared with Dad, and with the help of friends packed up everything she wanted, loaded a U-Haul, and moved in with Denny and me. Mom and Dad had split up for good.

Dad never asked—he just assumed I had sided with Mom. The truth was far more complex than that.

Kraig died when I was eleven, and I became responsible for myself. I had to find in me the will to live and the strength to overcome the challenges inherent in living. Mom struggled to do that. When she finally came out of her depression with interest in living again, she did so through me. She leaned on the foundation I had built for myself and found her bearings through my example. Now that Mom had left Dad and was venturing out on her own, I felt obligated to be her foundation again. Meanwhile, I longed for my dad's approval—I longed to be someone he valued. Though Mom was living with my family and me, I did my best to remain neutral and to keep my husband and children neutral as well. Dad didn't see that. We continued to keep our distance.

Dad eventually called again, this time at 2:30 a.m. "Kel, I don't feel well." Of course, he again was too stubborn to call 911. After he had talked to me, he called his brother Larry who drove fifteen minutes to get to Dad's house and then drove another fifteen minutes to get Dad to the hospital. This time Dad had suffered a stroke.

Mom was unmoved. She and Dad both had lawyers and were slowly working through a divorce. I responded to Dad's call on my own. This time I made the two-hour drive from Cleveland to our hometown, arriving at the hospital around 6 a.m., just as the third shift nursing staff was transitioning to the day staff. Nurses told me he had slurred speech; he had some short-term memory loss, and his right side was weak. I watched him roll from side to side in a restless sleep. At least he wasn't paralyzed. Within forty-eight hours, he regained his speech and the short-term memory loss dissipated. He had a few days of occupational and physical therapy and regained most of the control his right arm and leg had lost. After his release, he stayed with his mother for a while just to be sure he had fully recovered. I badly wanted to stay and help Dad establish a routine with improved eating habits and exercise, alleviate his stress and minimize the potential of overworking himself, do some of the farm labor, and take on the business bookwork. I just wanted to make life easier for Dad, but he didn't want this from me. He didn't want me to jeopardize my "better life." He didn't want me to get too involved.

By this point in his life, Dad had witnessed many children get involved in their parents' farming business and watched as friends lost control of their assets to their children. Dad didn't want that. He also didn't care for Denny's and my way of life. Our home and activities were typical of other young professionals in the late 1990s, but Dad felt we lived a life of luxury when compared to the one he knew. He believed we had overextended ourselves financially and feared we'd overextend the farming business as well. The separation and pending divorce agreement had put his way of life and retirement at risk—he would not risk it further by allowing me in. He wanted to do things his way. He wanted to be at the helm and in control, but without my questions, ideas, or opinions. Dad wanted me by his side in a crisis, but once he had determined he was fine, he wanted me to go home. So, I went back to my family and back to my job.

Just as before, Dad fully recovered. The only residual effect from the stroke was sometimes, just sometimes, when he was tired, you could see his right shoulder droop or his right foot drag when he walked. Quite frankly, it was amazing. Dad was proving to have this wonderful ability to survive serious health catastrophes and rebound with negligible lingering effects.

This ability became a way of life for many years: Dad experienced an event, called me in the middle of the night, hung up and called his brother. Larry would then drive to Dad's house and rush him to the local hospital. In addition to the two angioplasties and stroke, Dad had another angioplasty and a mild heart attack. Again, he bounced back from both with little or no permanent impact. After the divorce, Dad sold some land to raise the cash needed for the settlement and now had fewer assets, which provided less income. Under the strain of the divorce and medical bills, Dad settled for an even more conservative way of life.

In between Dad's medical crises, Denny and I made a concerted effort to include him in our family as best we could. We did this to ensure that Dad had some fun in his life and that he and the kids built good memories together. The extended family offered rides so Dad could travel to Cody's baseball games, Michaela's soccer tournaments, Morgan's dance competitions, and outings to see the Cleveland Indians play. Denny and I also picked Dad up so he could participate in trips to the Lake Erie Islands, Mackinaw Island, Disney World, and a week at our favorite vacation spot, the Outer Banks of North Carolina. We were careful not to burden Dad with expenses that would add to his stress. Mom was always with us, so Mom and Dad were together for these trips. They were pleasant with each other. Occasionally, Dad would sling a snide remark at Mom or me. "Geez, I wish I had the money to spend on all these sports and computer gadgets these kids have." For the most part, however, he put aside his distaste for spending money on travel and other luxuries for the sake of building family bonds. Then Dad began experiencing chronic health problems. Our family trips became less frequent than they had been.

First, he dealt with an ailment that made his joints hurt. These episodes were very unusual. The pain settled in his knee for a day or two, then moved to his hip, then his shoulder, and so on. One episode got so bad he couldn't get out of bed, but I was traveling and couldn't help him when he called. It was the only call I didn't heed, and I felt guilty for it. He was too proud to ask others for help, so he confined himself to his bed for forty-eight hours. When he finally managed to get up, he got around by pushing a chair through the house, but he didn't leave his house for five days. Dad's primary care doctor didn't offer a diagnosis. Dad just lived with the unnamed gripping pain and the unusual ailment for a couple of years. Eventually, he found specialists and learned he had rheumatoid arthritis. It took a while to discover the medications that worked, but he did find a regimen that minimized the pain and the debilitating nature of the inflammation.

Dad also dealt with cataracts and neuropathy, a numbing, tingling pain in his feet. I eventually learned that diabetes often causes neuropathy, but Dad wouldn't admit to that diagnosis, let alone that he was dealing with neuropathy. All I knew at the time was that this pain kept him from any event that required even the shortest of walks and kept him from joining in any activities we invited him to do with us. We again found ourselves at a distance.

Then came another call, this time from family. One hot, humid, sun-drenched Saturday afternoon, Dad was mowing the grass around his farm pond when he became ill and nearly passed out. Friends took him to our hometown hospital and needed me once again.

Dad was fortunate—the effects of this stroke were mild. He suffered the same short-term memory loss and slurred speech but recovered both within forty-eight hours. This time, however, there was permanent damage to his sight—the upper right corner of his field of vision was gone. He never regained it.

With this medical incident, I saw Dad exhibit an emotion that was usually present, but he'd somehow managed to keep at bay: I saw Dad get angry.

Though his eyesight was never bad enough to have his driver's license revoked, it was damaged enough to be a catalyst for him to curtail his driving. His world got smaller than before this stroke. After this second stroke, Dad drove equipment only in his fields and his pickup only on familiar back roads. He'd rely on friends to take him to doctor's appointments, or he'd stay home. Plus, when the farming season ended, Dad retired. He sold his equipment and cash-rented his land, ending a long career of physical hardship.

He never expressed it to me, but I know retirement was difficult for him. Farming was his everything. It was his education, the business that gave him life, and the one thing he had left of his father. He defined himself by the work he did and the dollar value of the business he owned. He threw himself into farming after his son died and he held on tightly to it when my mother left him. Farming was his life. It was hard to call an end to the multigenerational tradition and hard to allow someone else to reap the annual rewards from the land. Dad didn't get focused on the emotional aspect of retirement. He instead focused on the financial aspects. By filing for disability with the federal government, Dad could draw a higher social security benefit. He saw this as a good business decision. Also, he kept what he had left of his land, renting it out to other farmers. These two incomes allowed him to keep the house he had built, meet the financial commitments of his divorce, and live an independent but humble life on his terms.

Dad somehow continued to find a way to enjoy a few things—namely gambling. He continued to travel with his friends to Las Vegas. However, as his physical condition deteriorated, they began to frequent the nearby casinos in Windsor, Canada, and Detroit. His friends were understanding of his physical condition, and Dad found a way to handle the pain. Eventually, this too became too much. The diabetes was taking its toll. When Dad finally admitted he was struggling to walk a mere fifty feet, I convinced him to let me take him to the Cleveland Clinic.

I had a lot of respect for the Cleveland Clinic, and they didn't let me down. After a catheterization, we learned that cardiovascular disease riddled most of the veins in his left leg. They were, in effect, clogged, which restricted the blood flow throughout his leg. In the doctor's words, "Your dad's left leg veins are like a sausage, but his right leg had only some constricted veins. A vein should carry blood freely to supply oxygen to every cell. However, your dad's veins are diseased to the point that blood slowly soaks through the vein. The pain your dad feels is due to a lack of oxygen reaching the cells—the pain from dying cells. Getting the blood to flow through the main vein is the utmost concern." The doctor performed surgery and put in ten inches of stents. That opened the vein ever so slightly for the blood to flow again, but the doctor did not give us hope that this procedure would work for the long term.

Dad recovered and had less pain in the weeks that followed. Six months later, however, he was back in the ER again and quickly transported from the local hospital to Toledo via life flight. When I arrived, he was under anesthesia. The specialist that had been called in to treat him told me Dad's leg was essentially dead when they brought him into the hospital. There was no blood flowing anywhere in it. They had opened the main vein by inserting a clot-busting medication in his groin. They also performed angioplasty to push the fatty buildup back to the walls of the vein. They were now waiting to see how Dad would respond. A few hours later, an x-ray showed that blood was flowing again, but the cells had been without oxygen for a long time.

I spent the night in the hospital room holding Dad's hand, praying he wouldn't lose his leg or a foot or even a toe. I spent the night praying I wouldn't see the telltale deathly black skin that could mean an amputation was imminent. I listened to Dad telling me where I'd find the insurance papers, farm deeds, and safe combinations in the house. I weeded through all sorts of information, taking only a few seconds to say the most important thing, "I love you, Dad." Though the circumstances were grim, my heart felt full when he said the words I had longed to hear, "I love you, Kel." He didn't say that often. In fact, there were many years he couldn't say it at all.

There was a darkness in the room that night—Dad didn't think he would make it. For the first time since his initial health episode fourteen years before, I didn't think he would make it either. Our simple exchange of the word "love" was the only glint of light in that room that night.

Dad made it through those awful hours—and kept his leg, his foot, and even his toes. He began seeing a cardiovascular doctor on a regular basis, and as soon as he was strong enough, he had surgery. The cardiovascular surgeon removed a foot-and-a-half of smaller but healthy veins in his leg and used them to bypass the heavily diseased and fully clogged main vein. After surgery, Dad came to stay with us. We were now living in the Cincinnati area, and this was his first visit with us there. Though Denny was with him all day and I was with him in the evenings, he was very uncomfortable in the unfamiliar surroundings. He was eager to get home. Once again, Dad healed. He moved back to his house to live on his own and in charge of his own destiny.

Two years passed without incident, then a new challenge arose. As far back as I could remember, Dad had had problems with his right knee. It had started in high school after a basketball injury. He'd managed the pain most of his life, but now that he was in his sixties and overweight, the pain had become unbearable. Dad picked a doctor based on friends' referrals, cleared the surgery with his insurance, scheduled it, and completed the prep work before discussing it with me. "I'm getting my knee replaced next week," he said.

I was now living in Seattle. It wasn't a life-threatening surgery, and I didn't have much notice, so I stayed in Seattle to help my team with software challenges instead of making the trip to Ohio to be at Dad's side. On the day of his knee replacement, instead of waiting and praying in a waiting room in our hometown Ohio hospital, I waited and prayed in my Seattle office 2,500 miles away. The initial report was good—the orthopedic surgeon considered the operation a success. Twenty-four hours later, though, the situation deteriorated. Dad was now slurring words, having bouts of anger, and experiencing short-term memory loss. I turned to family to get answers to my questions, but I found few answers and more uncertainty. I called the hospital nurses in charge of his care, but they provided no answers to the cause of Dad's emerging symptoms—they would only review his vital signs. The deficient answers and the lack of responsibility for Dad's situation irritated me. The orthopedic surgeon refused calls to get involved, stating that he had filled his scope of responsibilities. Though Dad's primary care physician had an office only ten miles from the hospital, he had no rights there. Dad was alone and nearly lost in the hospital system, but a hospital staff doctor was finally assigned. It took some work to track down this doctor, but I did—I spoke to him while he was on a treadmill at the gym. I was relieved to learn he cared and wanted to do the right thing, but he couldn't answer his questions about Dad's developing situation, and he couldn't answer mine. I hopped on a plane as quickly as I could and made my way to my hometown.

I discovered that Dad's knee surgery had caused his kidneys to shut down and toxins to build up in his system. Presumably, the anesthesia from surgery combined with the damage from diabetes was too much for Dad's body to handle. Medicine was not my specialty, but eighteen years of on and off medical emergencies with my Dad had given me enough to know the hospital should have noticed there was a problem well before the forty-eight hours it took them to admit it. Standard urine output volumes, urine specimen tests, and blood tests would have shown that toxins were building in his system. Even after the memory loss, outbursts, and other symptoms were present; they could not determine the cause of the problem. Dad probably had a lawsuit he could win, but neither he nor I had the time to deal with that. I had just a few days away from my job to get him on a recovery path, and Dad had to use all the energy he could muster just to get better.

The hospital that performed the knee surgery couldn't do inpatient dialysis, so the Doctors there transferred Dad to yet another small-town hospital where they could do it. In this hospital, as well as the first, I could see the divisions in the many health care roles and responsibilities, and I failed to see the one thing that was needed the most—ownership of the big picture and a commitment to get Dad better. It was concerning and distracting from the real problem at hand—my dad's life. Thankfully, we met a young doctor from Africa who was now in charge of Dad's care. He was warm, intelligent, and reassuring. His heart was bigger than the heartless roles, responsibilities, and guidelines that drove the bureaucratic environment he worked in. He got Dad on a path to recovery.

Once Dad was stable, we had to surrender his recovery to the big business concerns of his insurance company and their government guidelines again. After just three days of inpatient care, Dad was transferred to a less expensive rehabilitation facility because he could no longer live on his own—he couldn't care for himself—he couldn't even walk a few feet. Because he needed dialysis, he was placed on a shuttle once a day to get outpatient dialysis on his own. The absurdity of this arrangement frustrated me. I'm not sure how Dad got through it. His will to live proved to be bigger than the list of senseless rules. After four weeks in rehab, Dad returned home and continued to take the shuttle to an outpatient dialysis facility three times a week. Then, just as his doctor predicted, Dad's kidneys began working on their own after three months. Dad had dodged yet another medical catastrophe.

For eighteen years, Dad just kept tackling medical problems. It was a skill, an art, and a gift! I learned that I was more like him than I ever knew. As Dad's medical emergencies would prove, I too am intelligent, stubborn, argumentative, witty, and bold—every characteristic that I'd inherited from him had gotten me through the medical challenges and our trying relationship. Emergency proved to be the only time when Dad and I would relate and work together without butting heads. Through our shared desperation, Dad and I would learn to share the same space and love each other without driving one another away. Dad needed me in his life, and he wanted and needed the love that had, in so many other relationships, escaped him—but neither of us knew how to let love happen until he called and until I put my needs aside to find a way to serve.

Now, Dad's cancer would demand that both of us find the grace to love again.

*Chapter 3*

# A Better Life

"And the day came when the risk to remain tight in a bud was more painful than the risk it took to blossom."
Elizabeth Appell

My five-hour wait in O'Hare came to an end, and I flew to Ohio. It was a relief to fall into my Mom's arms when I arrived. In recent years, I had most often been strong for her as she worked through her separation, divorce, and the move into a home of her own. I had almost forgotten how to let her be strong for me, but somewhere during the two-hour drive to her home and the night spent talking by the warmth of her fireplace, I allowed her to be the strength I needed, if only for a short time.

Her disposition was complex. Without words to say as such, I knew Dad's cancer had reawakened the memory of my brother Kraig's cancer treatments and eventual death—memories she had buried a long time ago. She was also dealing with the complex emotions surrounding her ex-husband. She had spent more than thirty years with Dad. On some level, she still cared for him, but at the same time, he had hurt her. She had endured a long separation and divorce process and learned to live without him. She must have also learned to protect herself and distance herself from him. Maybe she even resented him to some degree. Despite all that, she was a source of strength for me and managed to show compassion for Dad.

Early the next morning, Mom took me to see him.

There was no time for conversations, reassuring hugs, the catharsis of tears, or formalities of any sort. I got out of the passenger's seat of my mom's car and got into the driver's seat of my dad's truck. It was symbolic. I had traveled 2,500 miles with the help of my husband, flight attendants, customer service reps, and my Mom. Now I was alone with Dad, taking responsibility for his emerging crisis. I would be in the driver's seat for the next five months.

The day before, Dad and his brother Mike had met with his family doctor. Dr. Edgar had given them the devastating news. "Boys, this is very hard news for me to deliver. I've known your mother and both of you since I began my practice here over sixteen years ago. There is no easy way to tell you this. Jim, your cancer has metastasized to the brain. You have five brain tumors. There is nothing we can do—I advise you to get your affairs in order."

Dad had lived with that news for only twenty-four hours. I had lived with it for sixteen. For the two of us, this prognosis was unlike anything we had ever experienced. Neither of us would want to believe that our reactions fit any pattern, but at this point, we were both in denial. Perhaps the MRI had been misread? Perhaps Dr. Edgar was wrong—perhaps there was something the oncologist could do? I had a hard time accepting the fact that the CT scan in June and the PET scan in July didn't show these brain tumors. Perhaps the MRI belonged to someone else?

We were fortunate in that a well-educated and experienced oncologist based in Toledo spent one day a week in our rural hometown. We clung to hope as we waited in an examination room to meet him. However, after thirty minutes Dad became impatient; for him, the lack of timeliness translated to incompetence. He quickly blamed the female administrators and nurses. This reaction touched a nerve in me and drove my thoughts back to a time and place far away from the oncologist office.

In the years following Kraig's death, I overheard Dad talking to a fellow farmer as he contemplated the future. Referencing his farm, he wondered aloud, "What am I going to do with all this—I don't have a son to pass this on to." My immediate reaction was profound—"What's wrong with me? What's wrong with a girl carrying on the family tradition?"

I turned that question into a life-defining quest.

I left the farm thirty years prior because my parents wanted me to have a better life. Though most kids in my high school graduating class of forty-two could not or did not go to college, my parents expected me to get a higher education, and I never questioned it. Since my one and only sibling had died, I was my parents' only child—the only one to bring them pride. I went to college for them. I also went to college for me—I went to college to become more than my hometown environment would allow.

Thanks to my uncle, I had seen something that many people could not understand in 1982: a computer! I saw computer science in action at the distinguished Ma Bell Laboratories in Holmdel, New Jersey. I was intrigued. Leveraging my math skills, I entered college committed to pursuing a computer science major. Four and a half years later, I graduated with a degree in business administration and computer science.

By the time I graduated, my desire to succeed blossomed. I had started to like exploring the world beyond the farm. I liked showing the big city kids who poked fun at the farm girl in me that I could succeed on their terms. I liked that I was known for what I was doing, not just for being the daughter of the successful farmer, Jim Adelsperger.

Many Fortune 500 companies came to Ohio State to recruit because it was full of kids with good Midwestern work ethics, the business school was widely respected, and they tailored the computer science program to the needs of big companies. Four years prior, I had no reason to know anything about these companies. By the time I interviewed, however, I had done my homework. I understood each company, had my preferences, and used a combination of my knowledge and likable personality to get interviews with the ones that impressed me.

This process went well, and I had several job offers in hand by the time I graduated. I considered offers in several areas: insurance, oil, medical products, and paper manufacturing. Then my dream job offer came in. I went to work for a diversified chemical manufacturing company in Wilmington, Delaware, for a generous starting salary. My dad was proud, but a little sour too—it was more money than he earned at the time (or shall I say, more than he paid himself from his farming corporation). The money was nice—it stroked my ego, but I'd soon learn money wasn't my joy. The company hired me into its leadership development program, which provided a network of budding leaders, rotating job experiences to groom growth, and classes and conferences to grow professional skills. Through this program, I learned that I loved the education. My joy was meeting new people, experiencing new cultures, learning new business processes, and helping coworkers realize ways to make their jobs easier. I thrived when I was learning and growing.

I worked hard and was rewarded handsomely with awards, raises, and promotions on a routine basis. I became a leader quickly too, taking my first management position only five years after entering the workforce. After watching my father's wild farming success becoming obvious with a modern custom-built home, pool, upscale cars, travel, big parties, and high fashion clothes, I wanted, perhaps even expected, all the same. My salary reinforced my belief that all this would be mine too.

Denny signed up for success with me. He landed a job with a landscaping company, and we moved into a new townhouse-style apartment, then built a starter home a year later. Four years later, we built a bigger house on a bigger lot in a more exclusive neighborhood. I was clearly captured by the "bigger, better, more" philosophy and was willing to keep giving to my job to be rewarded more so I could acquire more.

As much as I loved learning and growing, I still loved the farm, and I loved my parents. I wanted to consider ways to be closer to them and to stay involved in the farm. Still, Dad kept me at a distance. He began to use my success as an excuse to keep us out. He never let me look back and consider moving home. I resented the fact that Dad didn't allow me that option. So, I stayed focused on the career that took my mind and my time further away from my roots. Though Dad didn't like our big appetite for spending money, I think he was proud of my ascent from the farm to what he called "a better life," even if he never really said as much.

After five years of building our foundation, our first child, Cody, was born. Our second child, Michaela, was born three years later.

I held primary financial responsibility for our family. Denny was contributing a salary, yet my health-care benefits and my 401K savings plan covered the whole family. Our big expenses—the mortgage and our good yet expensive childcare—also came out of my pay. Paying for two kids in childcare felt like bearing the cost of a second mortgage! To add to my responsibility, when my mother separated from my father, she moved in with us for a time. I was now responsible for providing my mother's food and shelter. I was proud and joyful that I could do well enough to support all of us and found it fun to accomplish more and more. A new emotion set in, though. It took me a while to understand this emotion because it was foreign to me. Eventually, I realized that I was feeling a sense of burden. The feeling came in like a cancer, ever so slowly eating at the joy my career had always offered. The prospect of a bigger, better, richer reward by being all I could be and working longer, better, faster, and smarter had steered me in a new direction. Now I experienced a slow drift away from joy to this new sensation—burden—quickly followed by another new feeling: obligation. These new emotions began guiding my career, driving me to make career choices for income, versus career choices driven by a love for learning and for helping the people around me.

For ten years, the company I started my career in was a firm and reliable source of challenge, growth, and income. Then in 1997, the company outsourced their information technology functions. The company transitioned my job and me to a computer science consulting company as part of this outsourcing arrangement.

For the first time in my adult life, I learned that giving everything the company asked me to give, adapting to change, learning to contribute in new ways as the company's expectations of me grew, and long-term commitment and loyalty to the company's success, simply wasn't enough to guarantee a job. The company would do what was best for the company, regardless of what that meant to me. I had to accept that my job security was often beyond my control.

I remained tough and learned to do what was best for me, but I never gave the consulting company a chance. I was simply discontent working for an employer that circumstance had chosen for me. I felt the need and the desire to make my choices about my job and steer my destiny.

After scoping out a wealth of opportunities and doing many interviews, I received several offers. Apparently, I had a gift for opening job opportunities! I also had ten years of experience in analyzing business needs, developing applications, and leading others to develop applications. This time, I chose to go to work as a project manager, implementing an Enterprise Requirements Planning (ERP) software package for a manufacturing company in Cleveland, Ohio.

At this point, Denny and I had two kids—we welcomed the opportunity to be closer to home so the kids could get to know their grandparents. We took the opportunity to restructure our lives too. In Wilmington, we had two careers and two kids in daycare with virtually no one to count on but ourselves and a few good friends. We managed our circumstances well, but parenting, our jobs, and basic living responsibilities consumed all our time and money. We longed for a little free time and a little extra cash to enjoy life. When we moved to the Cleveland area, Denny offered to leave his job to become a stay-at-home father. It was an opportunity to free up the time and money we desired to enjoy life a bit, and Denny wanted to commit to giving our children something he didn't have growing up: a parent at home. He took care of the kids and the house, and eventually, we had our third child, Morgan. My mom moved into this house too, living with us for five more years before she ventured out on her own.

That's how I became the sole breadwinner. My sense of obligation grew.

Though I was not in a development program like I was in my first job, I continued to work hard and earned different roles approximately every two years. The variation of work duties satisfied my need to learn and grow. I loved a good challenge. I loved building and implementing software. I loved analyzing data, finding patterns, and helping business partners make decisions with information. I loved applying technology to business needs to make other people's jobs a little easier. I had far more responsibility in Cleveland than I had in Wilmington and much more stress. However, I was a good soldier. I changed and adapted to the culture—I had a family depending on me, and I was enjoying my way of life.

In Wilmington, the primary focus of my role was to reduce costs to increase profits. That focus changed when I changed companies. My employer in Cleveland had ambitious growth goals. Sensible cost reductions remained important, but growth was central. Growth had a bright side: there was increasing room to contribute, new challenges and new opportunities. It resulted in generous merit increases and bonuses and created sustainable work. I saw a dark side to this growth too. The company routinely let people go to fuel progress. In response to downward economic turns, following acquisitions, and as a means of managing employee performance, newly acquired employees and long-standing employees alike were habitually released to meet shareholder's profit expectations, to adjust costs to sagging sales, and to make room for new employees with more suitable skills and experiences.

Employees immersed themselves in a culture with an ever-present threat of losing their jobs. They not only did the work they were assigned, but they also competed against their coworkers to avoid being caught in a downsizing.

Competition isn't bad. We see it everywhere in our society. It shows up in our schools in band competitions, science fairs, and debate teams. We choose entertainment in the form of professional sports competitions and competitive TV reality shows like Survivor, Dancing with the Stars, and The Amazing Race. Plus, companies compete for our investment dollars.

It's no surprise that competition among our colleagues and friends fills our places of work. A little competition often makes us better performers. However, unlike a high school basketball game that is governed by a set of rules and has referees to enforce those rules, competition in the work environment is highly unregulated. Outside of laws, it's up to each employee to define what they will and won't do to achieve their desired rewards and up to the values and ethics of leaders to determine the behaviors they will and won't tolerate.

I worked with a lot of good people at this company. As the company grew, however, I began to witness behaviors I questioned.

One business leader shredded the reputation of every IT leader assigned to partner with her—she tore into the first one because he was too soft to get the job done. A year later, she ripped the second one apart because he was too aggressive, and after another year chastised a third for trying to please everyone. She did all this to protect herself. She may have wanted to appear as if she was looking out for the best interest of the company, but she was just selfish and scared. It was calculated, and it was cold.

I watched a product executive heighten tension between his peers: the sales manager and the manufacturing manager. He convinced the sales manager that the manufacturing manager was a slacker because he didn't produce enough and that sales would be higher if there were more product in inventory. He then convinced the manufacturing manager that the sales manager behaved irresponsibly with company funds by demanding so much inventory. Then he just sat back and chuckled as the two leaders vehemently argued. When their arguments ended in deadlock, the VP got involved, and the product executive swooped in to resolve this constructed standoff in heroic fashion, getting kudos for saving the day. He then started to campaign for a promotion as the head of the sales and manufacturing divisions. It was nothing short of a cynical strategic plot to look good in the eyes of those that made decisions at the expense of his peers.

I also witnessed one technology group race to deliver cutting edge technology with a skunkworks project—a project that was not vetted, approved, or financed in the usual way. When they delivered the technology, the group sought attention and applause, not only for the good they did for the company but for their egos. They used their innovative technological know-how to take work and funds away from their peer groups. Instead of bringing others along, they let others fail, putting their colleagues on the chopping block.

I worked for that company for ten years. I strengthened my commitment to my morals and ethics along the way, believing the way in which to achieve success was just as important as achieving success; that the good of the whole company was just as important as individual success. Several tough situations tested me, but the good I experienced far outweighed the bad.

I eventually left that company to try my hand in a different environment. I took many good lessons with me and set out to make my mark in a job with more responsibility. As the head of the technology department for a mid-sized company in Cincinnati, I had the challenge of helping a privately-owned company go public by modernizing their technology. I was happy to be once again growing and learning while contributing. Still, the economy was unsteady at that time. The unexpected bumps and turns exposed questionable work ethics, and funding for my department eroded. It appeared to be a problem, but the problem gave way to an opportunity. Recruiters called, I listened, and I was shocked at what I was offered—an opportunity to be a technology leader working for a wildly admired company in the Seattle area.

Twenty years after I started my career, I had reached a peak few attempted to scale. I was far removed from my agriculture roots, working in technology—a field few women entered and fewer conquered. I scaled the corporate ladder like the mountaineers that climbed Mount Rainier, and I reached what I considered to be a summit—a great role with a great company.

Here in the oncologist's office, though, it was clear. My desire that had driven my life until now was to prove to my dad that I was just as good as a son. My career was rooted in the desire to amass enough experience and wisdom to earn Dad's approval and trust—to be worthy of the assets I stood to inherit. It's even possible that I subconsciously tried to fill Kraig's shoes—trying to live two lives—my brother's and my own. Now I understood: Dad's opinion of working women wasn't about me. They were about him. Wondering what he was going to do with his farm wasn't about my worth. Dad had trouble holding value for me—for most women, in fact—in a work role. Even my twenty years of business success didn't change his mentality.

The women in the oncologist's office this day were, in Dad's eyes, incompetent even though he knew nothing about them. I was tempted to confront his sexist disposition, but it was not the time or place. I simply tolerated his bias and tried to diffuse his welling anger. Eventually, the doctor joined us, and I chose to forget Dad's remarks.

Dr. Horvath was in his sixties, a short, thin man with a full, wiry gray beard. He was calm and had a presence much larger than his physique. Dad and I sat side-by-side, in a firestorm. First, I heard the news with my head: "Multiple tumors, I am sorry this happened to you." Later I heard the news with my heart. Emotions welled up then I pushed them back down to gain my composure enough to ask a question. We heard the answer; then the cycle repeated until we were sitting in silence. Scared. Sad. Confused—in shock, I guess.

Dr. Horvath was kind, patient, and gentle. When I pressed him to tell me how many tumors, he flipped through his records and stopped on a page that seemed to be one long paragraph. He may have wanted to give the appearance that he was reading; instead, it looked like he was searching for the right words. "Five main tumors, there could be other minor tumors." That answer broke every piece of armor I had left; it was a lightning bolt that struck my core. The countless stories I'd heard of other brain tumor patients swarmed through my mind. Not one of them had as many as five main tumors with additional minor tumors. Not one of them survived. I was forced further into this new reality.

As Dr. Horvath gathered himself and his paperwork, I looked at Dad for the first time. He never broke. His deep blue eyes stared blankly ahead—he looked like an unmovable mountain; a fearless soldier; a gladiator staring down inevitable death. I had seen that look in his eyes before. I retreated to a safe place in my mind, searching my memory. Where had I seen those eyes? It would take me many days to answer that question, but eventually, the answer would come to me. I saw those eyes the days following Kraig's death, as Dad propped up Mom and drew from deep within himself for the courage to accept his son's fate and to stand before family and friends to accept their sympathy. This time, Dad was finding the courage to accept his fate.

During our discussion, I asked Dr. Horvath to show me the MRI pictures. He reluctantly obliged. Dr. Horvath's radiation partner, Dr. Ankur, retrieved me from the examination room and escorted me down the hall to a room with a computer. Dad had declined the opportunity and sat in the examination room alone. An MRI is a compilation of many pictures, each one a different layer or slice of the brain. We started with a picture of the top and kept scrolling down, looking deeper and deeper into the brain. There were indeed five main tumors, each the size of a walnut, and countless small tumors that appeared as seeds—tumors ready to grow. These pictures confirmed what I already knew.

I rejoined Dad in the examination room just as Dr. Horvath returned. Just as the lung specialist had done before, Dr. Horvath threw us into action planning, distracting us from the news.

There would be no surgery. Dad wouldn't be able to handle anesthesia with tumors in his brain. The brain tumors demanded more urgent treatment than we originally thought. Radiation would start the next business day. Dad was to stop taking the medicine Dr. Edgar gave him for seizures and start taking a steroid to reduce the swelling in his brain. This steroid would exacerbate Dad's diabetes, though, so he also needed to start getting insulin shots. We would go to our hometown hospital, so I could learn how to administer insulin based on Dad's sugar reading. If Dad couldn't see the print on his electric bill, there was no way he was going to see the measurements on the tiny syringes. Further, rheumatoid arthritis had damaged his hands—there was no way Dad would be able to give himself insulin shots. Moreover, he lost his ability to comprehend these instructions as he struggled to accept his fate. The doctors, the nurses, and I just assumed that I was the answer.

I was also distracted from the weight of the news; I now focused on actions. I heard the word seizures. It seemed prudent to understand what could happen so that I could prepare. I pressed for more answers. "I need to know what to expect—who can I talk to about what's going to happen?" Everyone seemed to ignore this, however. I received no answers. I succeeded in life through research, planning, and controlling the execution of plans, but these strengths would not get me through this: no one knew what to expect.

I left the doctor's office strong and determined for Dad. I also left afraid.

## Chapter 4

# Finding Wisdom

*"Without the assistance of that divine being, I cannot succeed.*
*With that assistance, I cannot fail."*
Abraham Lincoln

As we left the oncologist's office, I couldn't help but notice it was a beautiful, peaceful day. The warmth of the fall sun was a sharp contrast to the emotional storm we were weathering. We retreated to the familiarity and comfort of Dad's truck. He sat in the passenger seat, staring blankly ahead. I ran through our task list, determined to be the intelligent, classy, well-educated woman that I had worked so hard to become. It never entered my mind that I could excuse myself from the responsibility the situation called for. I followed the instructions the doctor gave me, getting the medications, supplies, and training.

When we returned home, I prepared the house for the long haul, first cleaning Dad's bedding, then transforming my former bedroom from an empty shell into a cozy shelter just for me. I scavenged furniture, lights, bedding, and other useful objects from all corners of the house and barn—items that had accumulated over the last seven decades. I then made the first of many trips into town to get supplies. Having moved around the country, occasionally living in sparsely furnished temporary apartments while waiting for a big sprawling house in the suburb to be ready for us to move into, I knew it would not take much to establish necessities in my old but new temporary home. This shopping trip was for bathroom supplies to fill an empty bathroom and for food to fill an empty refrigerator and pantry. Before leaving, I made one purchase for the child in me—a soft fuzzy blanket, acknowledging my need for comfort. That blanket became a symbol of safety and a place to retreat from the trials around me.

That night, after ensuring that Dad was content in his bedroom, I settled into my old room alone and faced my demons. There truly were demons everywhere. My presence in my father's house, especially in my old bedroom, was a catalyst for this melancholy to emerge. Opening the closet doors, I heard criticisms over how much money I spent. Clearing a space on the dresser, I heard angry judgments about the time I spent on social engagements and not doing enough physical work around the house and farm. Walking into the bathroom that adjoined my bedroom, I heard "you're spoiled." Walking into the kitchen, I heard rage—pure rage—about the farm labor, machinery, weather, money, and business partners. I had internalized these disparaging ideas, and I felt responsible for my father's rage. I believed I wasn't good enough. Not good enough to have the pool, the car, the clothes, the trips, and everything else I had as a teenager living under Dad's care. Not good enough to help Dad farm in my twenties and thirties, and not good enough to help Dad with his current needs, especially the financial ones. I felt guilty that these feelings were rising in me now, for Dad was dealing with a terminal disease. How could I be so small, fretting about my issues when he was dealing with a life-ending illness? Still, it was the illness that forced all this unfinished business to the surface. The sense that this could be the end of Dad's life demanded that I acknowledge these demons and deal with the things that Dad, the house, and my hometown brought out in me and deal with them before Dad was no longer here. The weight of these demands felt crushing—I was facing my darkest hour.

I laid in bed feeling empty, lost, and scared.

Then something beautiful happened. Amidst my prayers for guidance and comfort, a strong sensation came over me—I knew I was not alone. In my mind's eye, I saw the golden figures of spiritual masters and guides, people unknown to me in this life. One by one they came into my awareness then quietly stood as if to honor the journey I had begun. I then saw friends and family assemble with them, encircling me. With each new soul I acknowledged, I released more anxiety and fear until I laid there in peace and filled with gratitude for their support. Their gift was the wisdom I longed to feel.

Others may have found this concerning, but this came as no surprise to me. I made my first connection to the divine spirit in this same bedroom over thirty years before.


When I was nine years old, my five-year-old brother Kraig, my only sibling, became ill. Halfway through kindergarten, an affliction in his hip struck him. He'd cry during normal day activities, and he'd cry in the silence of the night, waking himself and everyone in the house. Our hometown doctor assured my parents Kraig was merely suffering from growing pains. But he was in unrelenting agony, and my parents kept searching for answers. Ultimately, x-rays showed a mass in Kraig's hip, and he was sent to Mott's Children's Hospital, a part of the University of Michigan in Ann Arbor, two hours away from home. He received a diagnosis of Ewing sarcoma, a rare form of cancer that affects the bone. Before he turned six years old, Kraig endured an invasive surgery to remove as much of the cancerous mass as the doctors could. Chemotherapy and radiation followed. My mother, grandmother, and brother virtually lived at the hospital as his frail body went to the brink of death, a fragile space where cancer cells died off and healthy cells rebirthed themselves in the hopes of keeping Kraig alive.

Dad worked in the fields to support us and to pay the hospital bills because farmers did not enjoy the benefit of a corporation or the government paying for the kind of health care insurance many of us enjoy today. Farmers paid for their medical bills directly and footed the bill for subpar insurance on their own. Dad had to get us all through this catastrophe.

My parents chose to shield me from the hell of these months. I lived with my grandmother for some time, then with family friends. They loved me and treated me like one of their own, but I missed my parents and Kraig, and I longed to regain a sense of family.

Kraig had a rough time getting through the chemotherapy and radiation, but he did just that. His cancer went into remission. We enjoyed a normal childhood for a while—swimming at the lake, riding through the fields in the back of Dad's pickup, watching Ohio State football games, camping with my grandparents, and riding bikes. Mom and Dad were protective of their frail child, and they often had a fit when our play put Kraig at risk of getting a cut or bruise. We still made some lovely memories together. Then his cancer spread to his lungs. Kraig returned to Ann Arbor; I went back to living with friends, and my parents returned to the fight for

Kraig's life. This time he wouldn't overcome the cancerous beast. In November 1975, Kraig came home. He died Christmas Day.

Looking back, cancer, separation from family, and death were a lot for an eleven-year-old girl to endure. On the other hand, I didn't know anything different at the time. It was just normal. I didn't dare concern myself with my feelings—Kraig was deathly ill, my mom was overwhelmed, and it was all my dad could do to care for his son and his wife and keep our finances in order. I felt crushed when Kraig died. I was too young to understand it from my parents' perspective, but I understood it as much as an eleven-year-old could. It was heavy, it was dark, and it was destructive. However, as devastating as Kraig's illness and death were, it was the few years that followed that shaped my life.

After Kraig had died, I was ready to move on. I was ready to get my mom, my dad, and a sense of family back. I was ready to live. Mom was drowning in sadness, however. She sank into a deep depression and lived her days and nights sequestered in her bedroom. Dad buried himself in his work, leaving me lost and alone. Our family and friends knew how to help our family through cancer (they were quite generous too), but no one knew how to acknowledge and assist a family that was emotionally broken, and few dared to help us address the dysfunction that cancer had left behind. The three of us floundered. Born into this world with an innately strong desire not only to live but to flourish, I was old enough to understand this floundering as a kind of hell.

Like my mom, I too spent much time in my bedroom following Kraig's death. There I found peace and comfort—a gentle energy beyond my comprehension guiding me and loving me. It may have been angels. It may have been God. Whatever it was, it made me feel like a flower, pushing through the frozen ground; pushing through the bleakness of winter; pushing through the frost to find the sun so I could grow.

Basic forces of nature took over—I learned to take care of myself, and I, fortunately, had an abundance of resources at my hands. Dad's farming business was booming—we had just moved into a beautiful new and well-appointed house. I had shelter, food, clothes, a good school, the school supplies I needed, and a strong will. I learned to get myself out of bed every morning, make breakfast, get on the bus, and get to school. When I wasn't in school, I tried to spend time with my dad. I soon began to identify with him—he was living.

There is no doubt my dad influenced me and guided me to the career I chose. Even though he didn't have a college degree, he made sure I got one. Even though he didn't understand computers, he knew there was a better future there. He didn't understand Fortune 500 corporations, but he knew that working with my mind would be far more enriching for me than the physical exertion required by farming.

Mom eventually found her rhythm again too. I will never fully understand, but I will always admire what she did to find herself. In time, she became the sassy, fun-loving, adventurous woman that I love today. She would significantly influence my life down the road, but in the years following Kraig's death, it was Dad's influence guiding me—he catapulted me away from the farm to find that ephemeral "better life." The further away I went, symbolically speaking, the further I distanced myself from my spiritual connection—my internal guidance, intuition, and a keen sense of knowing how to manifest joy in life.

The first indications that what I wanted to contribute to the world were not expected from a woman came, ironically, on the farm. Dad had hired me to be a helping hand on the tomato harvester and eventually allowed me to drive the tractors or the semi-trucks in the field. Dad proudly drove the sophisticated machinery that pulled the tomato plants from the ground, shook the fruit from the vines, and then moved the produce across a series of conveyors as laborers assessed them and disposed of the diseased and rotten ones. I drove alongside the harvester to collect the plump, healthy tomatoes that would be shipped off to Heinz or Hunt's to make ketchup. I wanted to contribute with my mind, too. I had ideas about fixing machinery, managing finances, overseeing labor, and keeping the books. Dad, however, didn't want my opinion on those things—he just wanted me to work. In other summer jobs, I found something similar. Whether it was in the office at the local pipeline company or sorting cucumbers at a fellow farmer's processing center, I learned I was expected to be both the pretty young thing that was easy on the eyes and the worker that got things done. Again, I wanted more influence in the workplace—I wanted to discuss how we could do the task more efficiently or how I could contribute in more meaningful ways, but no one welcomed those conversations. I left the farm and the small community harboring a bit of resentment that my good looks and my ability to fit into the expected mold of a good twenty-year-old girl made me more welcome than my intelligence did.

Ohio State and the manufacturing company in Delaware were wonderful places for me. In both environments, I found the space for contributions expansive. Neither my looks nor my gender seemed to limit me—I could contribute whatever I had the courage and the confidence to offer as long as it helped the educational process or the business. In the leadership development program, I had the benefit of interpersonal skills and leadership training. I learned about personal styles and that there was no perfect style I had to conform to. Rather, I learned all styles were necessary. That gave me confidence as I contributed in ways that were natural to me but often unconventional to others.

There were some disheartening realities in Wilmington, however. In the historically male-dominated engineering department where I started my career, many men assumed I was a secretary. Thus, I learned to dress differently from the secretaries and set myself apart from them—I left the flowery dresses in my closet and began wearing suits just like the men. My contributions were, for the most part, not stymied by my age, upbringing, or gender.

When I made a career change to the manufacturing company in Cleveland, I found fewer female role models, and most high-level women were isolated. They had neither the interpersonal training nor an environment that encouraged them to be their authentic feminine selves. They had, instead, reached their position by conforming to the masculine style. I felt isolated. I did not want to give up my femininity to be successful in the job. By the time I understood this, Denny was well positioned at home, and I was well on my way to becoming a nontraditional wife, mother, and career woman. Before I knew it, Denny had adapted to being the only man home during the day and accepted the call when neighborhood mothers had a snake on their deck or water leaking in the kitchen. I learned to perform my role in the same way men did to survive in this male-dominated manufacturing company. I also learned to walk fast in three-inch heels to keep up with the men in the airport and restrain the natural desire to talk about potty training. Instead, I chose to talk about headlines in the *Wall Street Journal*. More importantly, I acquired the knowledge needed to talk about sports—like the weekend NASCAR race or the latest Indians outfielder trade.

Denny and I found another couple that had chosen to do the

same reversed role thing. I made friends with Beth at work, and Denny and I both made friends with her husband, Tom, who was a stay-at-home father for their two kids. The four of us found friendship and support in each other while Beth and I broke the mold for female leaders in our company.

There were still moms in my community that held me accountable to the traditional mother and wife role; teachers who expected me in the classroom and not my husband; PTO members that expected me, not my husband, to contribute food to classroom events. Fellow mothers expected me, not my husband, to be available for play dates. I learned to slough off the expectations founded in tradition from people that did not know us—people that did not have cause to challenge their stereotypes.

Sloughing it off became hard, though, when the expectations came from family. It stung when family not only didn't accept and support the roles we had chosen but also when they tried to mold us into ones more acceptable to them. I will never forget hearing one of our family members belaboring advice to Denny about a pension: "Just find yourself a nice little job, like a route truck with a potato chip company so that you can earn a pension." I was dumbfounded. "What's wrong with the pension I'm earning for us?" I asked. The man was downright horrified to think that a woman was earning a pension for retirement.

This lack of understanding was our reality.

Denny and I never re-evaluated our situation. We believed we had made the right choice for us. I eventually got over the fact that I was missing the day-to-day interactions with the kids and saw it as a blessing that I got to do all the fun stuff with them. After work, I carved pumpkins, baked cookies, went to baseball games, stood in line to get *Pokémon* tickets, watched their music programs, and made Halloween costumes. I decorated for Christmas, found pictures for their family tree school project, read bedtime stories, and did a little laundry and made curtains for every room in our home. Those that knew Denny well knew he never lost his manhood simply because he was not earning money and was, instead, taking care of his children. Denny became involved in the kids' sports programs by coaching the soccer, T-ball, and basketball teams. He eventually became the treasurer, then vice-president, and then president of the basketball league and contributed to the community in ways that were not possible when we both worked. It was a new way of life, and we all adjusted.

As I got promotions and new assignments, it was no surprise that work got harder than earlier positions. The art of being a woman in a manufacturing organization was tough. The art of being a woman in technology in a manufacturing company was even tougher. There were co-workers and leaders that loathed others' success and wanted to see, even help, successful people fail. They just helped to remind me to be grateful for the bosses that were part of my success.

One such boss took me under his wing and gave me assignments that enabled me to grow. The best thing he ever did was assign me to a strategic planning project—to help him develop the first-ever strategic plan for the information technology department. He hired two consultants to assist him with the effort, and he gave me the opportunity to learn from them in the process. He inspired me with vision and challenge and supported me through those challenges. It felt good to be trusted, good to have the opportunity to grow, good to give my creativity space on the job, and good to experience success at the same time. The board of directors loved the plan, and our company benefited from the projects that resulted from it.

On the heels of that experience, came a boss who represented the darker side of leadership. It was the same assignment and the same exercise in strategic planning, but this leader purposefully set me up to fail—as if I were a toy to tear apart and destroy and he was some powerful God. He was swift and curt with his words. He tore down decisions, tore down strategic directions, tore down groups, and tore down individuals. He tore me down as well.

He asked me to put together a proposal, which I did exactly to his specifications, and he asked me to present it in a public forum. When I did, he humiliated me. It was a scene like the one in *A Few Good Men* when Jack Nicholson delivers the very powerful and vengeful line, "You can't handle the truth!" Only unlike the movie, there was no Tom Cruise to save me. I was unarmed and alone. This man barked out degrading judgments of both my proposal and me in front of my colleagues—and then he smiled with pleasure. He did the same thing to others too, which made the workplace feel like a war zone—it was every man for himself. In his final act of destruction, he made me inform a good friend and coworker that she was losing her job. When I did so, he offered her a new job shortly after to save her.

It is amazing what a force of destruction a leader can be. With a few swift actions and a few darkly inspired words, this leader caused me to lose a good friend, my position, and my interest in doing anything good for the company. All my energy went into surviving his personal attacks. I was staring a decision in the eye: be an accomplice to the destructive forces to maintain my position and my income, seek shelter and hide in a new but safe position to maintain some semblance of income, or push back and meet this fiery force with a fire of my own.

I was grappling with the expectation that I perform my role in a masculine way; that I compete with my teammates to demonstrate my abilities, use fear to motivate and lead people, and let good employees go without mercy. None of this was natural. My strength was in creating teams to compete with other companies. My strength was helping people build the skills needed on the team. My strength was to define strategies and inspire people to pursue the goals. I had been prewired with these skills and had them groomed in my first job. I had also had countless mentors at Ohio State and in Delaware—I wanted to give back and be a good mentor too. The person I was when I was born and the person I was becoming to keep going in my chosen profession were worlds apart. In the chasm between those two spaces, I began searching for something more meaningful.

In that chasm, I found wisdom.

I'm not sure what motivated that devil boss to take his next action, but I will be forever grateful that he did. After he'd degraded me in public and cost me a good friend, he nominated me for a leadership development program called Influence. I was ecstatic when I got into the course. I knew very little about the program or what I was expected to gain from it, but my heart knew the experience was going to be just what I needed at just the right time.

The few training and development sessions I had experienced with this manufacturing company up until this point left me with the notion that something was wrong with me—that I had some deficiency to correct. I found the Influence program was different. This training celebrated all that I was in the present and all that I had the potential to become. It introduced me to new concepts and frameworks to explore and got me thinking about community, state, national, and global matters. Plus, after the long spiritual drought that had lasted nearly two decades, I began rediscovering my spirituality. We learned from the course facilitators, from each other, and from ourselves. After the first session, I looked past the ugly realities of my corporate world and the burdens of being the sole wage earner. After the first two and a half days, I was open to finding good in the work world again. Influence gave me exposure to feedback from my direct reports, colleagues, and bosses. It introduced me to Emergenetics (a framework for maximizing the creative, analytic, process, and social thought processes in an organization), Spiral Dynamics (human development and value systems), and the power of positive thinking. As the sessions went on, I learned that when I consumed my mind with complex matters such as national education, poverty, global economics, global health, and natural resource consumption, I had less interest in obsessing about the lack of female influences in the workplace and my ill-intentioned, devilish boss. I became more concerned about doing good in the world, despite my circumstances.

Probably one of my biggest "aha" moments was learning that the "bigger, better, faster" lifestyle I immersed myself in was called "Strive and Drive" in Spiral Dynamic terms. It's the basis of the United States' capitalist economy and the behavioral pattern that propels our country. My current pain was rooted in the fact that I was struggling to fit into the business community around me when my true essence was more than "Strive and Drive." My natural state was what Spiral Dynamics people called "Human Bond" and "Flex Flow." That is, I seek peace within myself and value the caring dimension of the community—I value being intuitive and creative to make the world a better place for all.

Education is a beautiful thing. I found solace in knowing there was nothing wrong with me. I was simply growing.

A new boss in the Cleveland manufacturing company and the Influence facilitators had yet another gift for me—more training—

in China! Travel to unfamiliar places, as it turns out, is one of the more effective ways to grow. The brain is presented with many new things quickly, which forces it to grow new neural pathways. Traveling gets our thinking out of the neural paths that we use every day—the ruts in our mind—and thus enables growth. This training, held in Shanghai, was called "Influencing the Global Economy." While I was there, I visited one of my company's manufacturing plants and met with colleagues in the company's Asia-Pacific headquarters. These were growth experiences in and of themselves. The training also included five days of exploration in Beijing, one day in a historic small river town two hours outside of Shanghai, one day exploring in Shanghai, and three days of class. The class brought together thirty women from China, six women from the U.S., two women from Russia, and one woman from Malaysia. Carol and Tim, the instructors from Influence, had a gift for effortlessly bringing strangers together and building a community where the individuals shine and form strong bonds based on trust and respect. It was no different in China. Thirty-nine women walked into their class as complete strangers from all corners of the world, and within minutes they were sharing their deepest strengths, concerns, and dreams. In this forum, I found a more authentic self under the layers of baggage I was unknowingly carrying. Also, I found a stronger self as I learned from others and explored the country and I found a desire to continue exploring and developing my spiritual life.

After the Influence program in Denver and Influencing the Global Economy in China, I felt as though I'd been cracked open and the real me was yearning to get out. I was not quite ready to emerge yet, for the issues I carried were hard to overcome, but I loved the learning journeys and the life support I got in both programs. I longed for more.

It wasn't long before I was invited to participate in a community of people who had graduated from these programs. The group called themselves the Wisdom Community. I didn't know much about them. I didn't know their purpose, beliefs, or intents. I just showed up with faith and the need to invest time in my well-being. They met twice a year and had a forum for people to share ideas and learning. I attended many of the meetings, made some suggestions for topic discussions, and eventually led a meeting. With this group, I was giving myself time to reflect on my life—and rejuvenate. I grew because of the diverse subjects we discussed, and the group kept me grounded while giving me time to envision the life I wanted for myself and my family. I knew from my interactions with the Wisdom Community that I was capable of being the peace-filled, intelligent, thoughtful and kind contributor that I intended to be. I knew I could do this without job status, without financial status, and without ego. I knew I could achieve a new way of life. I realized I'd go through change, and change might be hard if I let my ego pass judgment. A change was exactly what my soul was searching for.

My move to Seattle, however, was a move rooted in ego. I went for the status, the intellectual bragging rights, and the money. Just when I was craving to step away from the ego, I stepped further into it. Then the universe threw me another lifeline. Carol and Tim invited me to a program for graduates of previous programs—a coed training called "Bringing Spirit to Leadership" (BSL).

My new boss had training funds he had to use or lose, so my training request was approved, and I went off to the four-session program. In BSL, we dove deeper into Spiral Dynamics, learned the values of other countries and cultures, and simulated global business interactions. We read articles and books that opened our awareness to the human experience in other parts of the world, and as a by-product developed a sense of gratitude for all that we enjoy in the U.S. as well as compassion for others who don't have what we so often take for granted. Some of us developed a desire to better the lives of others who are less fortunate. Just as the name of the course suggests, we explored spiritual concepts such as Reiki healing, the medicine wheel, and—oh so powerful for me—meditation. In BSL, I broke that protective outer shell of mine open further, surfaced some deeply buried pains, and began the process of caring for my spiritual well-being. Most importantly, I began to forgive myself—and to heal.

I had been raised in a Methodist church and had regularly attended with my mother. When I went away to college and got married, however, I lost my desire to go to church. With a career and later, kids, I dedicated Sunday mornings to my relationship with my husband and the chores that the workweek didn't allow time for, like grocery shopping and laundry. I lost my connection to God. The church did not offer a compelling reason to return. Through Influence, China, the Wisdom Community, and BSL, I found a connection to the force I had known in my bedroom as a young girl. I found a connection to the energy that gives us life. I found wisdom, and I vowed never to let it go.

Now that I was in Ohio, in my old bedroom, it was no surprise I was experiencing a deeply moving response while praying with a heart broken open by pain. In my mind's eye, one by one, a golden figure representing familiar family and friends from across the globe came into the room, comforting me, and giving me strength. It was as if they were praying and sending their love and light to me. Without words, I knew they were all going to be with me on this journey. I knew I would be comforted when I was scared and guided when I needed direction. I knew I could trust myself, for I had access to all the wisdom and courage I would need. I knew I was "good enough" for this journey. I could let memories of the past rise and settle back into my being in a healthier way. I knew this would be a time of healing for my dad, me, and the relationship between us. Although I remained scared because I didn't know what events lay ahead of me, I took comfort in knowing that I had the strength and support of many to face whatever presented itself.

I slept soundly that night—as I did for the many nights to come.

Deb,

You were with
me via email and
text message helping
me thru this part of
my journey. Thank
you. Love you
my friend
Kelli ♡

## Chapter 5

# Love or War

"War is only a cowardly escape from the problems of peace."
Thomas Mann

The next day, I awoke before dawn. Through the east window, I could see the light breaking over the horizon and the sunbeams streaming into my room and my heart once again. Though the circumstances were heavy, it was a new day, begging to be lived. But I stayed in bed waiting to hear a sign of life from Dad. Finally, I heard him cough, and I felt a sense of relief. Fear that Dad might not have made it through the night had seeped in the day before. This fear kept me immobile in bed. Of course, it was fear of the unknown, but there was more. Perhaps I feared he would pass before I could work out all these complex feelings rising in me or before I could somehow convey just how important he was to me. Perhaps it was a fear that he would pass before the beauty of love could fill and sustain the space between us once more.

Dad got up on his own, got dressed, and went to the kitchen to start his normal routine—he was ready to face the day as if it were any other. I put my fears to rest, got up, and did the same.

We were discussing the football games we'd watch when Dad's brother Larry arrived.

Larry is the consummate businessman. Although he was casually dressed and tried to relax on this Saturday, Larry still acted as a deal-making business leader even in the comfort and familiarity of his brother's home. The three of us sat at the kitchen table, where Dad did most of his business. In some respects, this was the meeting of two souls, two lives bound in ways only brothers can know, consoling each other simply by sharing space. In other respects, this was a business engagement.

Larry asked what we learned from the oncologist and radiologist. At the sound of this question, I was aware that I was in my business brain too. I was not confident that Dad processed and retained all the information gained, so I longed to explain everything I had discovered about cancer in the brain, the medications, the doctor, and the treatments. I refrained from answering Larry's questions and from offering facts because this was Dad's deal. I let him describe his reality the way he wanted to describe it.

Dad was vague, leaving much to the imagination, but he made it clear he was going through radiation, after that he may see about chemotherapy. Dad resigned himself to the direction the oncologist and radiologist had given him. Then Dad's words faded, and he reluctantly held his hands up in the air as if to say, "I have no choice."

Larry launched a fiery challenge, "Don't accept this treatment plan from small town doctors. Who is this oncologist? Who is this radiologist? How do we know they are good? I'll ask all my contacts for insights. Let's get another opinion. Let's seek alternative treatment. Let's go to the Cleveland Clinic. Let's fight this."

I love Larry—he's family. I looked up to him when I was a little girl, and I still looked up to him that day. His words, "Let's fight this," reverberated deep within me.

Is fighting what Dad wanted? Is fighting what God had in mind when he put me by Dad this day?

I'd been "fighting" for a long time. Fighting to survive downsizings, fighting to finish projects on time, and fighting to maintain a good reputation in environments where co-workers strove to make others look bad. In fact, in the technology industry, we think so highly of a good battle, we've named aspects of our work in a way that honors a good fight. One of the revered terms is "War Room."

You can find war rooms anywhere software development is taking place. They are the unfortunate outcome of an environment or project that risks the quality of the software to minimize cost and optimize the speed of delivery. War rooms depend on the ability to commandeer swarms of intelligent people to rally together in a warlike atmosphere to urgently fix software flaws discovered after the software delivery.

Shortly before Dad's diagnosis with cancer, I had found myself at the epicenter of a software disaster and a six-month war room that followed.

It started shortly after Dad's knee surgery and kidney failure incident. I had stayed in Ohio for a week at the end of October 2009 to help Dad. When I returned to my Seattle area office, I was acutely aware of the position my one-week hiatus put me in. The high-tech industry and this company ran at an insanely fast pace. Though I had only missed five working days, I was one week out of touch with the rapidly changing status of a large project that was due to be completed the first weekend in December. As soon as I stepped foot in the office, there were four senior leaders anxious to know that the project commencing in December was all okay and that I was on top of any burning issues. Countless peers were eager to do battle to prove they knew more than me—that they were the white knights solving issues I knew nothing about because I had stepped away from the fight. There were seventy-five people on my team and tens of people on other teams eager to find me to explain their reasons why they could not finish the project by December; they had been looking to find that one person who would have the audacity to stand up to leadership and call the December completion date unrealistic. They predicted disastrous results if no one heeded their warnings.

I had gained perspective on the delicate nature of life while I attended to my Dad's life-threatening kidney failure. I was willing to listen to their concerns, but my team lacked proof of the doom and gloom they predicted. So, I did what my company (what any company) would expect a leader to do—I pressed my team forward in the battle to get more done.

A few weeks later, my team's concerns were beginning to be substantiated. Because of testing, we could see the new software was producing unusual and unexpected data. They suspected this was just a glimpse of a bigger issue, but they lacked time to investigate. Instincts told me to trust my team, and I did.

In the short time I had worked in this company, I had not seen any leader cast a vote to delay a software project, but I did it anyhow. It was an unpopular move, causing everyone to question my judgment. It was the right thing to do, but the other stakeholders soon overruled my vote. All other stakeholders gave a go vote; then they looked to my boss to validate or overrule mine. My boss explored the issues and ultimately overruled my decision. The company did not delay the project.

The implementation began as planned on December third. Like well-trained and highly motivated soldiers, we buckled down, never questioning how worthwhile the war might be, or what we'd be asked to give—never asking if the win was worth the fight. We simply sought to earn our stripes because we could, in fact, fight.

The project blew up.

"Kel, it's not good." One of my direct reports was on the other end of the phone reporting the status of the weekend software implementation. Just like the day the shuttle exploded, and the day terrorists flew planes into the Twin Towers and the Pentagon, I will never forget where I was and what I was doing when I got this call. It was that kind of an event, not for the nation, but for me.

It was December fifth, a Sunday. I was in our kitchen with my family, cleaning up from a meal after a weekend visit to a Christmas tree farm and a day spent decorating the house for the coming holiday. The software had been installed, but when they tried to run it, users experienced significant problems and couldn't keep it running. There was no going back—the software could not be uninstalled. There was no copy of the intricately complex databases, interfaces, and finely molded applications that the team had put together—there was no simple way to un-change the changes made to the one and only copy in existence.

It was already Monday morning in Asia Pacific countries—and employees and customer's business was constrained. No one could receive or fill orders nor could they send invoices. Distributors, partners, and customers alike could not use this software. Simply put, a large section of our company's business came to a halt.

The war room convened.

This war room formed in a small conference room in an inconspicuous office building. There were twenty or so employees there when I joined on Monday morning. The key players had spent the night in that room working—trying to make sense of the unusual symptoms.

There were times I felt intellectually inferior in this company; times I simply did not want to battle my coworkers to justify my rank in the company or to validate my position, times I simply wanted to listen and honor the intelligence around me because I knew I wasn't the smartest person in a room. But not today. There was something about this moment that was different. Maybe the project team saw me as an ally because I had voted to delay the project, proving I had the willingness to do the right thing, not just the politically correct one. Perhaps they were simply exhausted, for these were the people that had battled throughout the past five months, working extensive hours to build and test software to meet the December release date, and they welcomed someone who genuinely wanted to help. Maybe it was the sheer fact that I did not bust into the room dispensing blame and threats.

Whatever their reasons, they didn't seek to outsmart me, and they didn't carefully select their words to shield themselves from the fault (both typical communication attributes when projects of this size and importance fail). They didn't even point fingers at other individuals or groups not present in the room (something all employees at every company I had ever worked in knew how to do). They were simply human beings trying to do the right thing—they didn't want this software to be released, but since the powers that be determined they had to, they just wanted to get it fixed. They laid down their egos and their protective armor that was so necessary for the company culture to tell me all they knew. They shared the unpolished facts and allowed me to ask questions so I could understand the raw issues. When they had explained as much as they could, one of my direct reports looked at me with despair and said, "Really, Kel, we did everything we could to make this work."

Not many people called me "Kel." However, when they did, it was a sign of respect. They made it easy to set aside my frustrations with the overly competitive work culture and join the team. In fact, I was honored to help.

The twenty or so people present in the room and on the phone in other parts of the world found their way of contributing. It had been years since I had written a line of code, so I wasn't going to be any help finding and fixing bugs. Server performance was never my specialty, and there were plenty of people working on data issues. I could test, but no one needed a tester—they already knew what was broken. I took responsibility to keep upper management and other stakeholders informed. I told everyone in the room, "Every damn leader in this company will want to know what the hell happened and what we are doing about it. I'll keep them off your backs." Since joining the company, the word "team" had come to mean a collection of individuals working towards their personal goals. Here was a rare moment that I felt like a member of a true team—a group of individuals collaborating and working towards the same goal.

Regardless of how my brain-power matched up to others around me, I am a smart person. From the moment I defined my role as communicator, I started framing the technical issues in business terms, defining the consequences and reporting the impacts to our management, twice a day.

At first, the focus was on server performance. Soon the brilliant minds at work inside the war room and in other areas of the company were able to resolve the server issues and make the software available to our customers. Because many people across every time zone used this software, no announcement of its availability was needed. As soon as the software was available, someone somewhere attempted to use it. In the late afternoon on the Pacific Coast, we watched as customers from New Zealand and Australia logged in and put it to use. The software hit a maximum capacity of users, then broke again. As soon as the software became unusable, the war room performance teams scrambled to identify issues and resolve them. Again, the software was made available. As the user capacity increased, however, it would hit a new limit, and the system would crash again, starting the cycle over. With each additional cycle of issue identification and resolution, increasing numbers of customers could use the system. By Wednesday, the software was running for everyone.

Though the software was now working, the war room stayed intact, continuing to help the business get back to normal after an extended outage. A smattering of management began to appear around us, each one showing up with a personalized version of the same message, "I'm here to help." Still, there was no focus on blame and no intellectual wrestling. Everyone remained focused on resolution. I was still providing daily reports of issues, business impacts, progress, and expectations.

Unfortunately, we identified more issues. Because the systems went live with incomplete testing, we should have expected additional issues to arise, but we didn't. We had unconsciously hoped our issues were limited to system performance, but they weren't. What we had experienced up until this point was merely a warm-up for the real war.

Just as we suspected in November, there were data issues—and data issues were the result of flawed software code or even worse, overall software design. Given that this software was made up of thirty-five applications delicately woven together with intricate code, these data issues would be hard to unravel. One of the most intelligent men on my team tested, retested, and proved that the issues were real. Then he pulled me aside to help me understand just how significant these were. I volunteered to break the news to others.

I didn't create the problem. In fact, my team didn't even participate in the project that had. My team did, however, have the skills, experience, and knowledge to identify the cause and help fix it. I had shown up to help, and now I was sucked in. I held devastating news in my hand and was about to be at the epicenter of a developing crisis.

I shared the news with my peers gently yet unwaveringly. However, as the words slipped through my lips, the team environment I had enjoyed in the recent days evaporated. Fear touched everyone there. I had no intentions of hurting or blaming anyone—I simply intended to expose the truth so that a resolution could begin. Instead of working towards a solution, debates flared. People challenged the facts and my credibility extensively. Political posturing began. One VP stood up in a meeting, pounded his fist on the table, and in another *A Few Good Men*-style moment he barked out, "You cannot tell others about this!" Still, I held firm, making my case. It became clear I would not back down. I would ensure that inside the company acknowledgment of the problems occurred for quick and accurate resolution.

What had been one team working together in a single conference room gave way to small factions of people meeting in separate rooms. A single VP reached out to me to further understand what I knew. Everyone else looked for allies and formed alliances. Even the team I had stood up for found shelter in the storm. Soon, I had no one to trust. I had become a whistleblower.

My boss had purposefully kept his distance from the war room. He seemed happy with my work and chose to depend on me to represent him there. Once the deeper issues were exposed, he appeared. As I greeted him in the hall, I sensed I was passing my baton to him. I begged him to keep the war room operating as a team, unintentionally implying he wouldn't be a team player. Poor guy, it wasn't him—it was what he represented. I knew the war room had changed and his presence underscored it for me. It was no longer a team focused on issue resolution. It had become a microcosm of the company.

Company lawyers appeared. Closed-door meetings were held. PR specialists were enlisted. Twice daily conference calls took place with company leaders to keep them apprised of the business impacts and the efforts to resolve the problems. The issues were pervasive and complex. Issue resolution would be a lengthy process. It turned out to be the worst software implementation the company had ever seen.

At least eighty-five people and six layers of management were sucked in and consumed in this for months. Everyone worked excessive hours. At one point, just out of curiosity, I calculated how much time I put in: eighty-eight hours a week—that's what I was giving away. Eighty-eight hours of each week for sixteen weeks. One night I walked into my daughter's bedroom just to know she was there and know she was all right because I hadn't seen her for days. It was 3:43 a.m. She woke up, looked at the clock on her nightstand and asked, "Are you coming from or going to the war room?" That's just how it was—eighteen-hour days, seven days a week. I'm certain I did not see the worst of it. Countless others gave just as much or more time. Outside the war room walls, life happened. There were weddings, births, relationship struggles, holidays, funerals, and vacations. Those of us in the war room missed out on all that and more. We missed out on life for six months.

No one got a reward for the extra time or effort. The company didn't want to reward anyone who could have contributed to or been responsible for the debacle, so they simply rewarded no one. Eighty-five people gave up their lives, and the only reward was to continue working in the same culture and under the same circumstances that created the catastrophe.

War did not come naturally to me. I was wired to prevent wars—I was wired to create peace. My talents were best used to create schedules determined by well-defined plans, not by an ideal date for a leader's performance evaluation. I was a skilled cross-organizational collaborator that could negotiate plans and pave the way for success for all involved, not for the success of a select few individuals that cleverly worked at the expense of others. I wanted to launch a campaign to retire this exhaustively complex software. It only existed because the effort to replace it required vision, unwavering long-term commitment, and the ability to endure short-term setbacks along the way—and these were not the characteristics admired and rewarded in the technology industry. This software and the problems that went with it existed because wave after wave of intelligent people and their energies were herded in to fix, change, and add their version of brilliance in twelve months or less because it fit the company's timeframe for determining an employee's worth. I wanted to replace complexity with simplicity, so the company was no longer indebted to a slew of brilliant minds that could "fight" for the quickest, most innovative ways to further augment and patch the mind-bending suite of software every time the business changed.

The changes I wanted to make were cultural changes. I subscribed to Albert Einstein's philosophy: "We can't solve problems by using the same kind of thinking we used when we created them." However, there were no leaders present that shared this outlook. I was alone. Plus, trying to change the company culture on my own was like trying to reverse the rotation of the earth: it just wasn't going to happen.

So, I fought on like a good soldier.

Now I was fighting again.

"Fighting for Dad" was a noble cause. Still, no matter how noble the cause and no matter how respectfully the fight begins, the war would morph into something far from noble and respectable. "Fighting for Dad" meant debating doctors, nurses, insurance companies and hospital administrators, challenging doctors' credibility, standard treatments, and costs. Fighting meant defending myself from personal attacks, and waging battles with Dad's loved ones and lawyers for the right to set the fight's strategic direction. There would be losses along the way, and the fight would undoubtedly be ugly. I didn't want that for Dad, and I didn't want that for me.

Larry's challenge rang through my head again "Let's fight this." As I questioned the approach, I could hear my co-workers taunting me when I questioned the good "fight" at work. "You don't have it in you, do you, Miller?" I wasn't scared of fighting—I had the skill, I had a noble cause, and if I allowed myself to do so, I could be filled with anger and channel that anger into fuel for the fight. It wasn't a matter of if I could fight; it wasn't a matter of if I had it in me. It was a different question—a better question. Was fighting my best response?

When I was fighting in the war room, I gave up a lot! When I was in the war room, I missed my son's eighteenth birthday, my daughter's fifteenth birthday, and Christmas. I didn't buy one gift or decorate the tree. I didn't wrap the gifts or make the

Christmas treats. I showed up Christmas morning, but I promptly fell asleep. I stressed my marriage, and I also missed my daughter's entire basketball season. I did not see one game, didn't wash a uniform or a practice jersey, and didn't get the opportunity to sit at the kitchen table and discuss the challenges she faced and provide moral support. I was physically absent from life for six months, and I was emotionally absent much longer. Fighting meant missing special moments with the people I love—moments I would never get back. If I were to "fight this" for Dad, how could I be present for him emotionally? How would I close the gap that had grown between us? How would I recognize and savor those fleeting expressions of the love we shared?

For tens and thousands of years we have been "fighting" to grow the bottom line, "fighting" to gain market share, "fighting" for freedom of speech, "fighting" for religious freedoms, and "fighting" for survival, and we're still fighting. I had been doing my best to fight. But I had to ask myself, at what point does the fighting stop?

Maybe, just maybe, it was time to stop fighting. Maybe it was time to be led by the heart; to let love and compassion take the lead. Maybe it was simply time to be kind.

Welling up with love, I did my best to throw Dad a lifeline. "Dad, I'll do anything you want to do. If you want to go to the Cleveland Clinic, I'll take you there right now. I have the utmost faith in the Cleveland Clinic. They'll give you the best treatment possible. If you want to go to the Mayo Clinic, I'll get you on a plane, and we'll go there. Whatever you want, I'll do it. You just tell us what you want to do."

Dad appeared relieved. He always liked to be in control, so he had to be back in his comfort zone when I handed the decision-making back to him. Dad paused and said, "I want to be here in my home with doctors and hospitals I know."

Larry and I overcame our instincts to fight to respect Dad's wishes. We then focused on a matter of the heart: How do we use the time we have?

So, we retreated to the family room, taking our familiar seats to do what we always did on a September Saturday—we watched Ohio State football. Dad's ahead-of-its-time, 56-inch flat screen TV was the center of attention in this room. Like a Star Fleet bridge commander, Dad sat directly in front of it in his oversized leather reclining chair. Larry and I flanked him, Larry in a rocking chair, me on the couch. Though football filled our discussion, we were setting the tone for the time ahead. Dad would be in control of his fate. We would stand at his side in support. We would consume our thoughts with less frightening matters, like Ohio State football, and love each other through the challenges ahead.

*Chapter 6*

# Choosing Who To Be

"You need chaos in your soul to give birth to a dancing star."
Friedrich Nietzsche

That day, we started what would become our new routine—I took dad's blood sugar readings four times a day every day. I pricked Dad's finger, assessed his levels, then gave him an insulin shot and the right pills. I also made him healthy meals, trying to manage his blood sugar better, keeping him away from the starchy, sugary treats he had come to live on. If his blood sugar got too high or too low, he would die, so I took my role seriously. I followed the doctor's directions, and I followed my sense of right and wrong. Dad questioned everything I did: was I was reading the sugar level right? Did I measure the insulin correctly? Was I administering the right medications? Was the healthy food necessary?

Dad never questioned the doctors, the nurses, friends, and extended family, but Dad questioned me. Constantly.

Just like I had done in my formative years, I internalized his lack of trust as an indication that something was wrong with me; that in his mind, I still was not good enough. This thought triggered something within me. I wanted to challenge him. I wanted to push back and stand up for myself. I wanted to meet his questions with verbal force, undeniable logic, and a display of intelligence to show Dad once and for all I was good enough. That kind of response just fueled the fire between us. So, I choked back my feelings. I wasn't going to change my Dad's opinion, and I wasn't going to leave this situation. My only recourse was to accept his disposition. I chose to say nothing.

On Monday, Dad began receiving daily radiation treatments. Despite this, Dad's condition continued to deteriorate rather quickly. His eyesight remained poor, and his balance began to be affected. I knew he couldn't see small print and other things up close, but I believed he could still see at a distance.

I was wrong. One evening, as we sat in front of the TV, I asked, "Dad, how's that TV working for you, can you see the show well?" He had the biggest TV in the county. I hoped he could see that gigantic screen twelve feet in front of him well enough to enjoy the football games and ESPN sports talk shows. Dad was unusually blunt. "I can't really make out anything, Kel." I had nothing to offer, and we sat in silence.

By the end of the week, Dad was having trouble walking a straight line. One Friday in the pharmacy, while walking down an aisle, his center of gravity started to shift further and further to the left until he lost his balance and fell. I caught him. He stared at me, his deep blue eyes laced with fear. We said nothing, then he turned and kept walking. Later that day, stepping up one step into a store, Dad again lost his balance and fell backward into my arms. Once again, I caught him, and he stared at me with the same fear in his eyes, but he refused to acknowledge it with words. He collected himself and walked on.

Though Dad and I never talked about the fact that he was receiving treatments to give him time, not to cure him, he seemingly understood it. If he wasn't cognizant of what the treatments would and would not do, then he was simply following his family doctor's advice to "get his affairs in order." He took the initiative to meet with his lawyer.

Dad's lawyer was a woman. I found it ironic that Dad held such little value for women as workers generally, yet two of his closest business partners were women.

When I was growing up, Dad's accountant, Val, was a woman. She was intelligent, stubborn, argumentative, witty, and bold. Dad admired her, for she was just like Cecil and just like my dad. She advised him on everything from tax matters to equipment and land purchases. Val was different. In an era when women were burning bras to claim their rights, Val single-handedly made her way without the drama of protest. She had an educated opinion, and with a deep, raspy voice, she shared that opinion with everyone—taking control as a military commander would. She usually had a glass of liquor in one hand and a cigarette in the other when she was with Dad. Somehow, Dad always listened!

Val had passed away many years ago. Now, Dad was working with a new lawyer who was my age. She was intelligent, intense, authoritative, and passionate about her work—someone I wanted on my side of a legal issue. Even in this dark time, Dad's lawyer managed to get him focused on the work at hand. She worked through Dad's estate quickly, blowing away my perception that all lawyers work at an exhaustively slow pace, foreign to the insanely fast-paced high tech world where I had lived. I was not confident Dad comprehended every idea, alternative, and legal document presented to him, and I'm sure he didn't understand all the implications of his decisions, but he trusted his lawyer, and he followed her direction.

I was envious of Dad's accountant and his lawyer. They had Dad's respect, admiration, and confidence when I didn't.

I so badly wanted to be ultra-knowledgeable about things like estate structures, inheritance taxes, and power of attorneys so that I could guide Dad. I did research outside the meetings with lawyers, but the expectations that I put on myself were too high. The time I had available to study, and my capacity to take in complex new things were already stressed. In the end, my research served only to dampen my worst of fears and did little to improve my position with Dad. I had to trust Dad's lawyer too.

From time to time, I talked to Dad about his estate, but it was a delicate subject. I didn't want to push him into feeling that the end was near because I didn't want him to give up the fight he was waging. Further, I didn't want him to believe I was here only because I stood to inherit. There had been just too many instances in the past when Dad or his confidants expressed the belief that I only wanted the farm and his money. And that was the farthest from the truth. I was there for Dad's well-being, my well-being, and the chance to heal and enjoy the relationship we shared in the most beautiful way possible in the time we had left.


The week gave way to a beautiful fall weekend. Despite his failing condition, Dad wanted to be outside, in his truck, riding the backroads and inspecting the fall harvest.

Dad had lived with poor eyesight quietly for the past six or seven weeks. Without an accident to prove the point, Dad knew he couldn't drive. Still, depending on me to drive him where he needed to go irritated him. He had long been the master of his destiny. His life had been a series of challenges that taught him to trust only himself. He drove his own business, farming equipment, and life choices. Relinquishing the driver's seat of his truck, to me, symbolized a loss of control. Though I had driven the path to his fields countless times, he barked out directions and gasped when my braking, turning, or speed did not match his instincts. Directing me gave him comfort. However, I was strong-willed and liked being in control myself—being told how to drive irritated me. If I had gone on autopilot, I would have snapped back to protect my ground, but again I bit my tongue, so I didn't fuel the fire between us. By not fighting back and following Dad's directions, I gave him a gift—the sense of control he no longer had, even if it was at the expense of my personal power.

During Dad's radiation therapy, it became evident he didn't like waiting either. He didn't like waiting for me to get ready to go to his appointment; he hated waiting for the radiologists to begin their work; he disliked waiting for stoplights. He was conditioned to believe he could not afford to waste time waiting; that he had to use every waking minute to work. Though he was no longer farming, he maintained this belief. Every day, regardless of the time, Dad huffed in frustration when I came out of the bedroom to leave for his appointment. Then every day, he sat in the radiation therapy waiting room, discontent and impatient. After the radiation was over, we went somewhere for lunch. While we waited for our meal, Dad recounted the morning events, bemoaning the inefficiencies of the day, like farmers bemoan the weather. His lack of tolerance for administrative processes and lack of consideration for others annoyed me. I wanted to push back and make him realize his schedule didn't dictate everyone else's and he needed to learn to give and take without resentment.

However, I didn't follow that desire. Instead, I said nothing, for I had seen the volatile nature of his grievances—something his friends and acquaintances didn't see; something he saved for those closest to him. Pushing back might make me feel better, but it would ignite an explosion that would push Dad further away, and that was something I didn't want.

In this way, I was starting to make better choices around Dad. We had more work to do, but acting out of empathy, compassion, and love was a big step. I had lost touch with these values as I gained behaviors and values necessary to compete successfully at work. Empathy, compassion, and love were values and behaviors often modeled in my hometown—the community made it easy for me to claim them as my own again.

Then I had to find a way to own these values and behaviors as I went back to work.

I had taken a full week of vacation to be with Dad for this first week of radiation therapy. Those days gave me time to accept Dad's diagnosis, his treatments, my responsibilities, and Dad's disposition. I could now look out into the future and contemplate how I'd best use my remaining vacation and sick time to help Dad.

A piece of me just wanted to shut off work and be present for Dad—his crisis was just that demanding! On the other hand, Dad was my role model. I committed to my employers the same way my father committed to his farm. I was a responsible employee, and I would not allow myself simply to shut off work. I would find a way to balance my commitments.

It was 2010. Though cable had reached my father's farm many years ago, he had no Internet service. There were no Internet cafés in town, and cellular hotspots had yet to hit the market. My first order of business was to have an Internet service installed so I could connect to the computers in the Seattle office. Then instead of burning all my vacation time, I could do some work remotely in Ohio. I called my boss on Friday afternoon. It wasn't difficult to negotiate—I ended up with a good arrangement. Each day I would take a ½ day of vacation, giving me time to take Dad to his daily morning radiation treatments, then work a ½ day in Dad's house to attend to the most important needs of my job.

My employer had flexible work practices that would enable me to find the balance I desired; my boss made the negotiation easy, and the technology that enabled remote work was now at my fingertips. I was grateful for this.

As week two of radiation therapy began, Dad and I started another new routine. I took Dad to the clinic in the morning, got lunch, then he rested in the family room while I worked in a makeshift office fifteen feet away. My work didn't wait for me while I was out. It had only been ten days, but my colleagues were rushing towards their goals and had made considerable progress without me. It was my responsibility to catch up and make myself relevant again. It was like jumping on a treadmill that was already moving at twenty miles per hour. From my provisional office, I demanded answers to difficult questions and confidently barked out directions. My assertiveness blended with the culture on the other end of the phone, but my behavior was a sharp contrast to the compassionate, understanding, and, to some degree a submissive role I filled in my Dad's home. It was difficult for Dad and me to allow the intensity of my work to invade his home—a space that had started to become our sanctuary.

After a few days of work from Ohio, I realized I was gaining a whole new perspective on my work. With cancer living in the very next room, I had a waning tolerance for back-to-back meetings, political posturing, and overly complex processes that kept me busy, but not productive. Plus, I didn't have to tolerate five lane highways full of angst and hostility to get to work. I didn't have to hustle from building to building and conference room to conference room to get to meetings—all I had to do was phone into a meeting, so I had time to think about what I was experiencing. This change in perspective gave birth to an abundance of work-related insights.

When I took the job in Seattle, I didn't spend much time evaluating my employer. They ranked as one of the best, and they had a reputation for hiring only the best of the best. It played to my ego that they wanted me. I had no reason to assess the company, the hiring group, or the offer. I accepted on blind faith, moving my children to their third school in three years, taking a significant loss on our home, and significantly downsizing so we could afford real estate in the Seattle market.

Now, two years after moving to Seattle, what I saw in the workplace shocked me: things that had always been there, but that I only began to acknowledge when I gained this new perspective. Arrogance, greed, and manipulation filled the workplace—behaviors that were hard to admire.

Work had always demanded confidence. After all, who wants to make a purchase, invest in an idea, or collaborate with someone who fails to convey a sense of reliability and trust. From my Ohio office, however, I could see how confidence had mutated into unabashed arrogance. The phrase "the customer is always right" held no meaning. My co-workers believed that they knew better than the customer; they simply delivered the technology they thought the customer *should* want. Employees didn't listen to Wall Street about the economic conditions, didn't listen to customers about their needs, and didn't listen to each other. Sometimes this failure showed up subtly, other times it showed up in an irritatingly grand and boastful way, but it had the same effect. Those who listened were virtually run over. Only the brashest, most brazen, and irreverent survived.

And greed. Years before I joined them, the company had put innovative tools within reach of most everyone in the world. I admired that ingenuity and wanted to be a part of the culture of creativity that spawned it. However, instead of seeing this legacy, I saw the legacy of the financial rewards it had earned them. The "overnight millionaire" phenomenon of the tech world had dissipated many years before I arrived, yet the culture had a sense of entitlement ingrained in it. Employees not only expected stock awards that rapidly grew in value, they felt those rewards were their right. In rural Ohio, people made a living on an annual income less than my co-worker's yearly bonus, but my colleagues and I had lost sight of our prosperity. Instead, we built lives and debt structures around our ability to fight for higher performance review ratings and in turn, earn even better bonuses and the coveted stock rewards that went with them.

The ruthless behaviors I had witnessed in Cleveland were magnified in Seattle. Employees withheld knowledge in a grand form, making themselves indispensable to leaders. Leaders formed alliances only for the sake of making other teams look bad. Strategies were contrived to create diversions that hid project shortfalls. Marketing programs were designed to cover a product that failed. People acted like work was a cockfight—a high-intensity duel where multiple individuals displayed their knowledge until one person gained supremacy based on popularity and notoriety, winning the right to guide the work at hand while shaming the competition. It was a permanent struggle for power.

While I was working from my Dad's farm, it felt that my colleagues were begging me to behave in ways that felt unnatural to me—to manipulate circumstances and others to my advantage. If not to win, then to survive. It wasn't in my nature to convince a VP my colleague was wrong, and I was right so that I could enjoy his support during performance reviews. Rather, I thrived on collaborating with my colleagues, not competing with them. I didn't like the strategic maneuvering required to get a boss to align with me instead of a peer. I believed my boss could support both of us. I didn't like questioning the intelligence of others to prove my ideas were superior. I wanted my ideas to stand on their own, not to stand on politics. It wasn't my nature to challenge people to verbal duels—I prided myself on my ability to facilitate collaborative decisions. Also, I didn't like telling employees they weren't performing well, not because they weren't intelligent or they weren't capable, but because their efforts to prove it paled in comparison to their co-workers' efforts to disprove it.

I wrestled with my integrity as I struggled between doing what I believed to be right and doing what I had to do to survive.

The time and energy I gave to my job quickly came into perspective, too. I was beginning to accept that Dad's time on this earth was limited now, and I wanted to give him my time and an abundance of attention. I had worked fifty, sixty, seventy, even eighty hours a week for over twenty years, only taking a few short weeks to give birth to kids, a few days to mourn the loss of my grandparents and an occasional week of vacation. Now I wanted time to care for my Dad and time to sort through and deal with the emotions I was feeling. I did my damnedest to jump on that quickly moving treadmill, but after my half day of vacation and half day of work, I called the work day complete.

Many years ago, I developed a habit of working late. In the beginning, working extra hours set me apart from my peers as I single-handedly got more work done. Now that I was the sole caregiver for my Dad, I couldn't give the time. Dad depended on me for meals: Eating on time meant keeping his blood sugar from dropping and keeping his blood sugar from dropping meant keeping Dad alive for yet another day. I needed to administer Dad's medications, keep the house, and prepare for the next day's challenges. By then it was eight o'clock in the evening, and my colleagues on the west coast were still working.

I remembered a co-worker who had taken time away from the office to handle her father's estate and a man who had taken time away for cancer treatments. The job had not been kind to them. I knew the office expected me to work long hours despite my circumstances, and to show my commitment to the ambitious goals they were chasing. I quietly prayed they'd understand as I sat with my father for an hour each night, giving my compassion to a man who was fighting for his life. I resisted the implicit expectation to go back to work after dinner as my colleagues routinely did, and I resisted the temptation to work after Dad went to sleep. While many of my coworkers lived on three or four hours of sleep, I couldn't. When Dad went to bed, I did too. Getting sufficient sleep was the only way I still had to take care of myself through all this, and my colleagues were going to have to cope.

Now because of Dad's cancer, the way in which I spent my time was a crucial decision with deathly consequences.

I had been ignoring it for years, but I was indeed making a choice. I was giving my employers just a bit more every day—a bit more of my time and my bravado, believing I would soon earn the ability to live my life the way I wanted to; if I just gave a little more. However, each time I reached what appeared to be a peak, I'd find only a false summit; a plateau where a new set of demands awaited.

I gained perspective on "emergencies" too. One afternoon, while attending a meeting via phone, I listened to a colleague wage war to convince my team to take on an emergency project. I listened to his technical and financial rationale, but with Dad in the next room, none of it made sense. See, companies like mine raced to be the first to market. Though my group did not develop and deliver products directly, urgency was ingrained in our culture. So, we raced to reschedule our portfolio of projects, respond to software failures, find solutions for over-budget projects, and deliver on the VP's latest whim. It was as if this behavior would somehow give birth to the next game-changing gadget, send stocks soaring, render us all millionaires, and promise us that we'd retire with our names on the wall of fame to live happily ever after. We ran on adrenaline rushes: everything was urgent, everything was a crisis. Now, my Dad was living a true crisis, and at once it was painstakingly clear: there was nothing that was ever really a crisis at work. There was nothing there that would bring us a pot of gold or lasting happiness. We had merely *chosen* to work this way.

Suddenly, I regretted the nights I'd expected my team to stay late, the extra work I'd assigned them, and the insurmountable challenges I'd asked them to overcome. I regretted the nights I'd missed my daughter's solos in the school music program, was too busy to listen to my son's challenges in the classroom, demanded my husband's assistance to complete a power point presentation, or spewed expletives when everyone in the house was having fun because I had to work. I regretted treating work as a crisis that demanded my constant attention and in the process, created a crisis for those around me.

I realized that I wasn't just a victim, I was part of the problem!

This new perspective made me want to walk away from the job, but I had issues that kept me there—the debt cycle I had taken on from my "bigger, better, more" mentality and my ego, pride, and sense of obligation to my family wouldn't let me walk away.

I had built my life on the foundation of my job. I felt stuck; stuck in an environment where I no longer found the joy in a good business challenge; stuck in an environment where arrogance, greed, and manipulation prevailed.

I stayed strong and compassionate for my Dad, but every afternoon when I jumped on that speeding treadmill called work, I got angry—angry with others who had unabashedly taken excessive amounts of my time and angry with myself for giving so much of myself to work. I was angry with those who demanded I attend to their latest emergency and angry with myself for giving in to their emergencies. I wondered why I had waited until I was faced with death before I questioned the hours and urgency, the values my behaviors were modeling and why I hadn't given my time to my relationship with my Dad instead. I thought about all those times I wanted to be going to my kids' soccer games, hiking the Cascades, and eating a meal with my family without feeling the pressure to keep up with those at work. It was clear; I wanted a challenging and rewarding job just as much as I wanted to spend time doing things I loved with people I loved. I was angry, not with the company's policies or rules, but with the people that created these environments and the shameless, uncaring behaviors we employed to win.

Another weekend came, and I was happy for another day without appointments. I longed for an in-depth conversation to explore my new perspective, my welling emotions, and disjointed thoughts—a conversation suited only for those who knew me the best. That type of conversation would elude me for now, so I went for a walk in the fields directly behind the house, leaving Dad alone for the first time since I'd arrived. I searched for clarity and answers to tough questions just as I did when I ran in that same field with my cocker spaniel when I was twelve—the year after Kraig died.

I could not deny the dichotomies in my life. I had one foot in my hometown's modest, easy-going way of life and one foot in my employer's. Both environments were rich with issues, but the people in those environments dealt with their issues in completely different ways.

In my hometown, they were meeting life's challenges with empathy, compassion, and love—some of life's best gifts. On the job, coworkers were hammering the life blood out of each other, meeting their challenges with some of life's central vices.

As I walked the freshly harvested field, I heard combines groan in rhythm as farmers in the distance harvested the first mature soybeans of the season. Birds chirped as they basked in the warmth of fall sun. I remembered a presentation Wayne Muller, author of *How Then Shall We Live* and founder of Bread for the Journey, once gave where he described a teapot that had been used generation after generation and could make tea merely by adding water. That is, the teapot held the essence of the tea—it no longer needed the tea leaves to make tea, only water. The lesson was this: that which we hold in our lives day after day, year after year, become our essence.

I was now questioning what I would hold in my life. Arrogance, greed, and tools of domination? Or empathy, compassion, and love?

I was now asking myself the question: Whom are you going to be, Kelli?

Whom are you going to be?

*Chapter 7*

# Healing

"Anger doesn't solve anything. It builds nothing,
but it can destroy everything."
Thomas S. Monson

As Dad started his third week of treatment, he began to improve. No longer did he experience the occasional loss of balance when he walked and his spirits lifted. The radiologists confirmed the brain tumors were shrinking, reducing the pressure they placed on his brain and reducing the severity of his symptoms. Just as the radiologists had warned, Dad began to lose his hair.

Dad and his brothers were known for their thick, wavy mane. In their youth, their hair was jet black. Dad's hair started turning gray in his early thirties. He resisted the graying process by coloring his hair for many years, not always with good results. I remember taking supper to him once when I was a teen. I found him in the barn in coveralls and a black hat. I laughed and in the warmest way possible declared, "It's green. Against your black hat, your hair looks green". Dad didn't like it when I made fun of him, but I had the gall to continue, "Just let your hair color go natural, I bet it's beautiful."

Many years later, when he gave up coloring, his hair was pure white. Thick, wavy, beautifully white hair. When I was in college, a dorm-mate came down the hall and exclaimed "There's a man in the lobby with the absolute most beautiful head of white hair I've ever seen. I want hair like that!" At the county fair when people gathered and reminisced, someone eventually would talk about the men with the beautiful white hair—the Adelsperger brothers. It was the trait most people noticed first.

Now I took him to a barber shop to trim his thinning mane. As the barber combed and trimmed, gorgeous white strands fell from his scalp and landed on the floor in clumps. It was sad—it seemed a piece of Dad's identity was lost, swept into a dustpan and discarded in a flash.

At home, we found a white baseball cap with a red Ohio State football emblem. It was an item purchased with no intent to wear; meant to sit on the shelf like a trophy to boast about his team's national championship. Boasting no longer mattered. The white OSU cap became the permanent replacement for his beautiful white hair.

As he came to feel better, he wanted to be active, doing a few things he would normally do on an early fall day. I took him to the country market to get a cup of morning coffee, to the bank to make a modest transaction, and to his fields to observe the crops his business partner and friend would soon harvest.

Our community was kind. I saw a neighbor at the bank who told me a story about Dad plowing the snow out of their driveway in the winter. I saw a high school classmate, a guy I once dated, who wanted me to know he wished Dad well. Last, I saw a family friend. His eyes welled with tears as he looked me in the eye: "Ann?"

Most say I look like my Dad, but this man clearly thought I was my mother. He marveled over the years that had passed since he had seen me and gushed over the fact that I looked so much like my mom.

My relationship with my hometown was one of mixed feelings. I loved growing up in a small town. It was the definition of community—a happy place virtually untouched by modern day nemeses like crime, drugs, corruption, and poverty. The community was wealthy. If it did not have financial wealth, the community was rich with kind, caring, and helpful people.

Our family friend, John, was one of those great people. He owned the general store and ran the post office. When I was eight, I rode my bike to his store to get milk. John watched out for me, and as I grew up, John was sometimes the official coach and usually the unofficial coach too, of my sports teams. He taught me how to play ball and taught me to be a good sport. John kept an eye on me as I grew older and always ensured I represented my family and my community well.

In high school, I began getting exposure to bigger communities through various school competitions. Kids from other schools laughed at my high school friends and me. They laughed at our clothes, our lack of exposure to emerging trends like cable television and MTV, and our humble skills in every competition from sports to music to science fairs. When I applied to colleges, I learned my skills didn't quite stack up to other kids' skills. They'd had the opportunity to take advanced high school courses such as calculus and could participate in debate teams—things that my small rural school did not offer. I felt sheltered like there was more to the world than I could see. I wanted to know what I didn't know; to see what I couldn't see.

My parents had always planned for me to go to college, and now I had a reason of my own! I caught the competition bug—I wanted to show those who thought they were better than me and my small-town cohorts that they were wrong.

I remember the day I received my Ohio State acceptance letter. No one was home when I got the mail, but I'd see my parents later that night at the high school basketball game. At half time, I spotted my parents in the stands. In my cheerleading uniform, I ran up the steps, eager to share my good news. I handed the letter to my parents and yelled, "I got in! I got in!" My parents glowed with pride.

Later, a group of family friends sitting around my parents crushed my pride when they responded with "Why do you want to go to college? You'll be just a number on that big campus. You'll never make it. You'll be back."

The voices around me were begging me to rewrite my life into something more familiar to them; something like a local job, getting married and settling down into a traditional family, and giving my time and talents to my kid's activities while enjoying a modest lifestyle that honored the community's traditions and beliefs. I grappled with that for a while, but in the end, I took in all the negative energy around me and transformed it into fuel. It fueled me to break the bonds of our community's expectations; to go to college to disprove my naysayers; to see what I could do and who I could be.

I earned my college degree, got a job with one of the best companies in the world, grew my skills in a field that virtually no one in my community understood, and scaled that corporate ladder like a mountaineer. I occasionally looked back, wanting to see signs that the community acknowledged my success. If they measured success by income—I had it! If they measured success by title—I had them. If they measured success by the ranking of companies I worked for or by the number of people I led—I had that too.

However, that nod of approval never came.

Now I was back home with a broken heart, and those people were reaching out to comfort and support me. Now it was easy to see—money, title, and power did not define success. All that mattered was being a good person: being kind, compassionate, and understanding. When I showed up with these traits, they gave me kindness, compassion, and understanding in return.

Certainly, I was home for my dad. Somehow, though, I was also there for myself. Living in the house I grew up in, getting reacquainted with old friends, and visiting places I hadn't seen for many years was like traveling back through time, revisiting ideas and life patterns formed long ago. It was an opportunity to rethink distorted beliefs and self-judgments; to revisit old wounds, heal them, and let them go.

I thought back to the days after Kraig received his cancer diagnosis. Even though the events were horrible, I wanted to be a part of everything my brother, mother, and father experienced. I wanted them to trust me with the information. Even though I was ten or eleven years old and my parents and their trusted advisors deemed I wasn't old enough and didn't have enough life experiences to put the information into perspective, I wanted to know everything there was to know. I wanted them to include me in the army of people who were fighting for Kraig. I especially wanted to be with my mom and dad. Mom and Dad, however, had decided I was better off living with a family a mile down the road, keeping up a normal routine of going to school, sitting at the kitchen table each night eating dinner with family, and going to church on Sundays. Mom and Dad spent their nights sleeping in a visitor's chair in Kraig's hospital room 100 miles away in Michigan. On rare occasions, I got to visit him with my parents. I asked questions, only to receive ambiguous information.

Now, as Dad's treatments progressed, Michaela had taken to texting me every day during her school lunch hour, begging to know more information; begging for updates about Dad. I responded, giving only ambiguous information to save her feelings and avoid her having to worry.

Touching those memories now made me realize I did not like my parent's decision to leave others to care for me and to shield me from the truth. Now, thirty-five years later, I could see, Michaela was just like me. Michaela was experiencing that deep-seated need to know and need that I include her just as I had had that need all those years ago. I now saw my brother's illness through my mother and father's eyes. I now had the opportunity to handle this situation differently—not only for Michaela's sake but also for my sake—to heal the wounds born out of separation from my parents thirty-five years before. I vowed to keep Michaela close in my heart and to share information with her freely. I began texting her and called her to tell her everything. When the details were horrible, and she didn't have the life experience to put them into perspective, I explained the context and helped her learn.

Though radiation and steroids were reducing the size of Dad's tumors and the symptoms that went with them, there was still the issue of Dad's blood sugar levels.

For a healthy person, a blood sugar reading above 100 is concerning. However, the steroids Dad was taking caused his blood sugar to be unstable. Dad's blood sugar levels had been running in the high 300's since his cancer treatments started. This high level had long-term, damaging effects, but this wasn't the doctor's concern. They were only concerned about immediate dangers that could end Dad's life before cancer had run its course. It was the best we could do given his treatments. I was mindful of the types and quantities of food Dad was eating to keep his blood sugar as low as possible, and I took his sugar readings religiously: four times a day.

The doctors warned that Dad could also experience *low* blood sugar, and if he did, it would require immediate attention. I kept orange juice, strawberries, and peanut butter crackers on hand in case he had a low reading, but we hadn't seen anything below 200 since I'd started taking his measurements.

Until one Friday night. It had been a particularly busy day, with visits to two different doctors, a radiation appointment, a two-hour visit with the lawyer, lunch out, errands, and visits from five different friends and family members. After supper, his blood sugar was 54—it was very low. I noticed his hands trembling, so I told him he had to eat. He yelled back in a defiant, stern voice: "I will not eat more food!" Like a punished child, I retreated.

I never wanted to fight with my father, especially not now. Still, as I walked away, I knew I was right—I knew he had to eat. More importantly, I knew his life could very well depend on me to getting him through this moment. I called a friend to go over the facts and verified I was right. Together we determined what foods would best raise his blood sugar. I returned to Dad, giving him strawberries, orange juice, and peanut butter and crackers. Then I sat with him, observing his behavior, and retaking his blood sugar to make sure he was okay. My cousin Brad arrived for a visit while I waited. I told him what had just happened and he insisted on giving Dad a Coke. After a few brief moments, Dad was his usual self again. Now he was angry.

"You're trying to kill me!" he yelled.

I was shocked. It was the farthest thing from the truth—I was trying to preserve every minute I had with my father. I was trying to heal our relationship and trying to regain all that we had lost between us over the years. His words stung.

Dad's anger was not new to me. I was first acquainted with it as a kid when Dad came in from the fields for lunch growling. "Fucking machinery...Fucking Mexicans..." he'd unload with a fiery roar. I'd sit frozen in the family room watching my father let loose expletives in a way that made him nearly unrecognizable. After Dad ate and left the house, Mom found a way to explain his rage away, so I forgot the explosions I witnessed in my early childhood and the fears that they created. I remembered only the caring, loving man I saw more often.

Later in life, Mom had a harder time explaining away his blowups. As a teen, I witnessed Dad's anger in his office as he paid bills when all he could say in a slow dramatic drawl was "Jesus Christ" each time he picked up a slip of paper listing how much money he would have to spend. I also saw his anger in the fields—I was the target of his cursing and boiling anger when he drove the tomato harvester, and I drove the tractor and wagon beside him to haul the tomatoes he was harvesting. He would howl and yell from his driver's seat fifteen yards away from me. He apparently wanted me to go left, go right, speed up, or slow down, but clear communication was not forthcoming. As he worked himself up into a crescendo, his sentences would become laced with exclamations of "Jesus Christ" and "God damn." All he could do was grit his teeth, shake his fists tight in the air, then wave his hands until eventually, through trial and error, I did what he wanted. In my teenage years, I took his anger personally. I thought I was the cause and I tried hard to figure out what I did wrong so I could avoid it. However, I never could. It was all

I could do to laugh his anger off. Then in my twenties, his anger just drove me away.

I'm not quite sure where this rage came from, but it was clear Dad was mad at anything he could not control; that didn't go his way. Moreover, he seemed to be directing his anger towards those closest to him—his siblings, his mother, his wife, and me.

I can only surmise Dad's anger with his siblings was rooted in the overwhelming responsibility he took on when his father, Cecil, died. Dad was just twenty-six years old, and the oldest of four children—a young man forced to step up and farm a hefty 1,100 acres and fill the void his father had left behind. At the time, one brother was in college, the other was in the military, and his sister was just out of high school. When Cecil died, Dad farmed the family property and took over the responsibility of cash renting land from neighbors and friends. He took on the responsibility of working for young and old landowners, including his mother—people who depended on the land rent income as their means of living—convincing them he would be successful and able to pay the land rent. He dedicated himself to being that necessary success, but he seemingly was angry with anyone, particularly his siblings, who didn't also make the necessary sacrifices and dedicate their time and energy to the farm in the same way he did.

One brother, Larry, took a path that led away from the farm. His sister Martha married and was not involved in the farm either. When his brother Mike got out of the military, Dad welcomed him into the operation as an equal. They created a corporation, each holding equal shares, and they grew a farming business of their own beyond their inheritance. They both had wives and two kids and were a glorious success.

Then Kraig died. Dad surely experienced anger during Kraig's battle with cancer and after his death. I can't say I ever saw that anger—but it is one of the natural stages of grief. Dad undoubtedly suppressed it for the sake of his wife and me.

Then a few years later, Mike got a divorce. He and Dad were forced to split up the farm they'd built so that Mike could give his wife her fair share of assets from the settlement. Dad saw Mike's divorce and the subsequent business breakup as an unnecessary penalty he had to suffer for what he saw as Mike's mistake. To make matters worse, their mother granted Mike use of the land and barns at the farm she owned. This development shattered Dad. Together, Mike and Dad had farmed 1,400 acres. After Mike's divorce, Dad farmed 600 acres and had no shop to repair equipment and no barn to store machinery. Now he was angry with both Mike and his mother, and he directed his anger at his siblings. He was angry that he had to rebuild.

From a business perspective, Dad managed his predicament well and rebuilt his farm. However, he never recovered emotionally. He'd take another kick in the shins when his mother passed on. She left him a modest sum of cash but no share of land in the family farm. Dad was angry that he gave so much following his father's death and was left without any material assets from his parents to show for it.

A few years later came Mom and Dad's separation and divorce. Once again, he had to divide the assets with another stakeholder, leaving him with just a quarter of the value of the assets and a quarter of the acreage he once cared for at the height of his career. A lingering love for his wife would douse the fiery anger that boiled within him, but it was still there.

As Dad's health issues mounted, his physical ability to earn a living became limited. He had a profusion of healthcare bills draining the modest savings he had managed to keep since his divorce settlement. He flirted with a growing amount of anger every time he experienced a medical complication. Although he managed to control his anger in the presence of nurses, doctors, and visitors, when we were alone, his rage percolated. When he didn't get what he wanted, even a simple thing like the food he requested in the hospital room, he gritted his teeth and clenched his fists and tightened every cell in his body as he choked back venomous words. Sometimes he let the emotion and the words out—and he pointed them at me. I should have been happy he was releasing his pain; it was far better to release it than to hold it in, but I was not prepared to be the recipient.

Each time Dad had an emergency, I overcame my distaste for his anger so I could help him and love him, but each time I showed up, his anger repelled me when it came seeping out. He projected unkind and unloving judgments onto me when all I wanted was his willingness to be in my life and to be good enough for him.

The blood sugar incident was the first time since he'd received his diagnosis that he vented his anger. Logic would say neither his sugar reading nor his angry outburst was my fault. Everyone, even my cousin Brad and my dad, must have known that I was not trying to kill him. I reminded myself it was natural and denying him the opportunity to express his feelings just might make it worse. Besides, it was a chance for me to respond differently— better—than I ever had before.

That day, I listened to Dad yell and sloughed off his stinging words. I resisted the temptation to fight back. I learned to handle unearned blame and to resist the temptation strike back with my anger. I didn't pass my pain back to Dad, and I didn't hold on to it, for holding on would only create an emotional cancer in me. I simply let it go.

Eventually, a friend from Macon would exchange emails with me and would help me see that Dad was not angry with me, rather angry at his situation. The way Dad expressed his love and care was by providing for everyone around him. He farmed to provide for his mother, brothers, and sister when Cecil died. He farmed to provide for his wife and children. He offered the skills he'd learned on the farm to the community for volunteer projects. He gave his love by providing food, shelter, fun, and protective care to the people he loved. As life changes reduced his assets and health challenges restricted his ability to farm, Dad grew increasingly fearful he'd no longer be able to provide for his family and himself. Losing his ability to provide meant losing his ability to love. Fear filled the void, and fear simply slipped out as anger.

I came to accept that his anger and the pain it caused him was not my fault. This insight applied not only to my relationship with my dad but also with every relationship I had. I would learn to see that other people's anger was just that, something others owned, not something I was responsible for because I wasn't good enough or I didn't do something right. I would learn to accept that I was not responsible for other's pain, and I could not take their pain away. I learned I can love others, and if they want help, I can help them learn to release their anger in healthy ways so that love can fill the space anger once held, but I cannot make their anger go away. By resisting the temptation to meet other's anger with anger of my own, I could make my world better, and perhaps the world of those around me better, too. Though Dad did not serve as the best role model on how to bring love into the world, he could help me understand why it was so important.

Most days were difficult, but most did not involve near death experiences, and most were easier for Dad and me to be together. In fact, some days uncovered beautiful things if I was wise enough to see them.

One day, I had a few moments alone, so I went for a drive. When I saw the house of our lifelong friends, Tom and Irene, a wealth of memories welled up. My parents did most everything with them in the seventies, eighties, and early nineties. I even lived with them for a few months when Kraig was ill. They had been a great comfort in extremely difficult times. Tom and Irene were fun and hardworking, too. They prepared food and decorated the house for my high school graduation and turned a Memorial Day picnic into an engagement celebration for Denny and me. When they helped us move our wedding gifts from Ohio to our home on the East coast, they hung lingerie and "just married" signs on the RV, helping to turn a boring drive into an adventure. They were family. I made an impromptu stop.

When Irene saw me from her window, she immediately came outside and greeted me on the front porch, holding her arms wide open. There were no words. I simply buried my head in her warm embrace and cried, releasing much of the grief built up in the past days. I was blessed to have such special people who cared for me nearby.

On another night, my mom invited Dad and me to dinner. Spending time with my parents and eating dinner out should have been a normal, guilt-free event—a blessing. Nonetheless, as I flitted back and forth between the bedroom and bathroom I lived in as a teenager, getting dressed and styling my hair, so I looked my best, I heard my teenage friends condemning me: "You're spoiled!"

Some family and friends believed I had a challenging childhood, for experiencing the death of a sibling and living through my parents' subsequent depression and eventual divorce was not exactly a fairytale experience. On the other hand, it created a space for many extended family members and family friends to be compassionate and helpful during those difficult years. I became a little extra special to them.

Others believed I had an easy childhood because my parents fared well financially—I didn't have to work for life's necessities, and I enjoyed some of life's pleasures. People who struggled to put food on the table found it unfair that I had a pool in my backyard. Others raised in families where the children were expected to earn money to buy a car found it distasteful that I had a new car at sixteen without working to earn money to buy it. The two dynamics—extra attention and financial ease—combined to create the notion that I was spoiled.

I didn't want that label. It was not something I chose; it was merely the circumstances in which I found myself. I would have preferred my brother instead of the extra attention and to have the love of unbroken parents instead of a swimming pool. So, I resisted what I saw as an unfair title and defended myself when others kids claimed I was spoiled, but to no avail. The notion persisted, and I grew tired of trying to change the perception. I settled in and enjoyed the things my parents provided; I basked in the attention my parent's friends and our family gave me.

Now, all these years later, those old insecurities surfaced again. No one said it aloud. Maybe they didn't even think it, but I certainly did. Just being in my bathroom trying to look my best, that notion was back: Kelli was spoiled. I was forced to re-examine it.

All these years, I'd bought into their logic, even as I resisted the label. I subconsciously agreed that I didn't deserve all the fine things life had given me because I hadn't worked for them. I was still climbing uphill to earn all that I had, taking on big jobs, difficult goals, and non-traditional roles. I tried to lose the label through excess. The same logic applied to the attention and possessions I expected—they became rewards I thought I'd earned. Now it was clear—what people saw in my life was what they did not have. Those who did not have emotional distress in their lives saw that I did; those who did not have financial means saw that I did. I accepted the fact that I was guilty of expecting better as my right and in that moment, I chose to change. I now understood I created my life based on my beliefs. I would no longer believe in being spoiled—it could no longer define me. I unearthed memories, watched them replay, let other's perceptions of me go, and listened to my healthier thoughts.

So, that night I enjoyed a nice dinner with my parents—without guilt. It was a joy to feel like a daughter again; a rare moment in which I didn't have to care for dad or worry about Mom's reactions. A beautiful thing happened. Because I was no longer holding a defense against anything that could make me appear spoiled, I could hear my parents speak with love. Though unrehearsed, they both had a message for me. In unison, they agreed, "Kel, you need roots. You've moved your family around, but it is time for you to settle. You need roots." I didn't feel the need to fight back. I didn't slough off their message. I knew there was wisdom in their words, and I was blessed to hear them deliver their message in harmony. I was blessed to feel like a daughter once more.

Shortly after that night, I went to my cousin Laura's house and crashed the birthday party she and her husband Chris were having for their daughter. It was a simple gathering. No elaborate themes, no fad foods, and no outrageously expensive gifts as I had come to experience in Washington. There was a smiling, sun-tanned twelve-year-old at the center of attention, surrounded by four generations of loving family, and modest birthday gifts offered from the heart. I was awestruck by the joy that radiated from them.

All these things made me aware of the elaborate lifestyle I led and made me wonder—could I be happy trading the stress-filled job and the lush income for something simpler? Could I be happy living with less money and richer relationships?

Eventually, this trip and this time with Dad had to end. Before I left, Dad and I reviewed the doctor's advice again. Though he recommended hospice care, we hadn't pursued it yet. It was too hard. Accepting hospice care forced both of us to accept the notion that death was near. Our lack of action implied we weren't ready to accept that yet. When I scheduled my flight back to Washington, it seemed prudent to have hospice situated to help if needed. We soon met a nurse we liked and scheduled her for regular visits. Dad's sister, Martha, also arranged to spend a week caring for Dad while I was gone.

The night before I left, Dad and I enjoyed a glass of wine together outside on the deck under the full moon. It was a beautiful fall night. The sky was clear, the crickets were chirping, and a heavy dew hung in the crisp autumn air. We talked about the house and how much it meant to him. He gave his apologies to whoever would live there next—he felt he hadn't invested in its upkeep and that the new residents would have a lot of work to do.

I remembered the days when Mom and Dad built the house. After moving our belongings to Grandma's basement for storage, and moving the family to a small apartment for temporary living, Dad tore down the century-old farmhouse we had lived in to make way for our new home. He took care to save windows, doors, and posts—anything that could be useful in the future—then tore the house down with his bare hands and farm equipment. Mom combed through Better Homes and Garden magazines, gaining inspiration for the perfect design and décor. They took Mom's rough sketch plans to an architect for custom blueprints. Several family friends helped build the home—they poured the concrete for the basement, nailed every piece of wood in place to frame it, and laid the brick exterior. Mom and Dad and I spent hours staining and varnishing every oak trim board and every oak door. Dad picked out the windows and doors. Mom picked out every foot of flooring, every light fixture, and all the wallpaper. Dad and our family friend Tom designed and installed the landscaping. Years later, Dad, Tom, and my Godson Zack planted 93 evergreens by the house to serve as a windbreak. The evergreens were two feet tall when they were planted. They were now 20 feet tall. The house was a labor of love. How could I relinquish Dad's house, all the things it stood for, and all its potential—how could I relinquish that to anyone else?

With that thought, I began dreaming of living here again.

My cousin's husband, Chris, drove by that night, saw the two of us outside, and stopped to join us. Chris had a knack for irritating people. Maybe he stood up for himself and his family with a bit more abrasiveness than people expect, or maybe he joked about things that were uncomfortably close to the truth, or maybe he made that one raw comment that just gets in your craw and makes you uncomfortable. Whatever the reason, most perceived Chris as an irritant. This quality did not apply for me. Chris always minded his manners when I was around. If he slipped and said something inappropriate, I could shoot back in return.

I'm sure Chris had come from a cornfield down the road and had downed several beers while sitting on the tailgate of his truck shooting the shit with the guys. He wasn't the wine-drinking type, but he was kind and had a glass with us while we talked. Though he hadn't heard but a few sentences of our conversation, Chris seemingly knew the thoughts about Dad's house running through my head, and he encouraged me further. "You know, Kelli," he said in that extra deep voice and long, slow drawl that begged you to listen, "You and Denny could farm this farm. The farm would provide a good living. It's a good simple life here. You could enjoy it." He smiled with the joy he knew from his life on the farm—from the simple life that he knew. He raised his eyebrows as if challenging me.

He was like an unpolished angel with a message from beyond. Chris gave me something real to consider for my journey back to Seattle.


Years earlier I had left Dad to go to college, then to start my first job six hundred miles away, and then when he walked me down the aisle to marry my husband. However, this was the hardest departure of all. Had I done enough for his health and well-being? Had I taken care of his emotional wounds and my own? Had I used this time to its fullest and healed our relationship as much as I could?

The next day, my father-in-law waited in the truck, ready to take me to the airport. My aunt stood in the kitchen having agreed to stand in for me to measure Dad's blood sugar and to give insulin shots. Dad and I stood in the hall in a long embrace. A deathly thought ran through my mind—would I get to see him again? It saddened me to know that we both still had so much work to do on us—for our own good. I wondered if we would get the chance to continue that work. I cried. At that moment, Dad collected himself and became the comforting father I knew from long ago. "It will be all right, Kel," he said. "Everything will be all right."

*Chapter 8*

# Saying "Yes" to Life

"I will not die an unlived life."

Dawna Markova

Somehow, I left Dad, trusting his promise. I was numb during the flight but came alive again when I arrived home and saw my kids. Though my energy felt muted, I fell right back into the routine I left—right back into my harried lifestyle and right back into work.

I tracked how I had used my waking hours on my first evening back in Seattle. I spent one hour getting ready for work, two hours commuting to and from work, eleven hours working, and one hour at home with Denny and the kids. This schedule was a typical day. I did this—and my peers did this—to keep our jobs and our favorable positions with leadership. If we didn't put in the long hours and stay in good graces, leadership would find someone else that would. After awaking to the things in life that eminently mattered, I was sad we had created such an intense reality.

I was changing; the company was not. The demands, the deadlines, the intellectual antagonism, the meetings, the projects, the scorecards, and the people were still unrelenting. No one cared about my dad or what he was experiencing. No one cared about the doctors, the lawyers, the needles, and events I'd experienced. No one cared about my well-being, or that my dad could die. The feeling was mutual—I didn't care about work. I was living in another world where life and all its loving, healing, learning, and growing were in a fragile state. These were the things that mattered most—living, loving, healing, learning, and growing. I cared only to give my time and energy to these things. I now saw work for what it had become—a diversion from the things that mattered most. I showed up for work each day; I did my job, but I saved my heart for my kids, for I truly missed them, and of course, for my father, 2,500 miles away.

My heart was also hurting and needed a little TLC for the road ahead. I respected the need to be kind to myself, to heal, and to renew. I had given so much to my career over the past twenty-eight years. I had given extraordinary time and energy to my employer in the short two years I had been there, especially in the war room. Now, I cut back the extra hours I gave to work to save a little time for me.

Denny had always been there for me. He supported me when I struggled in college, listened as I adapted to new jobs and cultures, found my keys and badge as I rushed to get to work, and talked me through countless trying business situations. However, this time, with just a week together before he flew off to Ohio to take a few weeks to care for Dad, we struggled to connect. I'm certain Denny wanted to help me, but the months and years leading up to this moment had been increasingly difficult for us. Our marriage was still broken. In the few moments this week offered for us to be a couple, we simply looked at each other with emptiness, having no idea how to fix our relationship and no energy even to try.

I can't point to a single event or a single topic that caused our relationship to strain, but our marital challenges eventually manifested themselves in our personal finances. We were now in our mid-forties, a time in which we thought we'd be financially secure. We had been raised to spend conservatively, invest wisely, and save for our future. We did, to some extent, but we were far from secure, for with that big income came big dreams and big expectations. We spent big, and we lived on the edge.

Back in 2006, before Dad got sick and I was working in Cleveland, our financial stresses led to blows. Our lives were designed to live on my salary, and my bonus was just that, a bonus. I never intended my bonus for day-to-day living expenses. However, that year my very generous bonus was used up, spent, and gone within weeks of receiving it. Discovering this was an earth-shattering experience for me. I was stunned. I had dedicated so much more time, energy, and soul to my work than I expected when I first started working. I shouldered stress, difficult-to-handle personalities, extra hours, and time away from my family. It was natural that I looked to the bonus as a reward and I felt robbed of the benefit when it was gone.

I took care of the bills early in our marriage. Like my father, I knew almost to the penny how much money was in the bank, how much was owed, and how much we could spend. My brain was like a fine-tuned computer system, nicely keeping financial figures tucked into categories and quickly computed for balances. I knew where we stood at any given moment, and I guided my spending with this internal financial compass. When Denny became a stay-at-home-Dad, he took over the bills.

I didn't understand our issues at the time, but I eventually acknowledged we valued different things and those value differences manifested through our finances. I valued family adventures to new places like the beach and Disney World; investments that developed family bonds and enabled growth through experiences. Denny valued the development of family bonds too, but through hard work and household chores. I valued a modest but fashionable wardrobe and cars that kept us looking classy; he valued clothes and automobiles that functioned but weren't pricey. We struggled to reconcile these beliefs. Denny didn't manage us to a budget—he didn't say, "we spent more on vacation than we planned, so either we can curtail our spending on clothes, or we can stop eating out for three months." He just paid the bills and added debt when we spent more than we made. I didn't like this approach. I wanted a plan on how we'd spend our money and agreed upon adjustments when things didn't go as planned, but our unreconciled differences prevented us from creating a plan we both could live with.

Over time, I lost track of our financial position. I blissfully lived without the facts, and I lost my financial compass. We kept spending money. We bought a bigger home, went on vacations, signed our kids up for the best sporting events, took on home improvement projects, bought a plethora of clothes, and more. The debt we created became more than we could finance, and Denny carried the heavy truth alone. We were on a crash course. Only when my bonus disappeared in such a short time did the truth of our situation became clear to me.

Once the financial realities were exposed, Denny resented me for my carefree spending. "I didn't spend it," he'd innocently say. It was true that I spent more on the kids, the house, and myself than he spent on himself, and it was true that Denny pinched pennies when it came to groceries and car maintenance, but it wasn't true that he didn't spend. He went on every vacation, went to every sporting event, drank every bottle of wine, and signed the same mortgage payment plan that I did. I resented Denny for refusing to take ownership. I resented him for simply writing checks until there was no money, versus planning and keeping our actual expenses within the budget. I resented him for failing to hold healthy conversations about money all along.

After the truth had come out and we got past the initial fiery feud, we tried desperately to correct our situation. We made some smart financial adjustments, but we never really got to the cause of our spending issues. We let our mutual resentments grow instead. We unconsciously began perfecting the art of masking the issues. We improved our ability to put on a good face for others, showing up at fund-raisers, vacations, overnight sporting events with our kids, and Christmas as if nothing were wrong. We also improved our ability to put up the façade of a good marriage for our kids, family, and friends, and even each other. Most saw through it— they might not have known money was behind our tension, but they surely could tell we lived under a cloud of contention.

Denny and I broke and became emotionally raw. Our tense conversations turned into frequent fights. We fought in front of the kids, in front of our family, and I'm certain the neighbors heard us fighting from their homes. When we weren't fighting, we were edgy and terse. The fighting was never physical, always verbal, but boy, we were good, each in our personal way. Denny was passive aggressive. He simply didn't talk, didn't weigh in on a decision, and when a financial endeavor turned out poorly, he unleashed a storm of anger. He tucked his frustration into other subjects, like politics, too. He routinely disguised his anger about our financial situation as anger toward the Democratic Party.

To Denny, Democrats spent more than they earned, and Democrats wanted something for nothing. Denny identified with the political right, particularly conservative monetary ideas, much more than me, but we were both Republicans, so politics became a great cover for his anger. I used my intellectual strength as a weapon, going toe-to-toe on every spending issue. From Denny repeatedly shrinking my clothes in the dryer, forcing me to spend more money on clothing, to the monthly American Express bill that rivaled our mortgage payments, I went to war. I backed every position I stood up for with an infallible rationale. I developed a habit of flooding Denny with facts, figures, actions, and logic until he froze. Eventually, he learned to protect himself with a defense that met and often surpassed my offense: he deflected, justified, and defended every fact I stood on. We were in a circular war. I'd attack, he'd defend and attack, and I'd counterattack. We became extremely good at the art of hurting each other with words and blaming each other. All the fighting, blaming, and yelling got us nowhere. We were in a deadlock for years.

We never left each other, though. By the grace of God, we both knew that somewhere deep inside the person whom we resented, blamed, and to some degree hated, was the person we'd married—a person we loved deeply. We also looked around us. There were countless couples losing their homes and drowning in debt. We weren't the only ones. We thought we were simply chasing the American dream and the rewards we had earned. We thought we were chasing a better life. We wrongly rooted our spending in the belief that the more we had, the more the world would see, that we were indeed successful just like the co-workers, friends, and neighbors we compared ourselves to. We spent because we thought that more and better would make us happy.

I went to great lengths to make money at work. I had to, I thought. I couldn't afford not to. After working in Cleveland seven and a half years, I took a job assignment in Detroit, keeping our home in Cleveland. I left my family on a Monday morning, drove three hours to my Michigan office, worked there for four days, and then drove home to spend three nights in my bed and the weekend with my family. There was a nice raise, and I regained a little job security (something that was slipping away at the time). This adjustment made me happy for a while, but resentment set in again as I saw Denny and the kids enjoying everything about their lives while I was alone in a hotel. I wanted to be home enjoying the kids, my husband, our beautiful home, friends, and our community. I simply wanted to be enjoying my life. Still, all I had was work and a hotel room when I was away and anxiety and fighting while I was home. I put on weight, developed chronic back pain from excessive time in the car, and I became irritable and edgy.

After two and a half years of driving back and forth to the Detroit area, I found a way out. It was a familiar path that I had leveraged before—a new job. We moved to Seattle.

The west coast would prove to be our toughest challenge yet. We skimmed by the first year with the help of a hiring bonus, but pressure mounted as that bonus evaporated. There was the promise of an annual bonus, but I quickly learned the realities of my new company's compensation system. The percentages and targets looked nice in the offer letter, but the way the company applied those percentages and targets was shockingly different from most Fortune 500 companies. In short, my bonus was less than expected. We were worse off in Seattle than we were in Ohio.

I was disappointed in myself; I had broken one of my rules: I created a situation where I needed a bonus to meet my financial commitments—I treated a bonus as a "must have" and not the "nice to have" it should have been. Perhaps we should have curbed our egos more than we did—perhaps we should have bought a smaller house in a less prestigious neighborhood. However, we had established our financial footprint.

The sense of financial obligation weighed far heavier on me now. I had to be a player in the corporate game I loathed just to make ends meet. I couldn't see it at the time, but I had unconsciously begun adapting to the culture of topping my peers and letting the promise of more money dictate my actions. I was now a player in the corporate performance and financial reward system for my financial success.

My work life grew increasingly ugly. The company brought in bright and ambitious blood at a record pace. College graduates and experienced hires alike caught on to the system and started competing with their coworkers, positioning themselves for individual gain. Meanwhile, others suffered. They belittled coworkers while amorally selling themselves, finding weaknesses and exploiting their colleagues, and hardening themselves against one another. Everyone played to win. They rallied around the strongest alphas in the company, whether male or female. As one alpha fell from grace, they quickly attached themselves to another. Many sacrificed their personal power, their careers, their sense of basic human kindness, and to a large degree, their lives, to make themselves successful and to have a shot at the storied pot of gold this game promised.

I was stuck. Our society called this competition good. I saw no way out. The longer I stayed and the harder I tried, the worse it got. I hated myself, and I hated the relationship I had fallen into with Denny.

Over time, I developed a pattern of showing up late to work. I told myself that my habitual tardiness was due to the simple fact that I had worked many hours the day before and just needed more rest. To some degree that was true, but it wasn't the full truth. Most mornings I would lie in bed with a gnawing, burning ache in my stomach. The ugliness I saw at work was manifesting in my health. When I finally found the gumption to get out of bed and face it, I was ugly to those I loved—yelling at my kids and making my husband feel small. I virtually ignored my extended family and friends because I didn't want them to see whom I had become. For a stretch of time, that gnawing, burning ache led to coughing up blood. I addressed that issue with my doctor, and the bleeding subsided, but it occurred to me that lying in a hospital bed throwing up blood might be easier than going to work.

One of my worst moments came when I was driving to work on a curvy, two-lane road. As I saw a semi barreling down the road toward me, I thought, "If I just swerved to the left and let that semi hit me, I wouldn't have to go to work. I wouldn't have to keep up this charade of being a ruthless, uncaring, power-mongering bitch."

I passed that semi without swerving, and I went in and played the game to keep money flowing. The lesson, however, was clear: I was allowing my life, my days, and my moments to be determined by the pursuit of money. Money was just a means to an end; I wanted to be kind to my kids, and I wanted a loving relationship with a husband who was working with me side-by-side for mutual life goals. I wanted to like myself and be proud of who I was all the time, including at work. I wanted to enjoy life now—all aspects of life including work—not betting I could buy the freedom to live the kind of life I truly wanted in some elusive time in the future. What good was money if I sacrificed living joyfully? What good was money if I sacrificed loving my kids, loving my husband, and loving myself to get it?

Nonetheless, here I was with Denny, a few short days before he'd fly cross-country to care for my Dad. We stood face-to-face and empty. Like battleships passing in the dark of night, we silently agreed to share the same space without aggression. It was the best we could muster.

Denny soon flew to Ohio, relieved Dad's sister of her duties and settled in to care for my dad for three weeks. I stayed in Washington, attending to my emotional wounds, the kids, our home, and my job. Denny and I usually shared these duties; I should have felt overwhelmed. I was at peace with them.

Shortly into my stint as a single mom, our middle daughter made a plea: "Mom, can I have a Halloween party?"

In a flash, I remembered how I had reacted to such a request before facing cancer with Dad. I was edgy, snapping back at the kids' requests, scorning them for not appreciating money. I missed soccer games, school plays, an occasional parent-teacher conference, and countless family dinners to make money and I couldn't find it in my heart to spend it on them.

This time, I didn't snap. Instead of seeing a Halloween party as a financial drain and time burden, I saw an opportunity to change my habits. I didn't think of time constraints, the potential damage to the house, my stressed mental state, or the challenge of being the only adult in a house full of teenagers. I didn't even think about the unrelenting topic of money. All I thought about was living. "Sure," I said. "It's for my soccer team . . . seventeen girls," she clarified. "Sure," I said. "It's a sleepover," she added. I didn't hesitate. "Sure." Having heard this, my youngest daughter anted up, "Well, if she gets a Halloween party, I want one too." "Sure," I replied.

Five days later, I pulled off two wonderful Halloween parties. I treated seventeen sixteen-year-old girls to pizza, a night at a haunted house, a bonfire, a night of scary movies, then breakfast before they left the next day. That same day I cleaned up the house and pulled off an evening Halloween party for thirteen ten-year-old girls.

This new attitude repeated itself over and over. "Mom, can I go to homecoming with Michael?" I didn't look for reasons to say no: Is Michael into drugs? How much will the dress cost? How are you getting there? Instead, I said, "Sure, we'll go shopping Tuesday after work, and I can drive you and a group of your friends to the dance if you'd like."

When 5:00 rolled around each workday, I kindly said to myself, "Allow yourself to go home, work will be here tomorrow. No one will die if you don't get this done tonight."

The thing is, each time I had a choice, I chose to live. Even when I didn't think I had a choice, I discovered I did. I kept making a choice to live. Despite the money, despite the time. Dad's terminal illness was already changing my life. I was letting go of constraints. I was focusing on the possibilities. I was saying yes to life. I was allowing myself to do what made me happy.

I was looking my employer in the eye and saying, "You will not take what I love away from me." Instead of fitting my life to my job, I was living my life as I wanted—and if my life didn't fit my job, I'd have to change my job, not my life!

Denny had two wonderful weeks with Dad. The radiation had the intended impact—the tumors had shrunk, minimizing the effects on Dad's health. His eyesight was better than before radiation, he no longer experienced imbalances, his energy had returned. He was spending his time doing the things he loved: outside enjoying the fall sun, watching farmers harvest, and participating in activities to tidy up the farm and prepare for winter.

The third week, however, brought a different experience. Dad had chosen to try chemotherapy to treat the lung cancer. The last week of October, his oncologist gave him a very heavy dose of drugs to take his cells to the brink of death, where good healthy cells have the ability to regenerate and keep the body alive and cancerous cells simply die because they cannot regenerate. This dose of chemotherapy was strong and took Dad closer to death than anyone planned. Denny experienced some scary moments and eventually decided to take Dad to the hospital. Dad came close to death, but he survived, staying in the hospital for a week as the doctors and nurses cared for him. He came home just in time for Denny to fly back to Washington. I didn't know how bad Dad was until Denny got home and told me in person.

Denny and I spent one night together in Washington. Neither of us had it in us to care for the other. We were compassionate, but we were two individuals on two different missions that happened to land in the same bed on the same night, both of us hurting and wanting care, but neither of us emotionally able to give to the other. Without restoring my marriage, I hopped on a plane and flew back to Ohio to settle in for the long haul.

*Chapter 9*

# Ambition, Strength, and Courage

"You never know how strong you are until being strong
is the only choice you have."
Unknown

It was now early November. I had missed Dad's good days—
the days after radiation had shrunk the brain tumors and the
symptoms they were causing—the days after Dad had accepted
his diagnosis and his will to live was at its highest. By the time
I returned, his determination to beat his cancer was still alive
but not as vibrant. Our days and nights were filled with the little
things—making meals, doing laundry, running the occasional
errand, and visiting the doctor. Friends visited, some bringing
food, all bringing comfort in conversation. Dad and I often sat
in silence, both of us staring at the TV, working separately on our
emotions, beliefs, and ability to love each other. Each night, Dad
went to bed early. I usually followed close behind him, ready to
get lost in sleep.

One or two nights a week, I meditated before falling asleep. Most nights, it was difficult to quiet my mind. However, on other nights, I slid into a deep meditative state. In one meditation, I saw a vision of sand dollars in shallow water as a bald eagle soared above. I knew that Dad was giving me those sand dollars. Dad loved walking the gulf coast beaches of Florida in search of sand dollars, and he found many. In my mind's eye, Dad was giving me the treasures he loved in life. During my meditations, I would talk to Dad; I learned that I had loved my children in a way he could not love me. It helped me see that Dad was proud of whom I'd become, even if he couldn't tell me. Meditating was my only spiritual practice while I lived with Dad.

One of Dad's closest friends, David, came to get him every Wednesday night. They went to the local Moose Lodge for dinner and some light games of chance. Another friend, Bill, came every other Tuesday night to take Dad to the township trustee meeting. He enjoyed these nights out, and I came to enjoy them as well—my great escapes. They took Dad's older truck, so I took his new one, affectionately referred to as "Big Red." Dad had bought Big Red in May but had driven it only three or four times before his eyesight started failing. He reverted to the familiarity of his older pickup; first driving it, then riding in it. On the nights Dad left the house with someone else, I took the driver's seat in Big Red to get some shopping done.

Then there came a night that it all struck me. Here I was at the gates of hell, knowing my dad's life would soon end, driving a bad ass, bright red pickup truck down straight, flat, barren back roads fit for drag racing. I could see thousands of stars in the black sky as I belted out every word to Jason Aldean's My Kinda Party, a thunderous country rock anthem—I hadn't listened to country music since I was a teenager. This life was vastly different from the way of life I lived out West—a life that involved swarms of four-door sedans that filled the meandering mountain foothill roads or eight-lane highways that I would take to run errands. In that other world, I listened to lesser-known folk rock musicians like the Avett Brothers in my family-sensible SUV as I made my way to upscale shops and organic restaurants. I gasped as I realized my life was changing amidst all of this. My life was coming full circle. I was embracing my home.

I continued to work remotely, maintaining a delicate balance—I kept enough free time to care for and enjoy Dad while working just enough to be a solid contributor at work. On these days, I found my job a healthy diversion from the hell of the medical system. I truly enjoyed working with my colleagues, completing projects, and finding ways the organization could avoid future disasters. The distance continued to give me perspective too.

One day in November, there was a meeting for all employees in our division. Only a quarter of the division attended in person. Everyone else streamed in from around the world. Immersed in my hometown's way of life, I got to see leadership from afar. The VP looked dapper on a stage, covering various scorecards, applauding some projects, and holding the employees that worked on them on a pedestal for us to applaud. One-by-one, the VP's direct reports covered goals and their organization's performance against them. There were customized, fast-paced, morale-boosting music videos intended to intensify emotions. The videos were crafted in the company's film department and designed to emphasize key business points. During breaks, oodles of food and more music were available to keep the attendees happy. There was an open forum for questions with answers designed to enhance the company's image as an industry leader and stage lighting that made leadership look like a bunch of Hollywood stars. It was a finely crafted event.

The best leaders I had known had a clear and inspiring vision, effectively communicated that vision, recruited a team with diverse strengths, nurtured a highly functioning team, actively removed barriers to success, and motivated the team to achieve the vision. I didn't see that. I saw a scorecard, but not a vision. I saw a collection of strong individuals, but individuals that didn't know how to work together as a team—they often knocked their teammates behind their backs. Though there was some diversity on the team, they struggled to convince anyone to value these strengths and perspectives. They could tell us to remove barriers, but they couldn't model the behavior for us. And the only motivation I witnessed was fear: fear of missing a measure on a scorecard; fear of getting a poor performance review; fear of losing the job. On stage, leadership was a scripted marketing event. Off stage, leadership was spread thin so it could do nothing but drive people harder and manage the resulting crises.

It made me think long and hard about how I was showing up in the world and what kind of leader I wanted to be. Was the best leader the person that made the best speech, was the most admired, was the most feared, made the most money, or led the most people? Did method even matter if success was the outcome? Could it be that the best leader was someone that made a difference in the world—someone that made a positive difference in *others'* lives?

At that moment, I knew my ambition is to be the kind of leader that makes a positive difference in other's lives like I was doing for Dad.


I pushed all that from my mind. Soon I would set my sights on the holidays. I was determined to give Dad a wonderful Thanksgiving and my family beautiful memories. I also dared to look past Thanksgiving into December and made plans for Christmas and New Year's too. I would fly my family cross-country to join Dad and me not once, but twice. Given our financial situation, I didn't know how I would pay for four flights in November and four more in December, but I knew I couldn't live with myself if I didn't. I put the expense on credit and trusted my financial obligations to the future.

Denny and the kids arrived a few days before Thanksgiving Day. Dad's spirits lifted with their energy in his house. I had cleaned out the guest bedroom, which Dad didn't use as such. It had only been a storage space holding dreams of the life that could have been if Kraig had had the chance to occupy that room. It made me happy to make the room into a space for life and living—a space for my three kids. The room was small, but with a bunk bed and an air mattress, bedding on loan from family, and a nightstand, lights, and accessories found in Dad's storage areas, I managed to create a functional and comfortable bedroom for my three kids without spending a dime.

Again, I was finding new ways to live—I didn't go out and buy the highest quality and most fashionable bedding, I found a way to get what my family needed without the expense. This frugality was very different for me. I had always relied on myself—my ability to make money and buy for myself. I had always been the provider—for myself, my family, my Mom, and even at times, my extended family members. Being in the position to be provided for was new to me. I wrestled with it a bit, but I allowed it. I had to. I was emotionally spent and financially strapped by providing for a home and a way of life back in Seattle. Now I had to rely on family and friends.

I gathered all the kitchen furnishings needed to make a Thanksgiving dinner. I borrowed everything from measuring cups to dishes to a roaster for the turkey. It was just my family of five, Dad, my aunt—and in a beautiful gesture of forgiving and forgetting—my mother joined us as well.

This holiday was the first time our family had been together in that kitchen since the glory days of the seventies and eighties. The last time was in 1992 for Cody's first birthday party. Eighteen years had passed. Eighteen years of darkness in a kitchen designed to host family celebrations. Here we were, healing our wounds and gathering with the next generation, knowing this could be Dad's last Thanksgiving with us. Emotions were heavy, yet spirits were high. We had the courage to face the past and present for the benefit of the future.

It was tough to see Denny and the kids return to Washington. I enjoyed their energy, for it was a sharp contrast to the life I was living as I cared for my dad. My kids were, in fact, naturally "alive" while Dad was struggling to maintain his liveliness. I enjoyed knowing there were others in the house to handle whatever might happen—that I was not alone. I also enjoyed Dad's lifted spirits. Then, as soon as the kids and Denny left, Dad and I sunk back into our slow, low energy routine.

He was still taking chemotherapy at the local hospital. It was a much lighter dose than the one he received in October that nearly killed him. This session was a long shot, and it made him tired and weak.

I was still taking Dad's sugar readings four times a day and administering the correlating amount of insulin. Dad's sugar readings remained very high, always above 200, most often above 300, and sometimes in the 400s. I worried about these readings but never did I see the imminent danger with them.

Then there came a day in early December when I woke to a loud "THUD" from Dad's bedroom. It was 7:00 a.m., the time we usually got moving in the morning. I called out and darted toward his room. He didn't respond. I found him about eight feet from his bed, on the ground, trying to get up. He was on his hands and knees in nothing but his underwear. He had fallen when he got out of bed. When I entered the room, he looked up at me, his eyes glossy. It almost seemed as if he wasn't there—I didn't see Dad behind his eyes. He repeatedly pleaded, "Help me." I asked every logical question. "What is it?" "Do you hurt?" "Can you get up?" Dad didn't even seem to process those questions; he just repeated the words "help me." I tried to leave so I could get the sugar reader, but he tried to follow and tangled himself up on the ground again. I needed to get him into bed, but he couldn't move on his own, and he couldn't follow directions. I'm not sure where I found the strength in my body to move a 265-pound man that was all but dead weight—it must have been adrenaline. Somehow, I got my shoulder under him and moved him to the bed. When I got him into bed, he seemed to relax and didn't try to follow me out of the bedroom. I was then able to get the sugar reader. His blood sugar had dived to 35. He was in a dire situation.

It's amazing how the mind works. Though doctors had told me to give Dad orange juice, fruit, or peanut butter crackers in this situation, I didn't reach for that. I remembered the last incident when Dad's sugar had bottomed out. Brad had given Dad a Coke, and Brad was the perceived hero. I went straight to the kitchen and got a Coke. That didn't seem to do anything, so I tried orange juice and frosting from a tube. Nothing was working. I quickly called 911. When the two EMS units arrived, Dad was combative, flailing his arms and legs and talking in an eerily deep voice, demanding that people "get out." He wasn't himself, acting as if a demon had possessed him. Two people held him down while another person gave him fluids intravenously. A fourth person, whom I knew from my childhood, stood at Dad's bedside with his arm around me, helping me through. Somehow, he knew no child should have to see her parent like this.

Shortly after the EMS workers got fluids into Dad, the demons left, and he returned to himself. I was relieved when Dad looked up and calmly asked, "What is everyone doing in my bedroom?" He got dressed and was sitting at the kitchen table drinking coffee and eating Christmas cookies with extended family an hour later. He was a lucky man.

The days bled into each other. Dad continued to receive chemotherapy, and I continued to focus on the next joyful moment ahead—Christmas. Chris showed up again and offered to help by lighting the Christmas Star atop the 100-foot-tall grain silo behind the house. The star had been a tradition for Dad in the years following Kraig's death and extending into the eighties. It hadn't been lit for many years, presumably because he no longer wished to do the climb, discover what was wrong with the star, and fix it every year. Chris did the climb, fixed the lights on the metal star frame, and lit it. The rekindled star served as a beacon that drew attention to Dad's suffering and called out to the community to keep us in their prayers. Chris had given us a gift.

In mid-December, Dad became ill in the morning. Sitting in his leather reclining chair, he threw up. He hadn't been nauseous before. This episode didn't have the same urgency of bad sugar readings; in fact, his sugar readings were as normal as they got. He vomited until there was nothing left to vomit and then started dry heaving. He couldn't even keep water down. I called his doctors who advised me to take him to the emergency room. I called my uncles for help because I couldn't get Dad into a car by myself.

The fifteen-mile drive to the emergency room was the longest it had ever been. Dad was no longer vomiting, and he did not act lost like he had been when his sugar was low. There were no demons in the truck with us. It was just Dad and me, facing the fear that we were nearing the end. He stared out the window, and sadness surrounded him. I tried to be responsible and strong, but this gave way to stifled tears.

Once at the hospital, the realities of the business of health care and health care bureaucracies reasserted themselves. Dad sat in a wheelchair waiting for his turn to go back to an examination room. No caring souls were at work in the ER that afternoon—there were only processes and procedures. It was a cold environment for a man and his daughter facing the realities we were facing. I waited with Dad in the waiting room without questioning those in charge, like Dad would want me to do.

I grew restless. As I stared at the sterile waiting room walls, I remembered myself in a sterile business suit, sitting in a conference room, while a boss degraded me and I held back. I again saw myself frozen in a meeting with my colleagues, as the loudest, most obstinate co-worker barked out demands, holding back my thoughts because it was easier than prolonging the experience. I was again in a hospital desperate to get Dad better answers, but I held back my questions because Dad did not want to offend technicians and doctors. I held my words believing it was best. I held back to prevent difficult situations from snowballing into something worse. In my effort to make things easier for others, I was forsaking myself.

My restlessness grew. Finally, I pulled "the bitch card" and played it.

I had created and groomed the bitch card in my corporate life—something authority figures forced out of me for the sake of success. It's the side of me that doesn't cower to others in power. It's the part of me that doesn't conform to rules or social expectations for the sake of conforming. It's the intellectual part of me that leverages facts in an unrelenting argument to get what I believe to be right. It's a skill I've groomed over the years that proved my worthiness to corporate America leaders. A survival technique I've employed with coworkers after other tactics failed. I can argue with the best of them by questioning anything and poking holes in logic. I don't like to use the bitch card, but if ever there was a good reason to use it, this was it.

I approached the women at the counter and kindly asked how they determine when a patient would be seen. After we exchanged smiles and when I had proven I was a level-headed daughter concerned about her father, I dug in, and the bitchiness came out. "He received a lung cancer diagnosis in August, and shortly after that, they found five tumors in his brain. He wasn't doing well, but radiation turned things around quickly. I know you can see in your files that he was here at the end of October and we almost lost him then. He's been doing well since that time. We had a wonderful Thanksgiving, and he is looking forward to Christmas. My three kids, his only grandchildren, are flying in from Seattle in eight days. It's a shame they cannot be here now, but they're all in school. He's looking forward to it, and so are they. His blood sugar readings have been good—they were 285 last night and 195 this morning—his sugar is most likely not the cause; he is most likely dehydrated. Now, won't you and the rest of the staff on duty tonight feel foolish if the only thing standing between him and the last good Christmas with his grandkids is merely a bag of saline solution? Won't you feel foolish if you make him wait for so long that you make his situation worse than it has to be?"

I rattled through all this faster than that annoying voice at the end of a radio commercial reading the disclaimers. I was prepared to go further too and tell them about the "ball buster" lawyer we had on our side, but the saline solution comment seemed to be enough. I got what I wanted—someone immediately took Dad to an examination room.

He was suffering from dehydration with indications of pneumonia. The doctor, however, was uncaring and stuck in corporate rules and guidelines. Looking at the charts, he informed me what I already knew. As if to explain why I'd seen him sitting at a desk in the hallway for forty-five minutes instead of examining my father, he said, "Ms. Miller, your father is DNR, Do Not Resuscitate. If he fails, we will not revive him."

I found the bitch card handy again and went toe-to-toe. "I was with my Dad at the kitchen table I've shared with him since I was a kid when he made the painful decision to sign the DNR papers in September. I sat with him in the doctor's office when he signed the form. I cried with him in his truck after we left the doctor's office. I understand my father is DNR. You will not let my father fail tonight. The man will survive because Christmas is only ten days away. His grandchildren will be here to enjoy that Christmas with him. You will play God tonight."

Although the end was inevitable, I refused to let some ER process designed to maximize hospital profits determine whether Dad would live or die. The doctor admitted Dad to the hospital. Two days later, he came home, his health nearly the same as before the scare that sent us to the ER; his intent and his will to live seemed refreshed.

I should choose my words wisely, for it wasn't a "bitch card" after all. In the hospital, I was strong and courageous speaking my mind and standing up for what I believed to be right. I followed my heart with confidence and persevered for my Dad. I was his advocate, not a bitch. That night I struck the phrase "bitch card" from my vocabulary. I embraced ambition, strength, and courage as integral parts of who I am and realized these traits do not suddenly shift from admirable to distasteful just because I am a woman.

I brought Dad home to a house full of people. My mom, two aunts, my cousin Laura, and my friend Terie all gathered in the house that night. I played hostess, scrounging up enough food and drink to create a party atmosphere. Thankfully I kept more than a bottle of wine, a jar of dill pickles, and sour milk in Dad's refrigerator!

We watched the movie *Christmas Vacation* together, relating the Griswalds' experiences with our own. When the movie ended, Dad's energy shined. Stepping into the role of king of his castle, he began giving directions on what he wanted for his holiday celebration. Dad had lived alone for the last eighteen or so Christmases. Aside from the quirky fiber optic tree that had stayed in the dining room window for two years, Dad never really decorated for the season. This year he wanted a Christmas tree twelve feet tall with red ornaments and white lights and wanted it in front of the window so people could see it when they drove by the house. He even got out a measuring tape and asked Laura to help him determine just how tall the tree could be to fill the entire space. He wanted the family gathered just as they were, filling his home with joy. He was once again the host—the jovial man I remembered from the Fourth of July and New Year's parties in years past. I loved this part of my Dad, and I was happy to see it again.

I now had a mission and less than ten days to fulfill it. Although I'd borrowed some Christmas decorations from my friend, Terie, and had just enough decorations in the house to let you know Christmas was approaching, I didn't have a tree, or lights, or any ornaments. I didn't know until this moment that Dad would even want a tree in his house again.

In short order, I set out to fulfill his Christmas wishes, throwing my financial concerns aside and embracing my standards for quality. A snowstorm got in my way, but I had Big Red to get me through my shopping sprees. My in-laws learned that I was going out in the snow and icy roads on my own, so my father-in-law insisted on taking me shopping and accompanied me when Denny couldn't. He helped in the hunt for the perfect items, supporting me beyond measure. I bought ribbon and made bows for the tree. I bought a tree stand, lights, and red ornaments. I embellished on Dad's vision, extending the décor to the fireplace, getting a wreath and bough for the mantel, and poinsettias and candles for the kitchen. I made the house festive.

Denny and the kids soon arrived. Though we joked about cutting the top off one of the ninety or so mammoth evergreen trees beside the house, we continued our tradition of cutting a tree down at a local Christmas tree farm. The owners had been friends of Mom and Dad's through the years, and we left their tree farm with a twelve-foot tree as their gift to us. My dad had surely touched many people's lives—he was well liked. The kindness of the community was not lost in these hard days.

Throughout the week of Christmas people dropped by, bringing light and cheer with every visit. They drew us all closer to our Ohio roots and to the people who had supported and loved us all the years we were away. The Christmas Eve church service was difficult, though. This quiet, contemplative time reminded me of

Kraig's death—it had been thirty-five years since he'd succumbed to cancer. To some degree, I worried that Dad would choose to die on Christmas Day as a way of honoring Kraig; his death was something Dad never really got over—something that became the cancer that he was dealing with now. Now, more of me believed Dad would live through Christmas and New Year's and that he was determined to make memories for the rest of us.

We had a joyous Christmas Day through the hearts and souls of each other. The presents and the gifts were pure entertainment—a tradition. It was clear that true joy was not found in the Christmas gifts, but rather in the hearts of the people with whom you share the day.

Following Christmas, Dad found pleasure in playing cards again with a few friends at the kitchen table. I remembered the card game euchre from my childhood, but I didn't care to play it now. I was content playing hostess, making Dad his favorite drink, a Seven and Seven, and getting beer and food for the others. I also stepped back and watched Dad—he was experiencing times where he struggled with memory and sight—the impact of the brain tumors was beginning to show again.

On New Year's Eve day, Dad's business duties called. Despite his condition, he had to go to the golf course he owned with two other men and discuss financing with the bankers. It was not a happy meeting. Over the years, Dad had gotten to the point that he gave up trying to influence his partners. This lack of influence resulted in a financial drain, as they made decisions that required him to pour thousands of dollars into the business to pay for their ill-considered choices. At some point, and I don't know when, Dad lost track of the direction of the business. What was supposed to be a retirement income—a fully paid asset that brought an annual income in his retirement years—was now a fully mortgaged business that struggled to make ends meet. Dad couldn't articulate this. He felt shame over his inability to influence his partners and shame over the direction the golf course had gone. They purchased a second course that proved to be an over-extension of their management abilities. Unscrupulous business practices became normal, and they struggled to recover from them. At the same time, interest in golf was subsiding, further shrinking revenues. They were now overextended financially too. On this New Year's Eve day when I took Dad to the golf course to refinance a loan, I don't think he understood all the facts he needed to understand, but he felt he had no choice. He had to sign, and he did just that. There was a moment he began to unleash his anger, but he choked it back and didn't let it out in full force. His rage over this matter would stay with him until he died. I wanted to express it for him, but my energy needed to be held in reserve to care for Dad. His partners were lucky that day.

After New Year's, Denny and the kids had to return to their lives on the other side of the continent. It was one of the hardest goodbyes I'd ever experienced. Standing near the security gates at the Detroit airport, one by one I embraced my kids. Cody was strong. He was moved, but he felt the obligation to be strong for himself and me. He was stepping into the role of an adult, someone to count on for help instead of being helped. Michaela was strong in a different way. She was feeling deeply, interpreting those feelings, and releasing them into the world in the healthiest way possible. She told me she was learning the value of family and community that worked together for others' benefit from this experience—she was absorbing life's lessons and growing from them. I saw myself in her. She was dealing with Dad's illness in much the same way I had dealt with Kraig's illness thirty-five years earlier. Morgan was nine. Hugging her made my heart break. I didn't expect her to be strong. I didn't expect her to know how to handle these things. She cried, and I cried in return, feeling sad that I was not going to be with her to help her through the next steps. I cried because she made me realize I didn't know when I would see her, Michaela, Cody, and Denny again. I cried because I realized I didn't know what was next but knew it would be heavy and hard for all of us, and I longed for all of us to remain together.

## Chapter 10

# Dying

*"The fear of death follows from the fear of life.*
*A man who lives fully is prepared to die at any time."*
Mark Twain

The first days of the New Year brought yet one more gathering at our home. Family and friends gathered with Dad and me in our family room to watch the number six Buckeyes take on the number eight Arkansas Razorbacks in the Sugar Bowl.

Looking back, it was now easy to see that Ohio State football was more than football. We lived, we battled, and we died by Ohio State football. It made the good times in life more enjoyable, gave us a diversion when times were tough, and provided us a rallying point in our darkest moments.

Our attachment to the Buckeyes started in the fall of 1974. Kraig was eight months into his fight against bone cancer, recovering from surgery and the aggressive chemotherapy that followed. He had lost all his hair and a lot of weight. He had endured numerous tests, regular X-rays and MRIs, countless pricks of a needle, frequent hospital stays over one hundred miles away from home, and multiple rounds of chemotherapy. In many ways, he was a strong, strong boy. At the same time, the chemo treatments had left him frail. He couldn't partake in the typical six-year-old summer activities like playing baseball, swimming, or catching lightning bugs. However, he was bright enough to enjoy the Buckeyes.

Coach Woody Hayes and the Ohio State Buckeyes had enjoyed one of their best seasons ever, coming off 1973 undefeated. We were all excited for the new season to start. That August, Coach Hayes was scheduled to speak at the alumni association in our area. A goodhearted community man familiar with my brother's plight arranged for him to visit Kraig. It's amazing what a simple gesture can do for a brokenhearted family. Coach Hayes brought a football with the 1974 OSU football player signatures, a promise of football tickets for an upcoming game, and joy to a struggling young boy and his family. For me, he brought a lifetime memory—a memory that lives bigger and stronger than the fear, pain, and the heartbreak I felt while my one and only sibling was dying.

Of course, Coach Hayes came through with those football tickets. On September 21, 1974, we donned our scarlet and gray, watched the Ohio State Marching Band in their warm-up session, cheered for Archie Griffin and the team from our 50-yard-line seats, watched the band perform Script Ohio during halftime, cheered, and sang *Hang On, Sloopy* with 83,000 other fans. We stayed through the entire game as the Buckeyes rolled past Oregon State to win 51-10. It was a thrill for all of us, especially Kraig.

Years later, I was back in Ohio Stadium as an OSU freshman— same grand band, same winning traditions, a new coach, new players, and a new personal perspective. While I transitioned from a high school class of forty-two to a college freshman class of 7,600, struggled in classes tougher than I had ever known, and sorted through stranger after stranger in search of friends, Ohio State football was an anchor for me. Watching Keith Byars and the team beat the number-one-ranked Iowa Hawkeyes from the first row of C Deck, traveling to Michigan with ten friends to watch Ohio State win, and traveling to California to see the Bucks in the Rose Bowl defined my college experience. Ohio State football remained a joy, an inspiration, and a cause for enthusiasm.

Following my graduation from OSU, I moved to the East Coast. I took my love for Ohio State with me. It was part of my identity. When our kids were born, Mom and I cultivated a love for OSU—they learned the traditions and always had scarlet and gray in their wardrobes. Wherever we moved, Ohio State was a part of us. When we lived on the West Coast, we got up early on Saturdays to watch ESPN Game Day at 7:00 a.m. and the Ohio State game at 9:00 a.m. For night owls like us, getting up early on a Saturday is a mark of true dedication. We weren't quiet about it either—everyone in our Seattle cul-de-sac knew when Ohio State was playing.

Dad was happy and on a bit of a high, surrounded by people who loved him and focused on a familiar source of entertainment that usually proved to be rewarding. On this night, I stepped back and watched. The good energy we got from cheering the Buckeyes on generated the good energy we needed to carry on the battle for Dad's life.

That night I soaked it in, with one eye on the game and another on a project I was working on for Dad—I was creating a video, a slide show set to music, to commemorate his life.

With Denny's help, I found the artifacts that told Dad's life story. I discovered pictures in bedroom dresser drawers, kitchen cabinets, dusty boxes in the basement and in a few photo albums Mom had left behind. There were newspaper articles from the mid-seventies when Dad won the Young Farmer's Outstanding Farmer of the Year Award and certificates of election from Dad's Township Trustee position. We also found photos of his trip to the Caribbean, Hawaii vacation photos, high school yearbooks, my wedding pictures, pictures of the house under construction, pictures of Kraig yellowed from time, and pictures of newly purchased farm equipment. Thanks to a little genealogy documentation I found in a bedroom closet, I uncovered the names and a few bits of information about my great-grandparents and my great-great-grandparents. I was in awe when I found pictures of my dad on his honeymoon—he was so thin, toned, and tan! I laughed when I found the picture of Dad dressed up as the character from the 1970's Dunkin Donuts commercials, the Donut Lady. I cringed when I saw pictures that captured him with cigarettes—the apparent source of today's malady. When my aunt came to the house with an article she found, I was surprised to learn Dad's success reached back to 1967. Dad was just twenty-six years old when Monsanto published an article describing his near-record corn yields. That was news to me forty-three years later! I cried when I found the precious few pictures of Dad holding me when I was a baby. The further I went back in time, the more I learned. I learned that I'd never really knew the whole man—I had only known my Dad.

Putting together dad's life story in a video proved to be healing for me, and remembering all the goodness in his life helped wash away the pains I clung to. It also became a way to help my kids, and others who'd entered Dad's life in more recent years, understand all he was. For Dad was not the overweight, bloated, unhealthy, angry, and financially constricted man we had known in his waning years. Dad was a player—a risk taker, a giver, a fun-lover, a successful businessman, a community leader, a son, a brother, a husband, a father, a grandfather, and a friend. Dad was bigger than his health. Dad was bigger than this cancer.

The snow and cold of a typical Ohio January carried on. The days were shorter for Dad; he simply had less energy, as did I. Everything I did for him seemed to take more time and effort. I requested a leave of absence from my employer, then wrestled with and cleared the bureaucratic hurdles set by an unfamiliar HR rep whose sole purpose seemed to be blocking me. I kept my cool with yet another uncaring soul, and eventually, I got my leave. Of course, a leave of absence meant no income, and I didn't necessarily have a plan for covering our normal expenses without an income. Dad wasn't pleased—we had a fight about money.

I would eventually see Dad was projecting his money worries on to me, but at the time I didn't understand this. At the time, it was a continuation of an unrelenting argument about money. Dad didn't believe I managed my income and expenses well and never hesitated to express his dissatisfaction. Despite all my accomplishments in life, in Dad's eyes, I was failing because I didn't have a pool of cash on hand to tap into on demand and I carried debt. It was crazy to fight with Dad now, but I needed to stand up for myself. I didn't like his assessment that my lack of cash made me a failure. It didn't turn out well, and we went to our separate corners of the house, each nursing our wounds.

Dad still managed a couple of card games and evenings out, but it was more difficult for him now. One Wednesday night at the Moose, he fell in the parking lot. It was another sign that the effects of the brain tumors were back. On an unusually pleasant

Monday, Dad decided to go to the two banks he dealt with. Midmorning I got the paperwork he needed, and we got in the truck. First, we went to the small-town bank just two miles away. There we met with Doris, a longtime friend who made Dad feel like she was his personal banker. Doris had made cookies and a pillow for Dad and had dropped them off at the house recently to let Dad know she was thinking of him. She was caring and friendly, and when Dad explained what he wanted to do, Doris and I both took pause—neither of us believed it was the right thing to do. Dad calmly insisted. He was not interested in our opinion—he had a mission that day. He seemed to be acting with peace of mind, so I didn't stop him. He carried out his business just as he planned.

Outside the bank, in front of his parked truck, Dad said, "I want to go to the country market." I offered to help him into the truck, but he had another plan. "You drive, I'll walk." It was a distance less than a football field away, yet it was a distance I wasn't sure he could manage. Nonetheless, I complied. I drove to the market and waited for him there. As I stood on the sidewalk, watching him walk with a slight limp, he shined with the glory of years past and radiated everything that Dad was in life. It was beautiful. He seemed to glow in the sunlight. I knew it was a magical moment. The world stopped, and it was as if I was the only one there that could see. At this moment, I knew he was tidying up so he could leave this world. I knew this could very well be the last day of his life.

Dad entered the market, for what I don't remember. His walk still mesmerized me. We then got into the truck and drove to the second bank in town. Unfortunately, there was no kind and friendly face here. Dad had banked there since he started his business in the late sixties, but that didn't matter. There were simply bank attendants on autopilot as they adhered to the predefined processes and tasks for which they were accountable. No one working there that day tuned into what was happening in front of them. After waiting for twenty or thirty minutes and watching Dad's energy wane, I found the card formerly known as the bitch card and played it again.

I got what I wanted, though I didn't like that I had to play the card again. Someone finally saw Dad, and he took care of the changes he wanted to make. When exiting the bank, there was no glory, but there was a moment of healing. I had seen the balance of Dad's IRA and shared my observation—"Dad, I think it's completely ironic that the balance of your retirement fund is nearly the same to the penny as my retirement fund." Dad stopped walking, turned, and looked at me and with a disbelieving, forceful voice shouted, "You have that much saved in a retirement fund?" "Yes!" I proudly exclaimed. I went on to explain that the balance would be higher if the stock market decline hadn't bitten me in 2008. I told him that I'd started saving the moment I started my career because he encouraged me to do so and that I'd resisted the temptation to stop saving and take a loan from the account in challenging times because he taught me that. Dad heard none of that. He was still in shock and awe that I had safely tucked away a sizeable fund, and it had grown. There was a hint of approval, but mostly a huge sigh of relief. Perhaps we healed the scars of our financial disconnects. Perhaps it was bigger than that. Perhaps Dad could now relieve himself of the burden of being my provider.


The following Friday, Dad awoke at 3:00 a.m. with a sharp pain in his chest. Recently, I had started giving him morphine, but that day I couldn't get his pain under control. I called his hospice nurse, and she was at the house by 8:00 a.m. She stayed with me until the pain was under control. A family friend, Larry, also happened to visit that day. He'd been squirrel hunting on Dad's property and stopped to see how he was doing. My uncle Mike visited that day too. The two of them were a big comfort as I came to grips with the feeling that Dad was now slipping away.

Dad was lost in pain the remainder of that Friday and into Saturday. He couldn't even walk down the hall to the bathroom. He remained in his beloved leather reclining chair in the center of his house. My aunts and uncles started spending time with me in shifts to help me take care of Dad. Hospice arranged for a night nurse so I could get some sleep and recharge for the next day.

That Sunday, Dad rallied. It was just how others, especially hospice, described the dying experience. He had a day where he came up from the depths of pain, seemingly improving miraculously. He vacated his spot in his leather reclining chair, took a seat in a wheelchair, and laughed with family and friends. A hospice nurse came early in the day to give him a bath. Dad relished the attention, if only for a bath. Once refreshed, he joined the family and friends who had gathered at the kitchen table. My aunt and uncle brought one of Dad's favorites—Lake Erie fried perch and fresh-cut French fries. We spent the day telling stories and laughing.

Dad didn't always make sense and spoke with a muted voice and half-pronounced words. However, he understood us, and we understood him. He was joking most of the day, once ensuring us he knew the difference between a fork and a spoon and later stealing French fries from my mom's plate when she wasn't looking. It was a lighthearted dynamic that I hadn't seen in over twenty years.

Monday morning, a friend took me to a spa, something that Denny had arranged for me. Dad squirmed most of the morning, repeatedly asking the people around him, "Where is Kelli?" I returned home shortly after noon and assured Dad that I was there for him. A hospice nurse visited that afternoon and informed me that Dad was slipping further. She estimated he had ten days to two weeks to live and advised us to have family and friends visit for goodbyes. It was a sad task to share this news with others. Hospice provided a night nurse, and my aunts and uncles continued to help. We now had a hospital bed and set it up in the center of the house, right beside Dad's recliner. Dad moved to the bed Monday evening, filling it more than I expected. His body was bloating and growing. Hospice shortened their estimate of his time to four to six days.

On Tuesday, Dad had a moment during which he connected with us again. I held his hand as a nurse administered morphine. When the nurse asked Dad a question, he smiled and gave her a reply. It was the opposite of what I knew to be true, but it was what the nurse wanted to hear. Dad was simply complying. As I held his hand, I looked at him and said, "I think I've figured something out, Dad. I think I now understand that you could never tell me what you really wanted from me. You could never tell me you wanted me here on the farm carrying on the traditions and the life you built. You always told me the opposite of what you really wanted, didn't you?" Tears filled his eyes.

"Yes, Kelli."

These were the last words that I exchanged with Dad. Hospice shortened its estimate to two or three days. I called Denny, and he made arrangements to get Cody home from college and booked flights to Ohio for all four of them.

On Wednesday, Dad was receiving significant amounts of morphine. His body was getting bigger and more unrecognizable. In the short window of time that I had alone with Dad in the morning, I did what hospice had advised me to do—I gave Dad permission to leave this earth. I held his hand, talked through tears, expressed my love and gratitude for all he had done for me and promised to carry on in his honor. I told him I would keep the farm and the house yet live my life with the authenticity and flair that was uniquely mine. I assured him I would be all right and asked him to speak to me from time to time after he passed.

Later that day, Dad began to breathe laboriously. Hospice advised that he probably would make it through the night, but not through tomorrow. Family and friends began to gather. After supper, the house was full of those closest to us. Even my good friend from high school, David, appeared as if out of nowhere. Around 8:00 p.m., Hospice told me they were surprised Dad was still living. They asked if there was someone he still needed to see. I looked around the room and felt confident that everyone who could and should be there was there or had been there. Then it hit me—Mom wasn't there. Dad still loved her and never got over their separation. I called my mom to prepare her. I looked at David and said, "There was a time they thought of you as a son. Can you please make the drive to get my mom and bring her to my dad?" David complied. Ninety minutes later, she was at his side. I gave them time together, and then I joined them, the three of us united one last time.

As soon as Mom left his side, his breathing slowed. Dad was dying in our presence. Everyone gathered around him. I stood at his side, one hand holding his left hand, the other hand over his heart. Mom stood at his right side, holding Dad's other hand. Our family completed the circle, embracing each other as Dad slipped away.

James D. Adelsperger passed at 11:11 p.m. Wednesday, January 19, 2011.

## Chapter 11

# Falling Apart

*"Never be afraid to fall apart because it is an opportunity to rebuild yourself the way you wish you had been all along."*
Rae Smith

As soon as Dad passed, someone said, "Look at the time." It was 11:11; I knew this was a message to me.

After Kraig had died, I spent a lot of time in my bedroom listening to Fleetwood Mac on my stereo, doing homework, writing—anything to pass the time. Dad was in the fields working, and Mom was in her bedroom. On my nightstand sat a digital clock radio with lime green numbers that glowed in the dark. Late at night and during the day when I was not at school, I found myself staring at the clock at 11:11. The more I saw this number, the more curious I became. Why was I so often mesmerized by the clock at the same time? More recently, I saw these numbers again. When I was contemplating a job offer, I saw 11:11 on my computer screen. When worried if Cody was safe after he started driving, I saw 11:11 on the microwave clock. When I wondered if we'd have enough money to pay the bills, I saw 1111 on the invoice. I had come to believe the number had to mean something—that it was a sign of a greater force in life and that everything was okay just as it was.

Dad having left this world at 11:11 was clearly a message to me that all was right—that he had chosen to leave this earth, that I was supposed to be exactly where I was, and I was doing exactly what I was supposed to be doing. It was an affirmation that everything would be all right.

When Dad left, I felt an unexpected sense of happiness within the sadness. I felt I had done my job, and done it well—that I had helped him move on. It didn't feel as if his life had ended. Instead, I felt that he had gone somewhere else. I was sad that I wouldn't be able to see him and talk to him, but I didn't feel our time together had ended. I only felt that our time together on this earth had come to an end, and one day I would see him again.

The moment after all my aunts, uncles, cousins, and friends left the house I fell to the floor in tears, like a marathon runner at the end of a race. Although I'd given everything I had for the last five months, I wondered if I'd given enough. Every cell in my body simply caved with the weight of the question, and I collapsed. Finally, with my mom's help, I rose, moved to my bed, and fell into a deep sleep.

Waking up says a lot about life. In that short fraction of time between sleep and awareness and knowing, the heart is at peace, and the mind is empty. In those seconds, I experience pure, untarnished joy—our natural state. Then the mind wakes up and asks, "Where am I? What's going on?" Like a movie running at an unrelenting speed, the mind recalls all senses—visions, sounds, smells, emotions, learnings, truths—and it puts you right back where you left off in the moments before you fell asleep.

Waking up the next day, seeing the sunlight beam through the windows, feeling the warmth of the light on my face, and just feeling alive—I felt joy. Then I remembered what had happened the night before. The clouds rolled in, thunder pounded, and I felt a profound sadness. As if on autopilot, I took a shower to prepare for the day, completely unsure what a daughter was supposed to do ten hours after her dad had passed away.

Mom had stayed the night with me. She was up and about and had resumed the same spot she'd held in the kitchen all those years ago. She glided through the house cleaning, organizing, and preparing. When guests came, she didn't greet them as the head of the household—she referred them to me.

Anna and Jerry were the first to arrive. I remembered Anna as my 4-H advisor from thirty years before and her husband Jerry as the father of kids I looked up to in high school. They brought an apple strudel along with their condolences. How they'd known that Dad had passed and found the time to bake a strudel, I'll never know. The beauty of living in a small town was that everyone was there for everyone. Everyone pitched in. Everyone cared and expressed their concern in a way that worked for them.

The owners of the local country market, the place Dad had coffee every day while he was healthy, arrived with a cold cut and cheese platter. Denny's aunts brought cookies and muffins. More visitors came, delivering more condolences. To my surprise, Chris also came.

Today, Chris didn't present the hard persona most men in the area usually show. With genuine tears in his eyes, he hugged me. As he wrapped his arms around my shoulders, he looked me in the eyes and said, "Kel, what you did for that man was just ..." He paused, and his voice cracked as he searched for a word and controlled his emotions, "... was just wonderful." Choked up to the point he could barely speak, he continued. "There aren't many people in the world that would do what you did."

My emotions rushed in, and my truth came pouring out. I was happy that someone acknowledged that I had a choice in how I handled the last five months and happy that someone noticed that I made a good decision. I chose my relationship with my father over my income. I chose to face and heal old wounds and to spend the past five months of my life with my dying father out of love. At that moment, I was acutely aware that I had likely lost my position in my company. That meant I'd given up my lifestyle and status. By giving Dad everything he needed to live the last five months of his life in his home with his pride and dignity intact, I'd given up an entire way of existing. Even if I hadn't lost my job, I'd lost my desire for it and instead had rediscovered a love for the community, a love for close relationships with family and friends, and a less complicated way of living that was more important than the constant corporate warfare I had come to know.

Perhaps Chris didn't know what his comments meant to me, but his words held deep meaning. With the last words exchanged with my dad on my mind, I replied, "I would have done it a long time ago if he would have let me." That was, in fact, true. If Dad hadn't pushed me towards that "Better Life" and hadn't resisted me farming with him, I would have found my way back many years before. However, we had lived worlds apart—physically, emotionally, and spiritually—for twenty-five years. Only through his death were we reunited. I was thankful for the past five months.

Chris and Laura realized I needed to go the funeral home to begin arrangements long before I did. I was drifting through the day, and the thought hadn't yet occurred to me. They made the appointment and filled in for Denny, driving me through the snow to the funeral home. They supported me through the decision-making process, then listened to me babble as I talked off the stress. From time to time, they even helped me with decisions. Chris and Laura both held my dad in good esteem—they looked up to him and admired him, not only as an uncle but also as a man who did good things for the community. Their input helped me create a tribute fitting for the man my dad had been.

Denny, Cody, Michaela, and Morgan arrived that night. We went through the stories and the emotions as they came to grips with the fact that their grandpa had passed. Together, the five of us prepared for visitation, the funeral, and the celebration of life. I put the finishing touches on the video I had created and wrote a eulogy for the Pastor to read at the funeral. Then I wrote a deeply grateful thank you and made copies for each table at the celebration of life—I wanted everyone to know just how much I valued the support each had given Dad and me throughout the last five months.

Two local papers printed Dad's obituary and announced visiting hours would be at the funeral home from 2:00-8:00 p.m. on Monday with a funeral service at 10 a.m. on Tuesday. On Monday, I arrived at the funeral home at 1:00 p.m. To my surprise, several people were already at the funeral home to pay their respects. I started greeting people shortly after 1:00 p.m. The funeral home owner advised me to prepare for a lot of people, but I never expected I'd be standing for eight hours straight, accepting condolences from a steady line. Each person reminded me that Dad had touched many lives and how much they liked him. Memories rushed in as I greeted men and women who served in the Lions' Club and on the school board with Dad, fellow Moose members, business partners, and fellow farmers. Neighbors who were grateful for all the years Dad plowed out their snowy driveways, couples who'd traveled the continent with my parents, Dad's high school friends, my high school friends, extended family, friends who gambled with Dad in Vegas and Detroit, and people my dad had employed also attended. There was unending gratitude offered through handshakes and hugs and an unabated flow of love.

I cried a lot that day. I held my head high and was as strong as I'd been the entire five months I was caring for Dad, but I cried. I've always wondered why we cry at funerals—is it sadness for what could have been but never was or for the opportunities that once were but are now lost? Is it sadness for ourselves in that we have lost a source of love? For me, I had no regrets. I had worked out everything I needed to with my dad. I had unearthed the pains and processed them, addressed the misconceptions, and rewrote our history. I had loved my father with all my heart. Nonetheless, I cried for myself, knowing that experiencing Dad's death was in many ways the death of the person I once was; the end of a life that had gone off track. By sharing in Dad's death, I received a second chance to get things right. I cried as I let go.

The next day, we gathered for a funeral service. Because the funeral home wasn't big enough to hold the number of people expected at the service, we gathered at Dad's church, though I doubt he'd been there since Mom left him in the early nineties. Rev. John Alice delivered the message, recognizing my father in a very fitting way. He likened death to a child playing on monkey bars. The child must let go of the rung behind him to grab the bar in front of him so he can move forward, just as Dad had to let go of this life to move forward. Rev. Alice also didn't look at this event as a death, but rather as a passing from one form of life to the next. He too took solace in believing we would all reunite with Dad someday.

After a short service at his grave, our close family gathered at our home for lunch, and we previewed the video I'd made to commemorate Dad. We then moved on to the golf course for the celebration of his life. When I arrived there at 5:00 pm, the published starting time, it warmed my heart to see the parking lot overflowing with cars. The golf course held 250 people, and the caterers had made enough food for 275. Every spot in the bar, restaurant, and banquet room was full, and every ounce of food was getting eaten. We showed the video; we laughed, and we exchanged stories and memories. Dad had lived a good life, and he had made an impact on many, many people around him. It had never been so evident to me as it was that night.

I am not sure how one goes through such a traumatic experience and returns to life unchanged. Still, that's what I tried to do. That's what we all tried to do. The kids had to be back in school, and I had to be back at work. My leave of absence ended the moment my dad died. I had a maximum of two weeks of bereavement time, which is generous compared to most companies but not nearly enough in reality. By the time we'd held the funeral and celebration of life, I had little time to secure the house and travel back to Seattle. There was no time to nurse my wounds. Somehow, some way, we had to carry on.

I was away from our suburban Seattle neighborhood and our home for nearly three months. I had no idea what I'd find when I returned. However, there in our neighborhood, I was met with another joyful expression of love. Our neighbors had decided to ease our transition back home by stocking us up with ready-made meals and snacks. They had a nice bouquet of flowers and food waiting on the counter and more food in the fridge. That allowed Denny and me to scratch grocery shopping and food preparation off our to-do list and instead use the time to tend to the hearts and minds of our kids and each other. I so loved our neighbors and friends for this gift.

Denny drove Cody across the state, back to his freshman year of college. It was hard saying goodbye to Cody not knowing what he would be feeling or how to support him across the distance. Morgan went back to fourth grade and soccer practice. Michaela went back to her sophomore year, twice-weekly soccer practices, and weekend games. They all had a considerable amount of schoolwork to make up, too. Denny kept busy with housework, paying bills, and shuttling kids back and forth to events. For a while, I just sat numbly on the couch, busying myself with something forgettable on my computer.

I eventually eased myself back into work, first meeting my best friend Beth at a Starbucks. Beth and I had worked together in Cleveland, and she had moved to Seattle a year before me. I was fortunate to have her help me get re-acclimated to the obsessive buzz of the work environment. When I ventured back into work, I discovered that my group had moved to a new office while I was away. In fact, the organization had gone through almost a complete overhaul, with new leaders and team members. I had a new boss, and my team had shrunk from forty-four employees and thirty contractors to four employees and three contractors. On my first day back, I found my new parking lot, new building, and new office and proceeded to unpack the two crates of things moved from my previous office. A few kind coworkers stopped to welcome me back and express their sympathy. Most said nothing. I suppose some didn't know what to say—saying nothing was easier than finding the right words. They simply avoided any interactions with me. For others, there was a message in the silence—foreshadowing what was to come. My organization had clearly moved on after the war room episode, and I had lost my place in most of these people's professional or personal lives.

It was now February—midyear review time. A time when bosses told their employees how they were performing. It was a preview of the annual review later in the year, which determined raises, bonuses, stock rewards, and an employee's future with the organization.

Every company I ever worked for employed a stack ranking performance management process to evaluate and reward employees. For over twenty years, I went to the table, sat beside my peers to keep the obvious good performers in good light, market the good deeds of other less obvious performers, and protect some employees from unjust criticism. If those around the table engaged in the effort with good intentions, the process could surface feedback every manager could use to help an employee grow. More often than not, though, the feedback was designed to tear an employee down—a process designed to gain better financial rewards for a precious few. My experience in the past few years was a gross exaggeration of the process pros and the cons. The rewards for the top performers were amazingly high. Management took money away from the bottom and middle-tier performers to give to the top few, while the bottom performers were "managed" out of the company. Lost was the intention of giving employees feedback to improve organizational alignment and to help employees grow. All employees knew that completing all their performance goals was not enough. They also had to prove themselves better than their peers and win a favorable opinion of other managers. The work year became a strategic political effort for employees to stage themselves for the ranking process. Employees used their knowledge, strategic partnerships, self-promotion skills, and intelligence to win the game and to defeat others like players in a computer game. Some might call it a culture of professional bullying. Every company I ever worked for did not, in theory, tolerate employees making progress at the expense of others, but every company cared more about getting stuff done than they cared about how.

With twenty plus years of "stack ranking performance management" experience, I had promoted and demoted countless employees. I had fought for and secured good performance scores and sizable bonuses for many employees and accepted constructive, nonetheless hard to deliver criticism for many others. The hardest messages to accept from the process were the poorest performer messages. They were also the toughest to deliver. I never got used to delivering the "shape up or ship out" message; it was always difficult. Personally, the system nicely rewarded me—it was a process that I'd used to get to the position I currently held. Now, I had grown to see the dark side of the process: it was difficult to rationalize why intelligent, well-performing employees were forced out just to meet a predefined ratio, and it was often difficult to give feedback that could justify an employee's place, versus feedback that could help an employee grow. The process kept organizations from becoming stagnant, as bottom performers moved out and new players were brought in at a record pace. The process also excused the organization from being responsible for recruiting—the doors were open to a broad field of recruits in hopes of finding a new superstar who could successfully shoulder out the weak. In the course of action, the organization sacrificed continuity and institutional knowledge. In an organization where it took six to nine months for any recruit to learn the culture and become productive, it was an inefficient and costly recruiting and performance management process; one that got in the way of people doing their best work and thriving. The stack ranking process drove employees to optimize their performance management game, not to optimize what they accomplished for customers, the company, or its shareholders. Nonetheless, it was the process I drove.

Shortly after returning to work, I attended the mandatory training where HR and Legal told managers how to deliver midyear reviews. In recent years, the process had become so controversial that the company had fielded several disputes and responded by training managers to message better. However, the content didn't change: a precious few employees would hear they walked on water, most would hear they were on target to meet their goals, and a small percent would hear they were poor performers.

Two weeks after my return to work, I was sitting in my boss's office for my midyear discussion. My boss had a frat boy smile and the gift of gab. He filled the opening minutes of our discussion with the kind of niceties that would make any employee at ease with any message he had to give. Soon I heard, "You are not performing well," and then I heard all the phrases HR and Legal had taught us to say. I was getting the "shape up or ship out" message.

I learned many years ago that professionals are not supposed to cry. Over the years, I worked hard to develop the ability to get through trying circumstances without crying—I got very good at stuffing away emotional reactions to being the good business person big company employees are supposed to be. But I lost my ability to hold back my tears the day I'd broken down in O'Hare Airport—the day I learned to feel again. So, I cried as my boss looked on. My leaders undoubtedly saw my tears as weaknesses, which probably reinforced their decision to label me a poor performer. However, they didn't understand why I cried.

I cried because the wisdom I had acquired in that split second was beginning to act in my life—the wisdom I needed to walk away from my twenty-five-year career. If I'd had any reason to question that path, my review was now reinforcing it. I cried for everyone who had ever been told they were at the bottom of the stack. I cried because some of them probably believed it. God had worked miracles through me while I was with my father—proof that I was not incompetent as the process now labeled me. Moreover, I cried for the audacity of my boss, his boss, and his boss's boss. What kind of people had the gall to tell someone that they weren't performing well just a few weeks after burying their father? How could there be three persons in this chain of command that didn't have the sense to stop another from being inhumane? So, I cried for the people who defined the system, and the people that bought into it. I expected more from a company with an overabundance of financial and intellectual resources. Where were the humanity and compassion? Where was the inspiration, guidance, and leadership to be more than we were at the moment? I bought into the notion that I could achieve success and prosperity through hard work and determination. I bought into the stacking ranking process. However, it was a lie. I cried because this is how a twenty-five-year career chasing the American Dream would end—realizing I was adrift in a sea of people motivated by their self-interests.

I didn't want to be the person corporate America was telling me to be. I didn't want to be a heartless, soulless shrew for the sake of market share. I wanted to rise above that. I wanted to be a better human being in each moment in my life, not guided by the pretense that I was better, smarter, or stronger than the person beside me. Not guided by the position, power, and money that could be mine if I chose to play the game. I wanted to play a different game. I wanted to be the best person I could be physically, emotionally, and spiritually, and I was learning that money was just a means to this. The only thing the stack ranks and my company had to offer was salary, benefits, bonus, stock, a choking environment, and all the ego that went with them.

For the first time in twenty-five years, I looked past the dollars—other things now mattered more. For starters—me—I mattered more than money! The way I lived mattered! Living and working in an environment aligned with my personal values mattered. Being my true authentic self and working with a sense of purpose beyond financial gain mattered. Living a full life and not just a work life—spending time with my kids—having a healthy relationship with my husband—these were the truly important things of life.

Though I'm sure my boss wanted the "you're not performing well" message to motivate me to get back in the game, the message fell flat. I heard my heart say, "Thanks, but no thanks," and I heard the angels cheer. It was time to choose something different in my life. It was one of the most freeing decisions I had ever made. I felt like a newborn child, closing the door to a life I no longer cared to live in and standing at the edge of a world of possibilities.

So, I went back to my couch, busied myself with computer games, and wrote 265 thank-you notes to people who had donated to Dad's memorial. I took care of my kids, and the estate Dad had left me.

Then one day in April, my middle daughter Michaela found me in a fog sitting in my favorite spot on the couch. She knelt down, looked me in the eye, and said, "Mom, it's okay if you want to be in Ohio, near the businesses and the home Paw Paw left for you. Just give me two years in the same high school."

Her words sent a jolt through me. They made sense. I had ruled out a move to Ohio because I didn't think it was in the kids' best interest to move again. However, Michaela was giving me permission. I soaked this in for a few hours, and after supper returned to her and said, "That means we'd have to move this summer." She stared at me awhile, then smiled and said, "Duh!"

Financially, moving seemed like a mountain of a challenge. Our home had lost considerable value due to the falling real estate market. Selling it meant losing everything we had paid into a mortgage for twenty-one years and finding a six-figure sum of cash we'd owe the bank. Bankruptcy or default were options, but Denny and I chose to do neither. We would handle our transition in a stand-up way—sell the house for a loss and find a way to pay the bank what we owed.

So, that became our plan. My father had left me plenty of assets, but very little cash. We needed income in Ohio, and a generous one to also pay down the debts we were carrying. I checked in with a few recruiters, and each told me that finding a position in Ohio similar to the one in Seattle would be hard, but they also told me I had great credentials—any company would be lucky to have me. I just needed to be patient.

Denny began looking for a job too. Our hometown network certainly helped us out with this. Chris showed up again at a key moment. He recommended Denny for a job, Denny interviewed, and he started that summer. I found humor in the fact that I had been working for twenty-five years in top name companies, but couldn't land even an interview while my husband had been a stay-at-home father for fifteen years and had been away from agriculture for twenty-five years, yet landed an interview and a job immediately.

The realities of my job search were at best humorous, and at worse frightening. As my search kept turning up empty, I realized I had some work to do on my ego. I had come to define myself by the company I worked for and the position I held. Though my head understood that I was not my job, I'd never actually been without a big company and a big title. I was going to have to help my ego through this transition!

Five months after Dad passed, Denny packed up much of our household, rented the largest U-Haul possible and drove our belongings cross-country. This truckload was the first of three loads (we owned a lot of stuff, and I was in no frame of mind to donate, trash, or sell any of it). Once Denny arrived in Ohio, he started his new job. Michaela was the next to make her way to Ohio, arriving in time to begin soccer practice with her new high school team. Morgan quickly followed, but Cody made a difficult decision to stay in school at Washington State. I set him up in an apartment there; then I got used to living alone in a large house. I packed up more of our belongings and kept working. We planned for me to stay at my job to cover the big mortgage until the house sold. Soon, it all weighed too heavily on me. After making the decision to lead a more authentic life, I had a hard time maintaining my corporate charade. I had friends and all the great things Mother Nature had to offer in Seattle to ease my pain, but it wasn't enough to overcome the ugliness of my job. I had to move on, whether we sold our Seattle home or not.

First, I went to the mountain.

On an amazingly beautiful, blue sky sunny September day, I got up and got ready, just like for any other workday, but when I got outside, I looked at the sky and knew it was not a day to waste in an office doing a job I had come to loathe. So, I packed some food, a journal, my favorite pen, and pointed my car south to Mount Rainier. It was uncharacteristic of me, but it turned out to be exactly what my soul needed.

Denny and I had made the journey to the mountain many times. I'd crawl into the passenger's seat and immediately let go of responsibility, sinking deep into the depths of my soul as Denny drove. On this occasion, however, Denny was 2,500 miles away; I was on my own. Today, I was alert and attentive to my surroundings as I drove through wealthy suburbs, industrial communities, honkytonk neighborhoods, bohemian enclaves, naturalist homesteads, as well as the characterless communities full of people on autopilot. After two hours on the road, I arrived. It was like returning home. Without much thought regarding where I'd go or what I'd do, I parked the car along the Nisqually River.

The peace and tranquility in this space were far away from the contentious business I would soon leave behind, and even further from the turbulence of transitioning to a new life in Ohio. I welcomed the peace. I walked across a dry riverbed filled with basketball-sized rocks to a bridge which park rangers had handcrafted from fallen timbers. I crossed the water and found the perfect spot. Sitting on a flat rock with a second behind my back for support, I was right beside the water and facing Rainier. The sound of the rushing water chased away my pains and fears and opened my senses to the beauty around me. Evergreens flanked the river bed and reached high to meet the deep blue sky. They formed a glorious bed of green that framed the picturesque Mount Rainier at the end of the valley. The mountain jutted out from the surrounding landscape and glowed purple—a sharp contrast to the pure white glaciers that graced, but did not cover the mountain. Both the rock and glaciers seemed to glow in the sun. Although I was grateful for the peace and solitude, I couldn't explain why I was the only human being lucky enough to be in this exact spot taking in this amazing sight.

Words rooted in deep emotion came easily to me that day. From that perfect spot in the riverbed, I wrote:

### For My Soul to Thrive

Maintain balance in all chambers of life;
Especially the chambers you deem important
Listen to your heart
Meditate
Be in nature
Nurture your free spirit
Love
Be loved
Laugh
Let go of emotional anchors
Experience
Trust intuition
Don't wait 'til it's convenient, heed the call
Let go of stuff—live light
Connect with people
Connect with people who are not like you
Travel
Trust in the good in others
Let go of expectations
Make room for new
Invite and allow the good stuff in
Expect the best to happen
Give

I will always remember that day as a gift from God. The following day, I went back to the office and quit.

I didn't have a job in Ohio; we knew Denny's income wouldn't be enough to sustain us, but I trusted that the universe would show us the way to pay for our oppressive mortgage without my income. I quit the job, the way of life, and trusted God would show us a way to get our lives in order. I walked away from my career and moved back into the house I grew up in—the house my mom and dad built. I went back to the farm. I started over.

## Chapter 12

# Transition

"I can accept failure; everyone fails at something.
But I can't accept not trying."
Michael Jordan

"Get out of your head and into your heart." I first heard this phrase from Maria Shriver at Tim Russert's memorial service. The words lingered with me for a long, long time, and now they called to me. They were words of inspiration.

Over the course of my career, I had developed a strong mental capacity to understand and analyze complex problems. Having taken a lot of math in college, and furthering my problem-solving skills by conquering more and more difficult and complicated real life situations, I grew day after day. I not only saw every challenge the world presented to me mathematically, but I also lived in my head and let my brain take the lead in most everything I did. The phrase "get into your heart" invited me to see life differently. The truth is, I had been longing to follow my heart for a long time, but my head had been too strong, it drowned out my heart's voice. I spent the first few months in Ohio learning to listen.

To some degree, you would have thought I was a teenager after high school graduation. I was full of energy and determined to make something happen, but I wasn't quite sure what I longed to do. I was in a position to try, err, adjust, and try again, so I allowed myself to try things without expectation of success. This trial and error approach was how I was going to determine what I was going to do with my newfound freedom.

As we settled into our somewhat familiar, yet new surroundings, we had a lot to learn. The culture was certainly different. Things that came naturally to me were not always well received in my new home. For example, when I met someone new, I confidently said, "Hi, I'm Kelli," and held out my hand to shake. Puzzled looks most often greeted me. I would get a hesitant and uncomfortable hand but no introduction in return. Some people simply stared at my hand, frozen in disbelief that I was introducing myself with a handshake, and in effect, refusing my greeting. My work experiences taught me that such a refusal was rude, but in our new surroundings, this behavior was simply evidence of a different protocol. My aunt eventually said, "Kelli, everyone knows who you are—you're the family that moved from Washington. Everyone knows everyone here. It doesn't even occur to them that you don't already know them."

Our living conditions were much different than they had been, too. In Washington, we lived in a liberal, progressive county where constant change was normal, and our neighbors hailed from every country on the planet. We enjoyed a strong local economy built on the back of the high-tech industry. There were geniuses on every corner. Our kids went to school in generously furnished buildings that were less than ten years old. We lived in a neighborhood where the average home price was over $700,000, and average incomes were over $200,000. The community had hope. They believed in themselves and believed they could handle any challenge life threw them.

In contrast, in Ohio, we lived in a conservative county that did not embrace change. The local economy was based on agriculture and had been since its founding in 1820. Ninety-eight percent of the residents were white, and most were the third, fourth, and even fifth generation. People moved out of the community all the time but rarely did anyone new come in. They lived in houses that had been in the family for seven generations and had always made their living with their hands. Our kids went to school in the same building where our relatives went sixty years before with the same old wooden doors on the closets and green tiles on the walls. The average home price was under $40,000, and families got by on $11/hour jobs. They might not have known the difference between a merlot and pinot noir, but they prided themselves on helping their neighbors when they were in need. They recognized that everyone needed a little help sometimes but didn't think it took a liberal governmental program to provide—just a kind heart and a helping hand.

While I didn't mind the differences between liberals and conservatives, or new or old school buildings, I did mind other things. For one, I missed good food. In Washington, I routinely ate sushi, purchased fresh halibut at the fish counter, and regularly indulged in fish tacos with mango salsa or Thai chicken. In rural Ohio, the most interesting thing to be had was a good burger. Most restaurants just served everything deep-fried (deep fried veal, deep fried hot dogs, deep fried cheese sticks, deep fried pickles, and the like). Seafood was just as foreign as Thai or Greek. Pizza was considered a "diversity food."

I had already explored my hometown thoroughly as a kid. I knew every back road, every field, every pond, and every creek, and they were all the same as they had been thirty years prior. There were no professional sports teams, no upscale bars, and few musicians came through town.

We received invitations to parties with other couples. However, these often turned out to be difficult, too. Our new circle of friends didn't share many of the things we knew and enjoyed. They didn't like wine and didn't want to hear about the great Cougar Crest we'd found, nor the story of how we met the vintner. They weren't intrigued by trends in technology and didn't care to hear about the latest Xbox features or our insights into the mobile phone wars. One of the most poignant moments came during a girls' night out. I couldn't talk about the cool recipe I had found or talk about the latest scandal at the high school. So, I talked about what I knew, describing my challenges finding a job in Northwest Ohio. After I had finished, a woman across the table looked me dead in the eye and asked, "Do you need a college degree for that role?" She didn't know what she had said.

Nonetheless, I felt the ground beneath me crumbling. Life just seemed to keep telling me that I had more to let go. It was becoming clear that it was time to stop looking outside myself for entertainment and direction. Life was begging me to explore the one thing I'd had with me all along—my heart. I had to stop distracting myself with the world around me, whether with the culturally-rich Seattle, or cornfield-rich rural Ohio. What did my heart want to do? That was the question I struggled to answer.

First, I explored my role in the family again. I tried to do the things that most mothers do but rarely had needed to worry about for the last fifteen years—I'd worked while my husband stayed home. Now, I got the kids around in the morning and off to school, then cooked, cleaned, and unpacked boxes until it was time to get kids home from school and off to their sports practices. In truth, I cleaned as little as possible. I still didn't much care for that. I tried challenging myself in the kitchen again, but I quickly rediscovered that while I liked cooking for large events, mastering the art of daily meal preparations was not going to satisfy me. I heard a voice inside me say, "Kelli, you're *supposed* to cook, clean, and do these things for your family," but it was the voice of guilt. I learned to let that voice go. My heart was still calling.

What I wanted most was to be present at my kids' extracurricular activities and share the mornings with them without the stress from work. I wanted to spend time with extended family occasionally and now had an opportunity to be a part of their lives, something we couldn't do when we lived at a distance. Time was like a blank canvas begging for me to paint it.

I saw the golf course that my father had owned as an opportunity. Dad's partners' way of managing the business required them to throw large sums of money into the golf course just to make ends meet. Now that I had inherited my dad's shares, I thought it wise to learn more about the daily operations. If I couldn't make the golf course profitable again, perhaps I could at least get it to the point that it broke even so we could avoid having to sink more money into it. I got involved and did nearly every job in the place—tended bar, cooked, waited tables, sold outings, purchased supplies, balanced the books, replaced the point of sales cash registers, acquired a less expensive credit card processor, and marketed the business. About the only thing I didn't work on was payroll and grounds keeping. I poured forty, fifty, and even sixty hours a week into the business and never once took compensation for my work. But nothing changed. To my partners, the change was harder than simply putting more cash into the business. Eventually, I wondered why I was giving so much of myself away to all of it. So eventually, I walked away and let a lawyer represent my interests.

Creating a new business also interested me. I worked with a local organization to develop plans for a restaurant and microbrewery in town. My personal tastes colored the business plan—I proposed that we offer a healthy food choice in town. And most would agree that a microbrewery could be a success in a town with two growing colleges if managed right. So, I put pen to paper and drafted plans for a new business. I met with local business men and women, the college leadership, and the mayor for advice. I even reviewed the plans with the city's development team. The golf course had jaded me, though—and the food business was tough. My heart was really into the process of defining and developing a new business, but I wasn't really into beer and day-to-day restaurant operations. I moved on.

Unfortunately, responsibility was calling. The checkbook balance was decreasing, and the credit card balance was increasing. An oppressive mortgage on an empty house 2,500 miles away had done its damage, and Denny's income was only able to sustain the modest lifestyle we'd adopted in Ohio. I felt increasing pressure to make money, so I did what most people in my position do—consulting.

I realized my network of the "who's who" in my hometown was quite strong. Plus, I didn't lack the confidence or the guts to approach anyone and everyone. I took the advice of countless job coaches—I engaged my network, informing them of the services I had to offer and asking for introductions to two or three people that might be able to use them. It was in these conversations that my career took an unexpected turn. I was offered a sales and marketing position with a physical therapy company that my uncle owned with his brother-in-law. Believing that I could do anything I set my mind to, I went through the interview process, without telling anyone that I was the owner's niece. Though I didn't have experience in the healthcare industry or a depth of experience in sales and marketing, my professional experience shined through. I was offered the job and began in June 2012. My checkbook was relieved, my ego pleased, and my need to have responsibilities and grow and learn was satisfied.

My spirits soared as I learned the healthcare industry and began executing marketing plans. I once again found career satisfaction. Though my income was not even half of what I'd made in Seattle, I began paying down debt as we learned to live within our means. Plus, I could be more involved in my kids' lives. I attended every sporting event my daughters played in. I even helped feed the team. Because this was the first time in eighteen years that Denny and I both worked full time, we rebalanced household chores as well. I paid the bills, did the laundry and grocery shopping, and on occasion, I cooked. I carried far more household responsibility than I had in the past. Denny and I continued to combat each other as we worked to get the balance right, but we were on a better path.

Until that fall, when trouble reared up again.


On a Thursday in mid-October, I was sitting at my desk in a little corner of our small but open office space. Having not eaten breakfast that morning, I had lunch on my mind. That's when Mom called. She'd had her annual mammogram in September. The radiologist found something on it; the doctor had scheduled a biopsy, but I didn't think much of it—I thought the doctor was being overly cautious. Honestly, I thought the odds were on our side—my brother had cancer, and my dad had cancer. Certainly, Mom would be spared.

I was still feeling bad that I had missed her biopsy appointment earlier that week. It was an honest mistake. I'd put it on my calendar for Tuesday instead of Monday. Thankfully, my aunt was scheduled to drive Mom to the hospital. I was supposed to meet Mom and my aunt there to help her get on the table for the process. I was supposed to be there for moral support too, but I just plain missed the appointment.

I picked up the phone expecting a casual chat, but I heard the urgency in her hello. "Kel, I have cancer," she blurted.

The world stopped for a few seconds, and there was nothing but void. Mom rambled on about the doctor, how she got the news and more. Nothing registered. I was conscious enough to recognize there was a phrase for me to digest—Mom has cancer—again my brain froze up. I had been so certain she would be fine. But here she was, awakening me to the unthinkable—Mom had cancer.

Somehow, I came out of the fog and found that familiar place of strength that I'd developed when my brother was ill—a strength I'd built on when I was my dad's primary caregiver during his illness. I kept all other emotions in check. They had to be; Mom needed that from me. "I'm sorry this happened" was the only thing I could find to say. Geez, I'd hated that phrase when Dad's oncologist used it two years ago. It seems appropriate for when you say words that hurt, or when you miss a birthday party, but they seemed terribly inadequate for this. I repeated it again: "I'm sorry." It's all I could say.

When I got off the phone, a rush of emotion overcame me. A wave of chills and heat started in the pit of my stomach and moved through my limbs. I cried. I followed my instincts and got to Mom's side quickly. We simply sat together, individually processing the information and finding strength in each other for the road ahead.

Soon we found ourselves sitting in a doctor's office listening to the details of her cancer diagnosis. As I sat with Mom, I had flashbacks to Dad's doctor visit, which made this new experience terribly difficult. I was thinking back to her experience with Kraig, too.

Mom had a new family doctor, and I knew very little about her. Mom spoke highly of her, but I wanted to dislike this doctor and find fault with her even before we met. My hatred of cancer and Mom's diagnosis just spilled over onto her. But she was young and intelligent with a warm and empathetic manner. She explained things well, accepted questions with grace, allowed us time to work through emotions, and helped set expectations for the course ahead. I still disliked the topic at hand, but I liked her.

She told us Mom had two types of breast cancer: cancer in the milk ducts and cancer in the lobules (the part of the breast that produces milk). She described the cancer as invasive, meaning the cancer had moved beyond its place of origin and into surrounding tissue. We asked all the questions: did invasive mean aggressive? What stage was the cancer? What size was it? What were the treatment options? Was it genetic?

As the doctor spoke, my mind was a runaway freight train as I processed the implications, unlocking the door to a flurry of emotions. I worked very hard to stop the rush of thoughts, to stay present and centered, to hear and digest all the information. Still, I was hurt, lost, sad, broken, angry, and eager for information all at the same time. I just wanted to break down and cry. I wanted to scream!

I didn't.

Later, when Mom wasn't looking, I sank into a dark place. It was an ugly, desperate place, and it didn't take me long to find my way there; it was familiar—I'd been there with Dad just two years ago, and I didn't want this for my mother. I didn't want to see her suffer physically or emotionally. When I'd faced situations like this before, my response had always been to extend myself, to carry as much of the load as I could, so that my loved ones didn't have to. With so much experience, I'd become quite capable of carrying a very heavy load. Needless to say, the thought of doing this again was overwhelming. The thought of giving Mom daily care and helping her through chemotherapy—taking her body to the brink of death so that the cancer cells would die—was devastating.

I'd been at my job only five months. I didn't have any vacation time, and I couldn't take a leave of absence because I hadn't been with the company long enough. I had no idea how I'd get time away from work to help Mom, and I couldn't afford to be emotionally absent from my job like I had been when I cared for Dad. Nor could I bear to suffer the helplessness I felt when I witnessed Dad's pain and emotional distress. I was simply tapped out.

Looking down the dark road ahead led me to only one conclusion—I'd have to quit my job. I'd simply have to find a way to live without the income and the benefits.

Mom had the choice of seeing surgeons in town or stepping outside that system. Staying meant she'd have a general surgeon, but the radiation would be nearby. Going outside meant she'd see a breast surgeon but would have to drive for radiation. Mom decided to make the one-and-a-half-hour trip to see a female surgeon who specialized in breast surgery at the Cleveland Clinic.

We made our way to downtown Cleveland on a chilly, windy, rainy Halloween, driving through the outer remnants of Sandy, the hurricane that had just devastated the New Jersey coast. Getting to the Cleveland Clinic main campus puts some people off—not everyone feels comfortable driving in East Cleveland and trying to find their way around the maze of buildings and parking garages that make up the clinic's main campus. However, I'd been there before—for mammograms when I'd lived in the Cleveland suburbs and for the birth of our youngest daughter, Morgan.

We arrived fifteen minutes early, and someone promptly took us to an exam room. A nurse guided us through a forty-five-question health assessment and then left. Soon another nurse joined us. Convinced that mastectomies were the best answer, Mom started by saying, "I don't need them. Take them both off, and if you can get me in, let's do it today—seriously!" The nurse smiled. We had to love Mom's approach—there was no anger, no resentment, and no blame. Mom loved life, and even without the benefit of the Cleveland Clinic's advice, she'd found an answer that got her back to the life she loved.

The nurse acknowledged Mom's eagerness to proceed, but she stayed on course to assess Mom's situation. She was pleasant and listened to everything Mom wanted to share, even off-topic information. Mom felt important, just as a patient should. The nurse explained Mom's diagnosis thoroughly, answered questions, and assured Mom she was going to be all right. Once she was sure we both understood the diagnosis, she explained typical treatment options. Before she completed her work, she asked Mom to define her stress level on a scale from one to ten. Mom looked puzzled, but eventually answered, "Two—because I have such a good support system with my daughter, sister, brother, extended family, and friends."

I had stayed calm and unemotional most of the day, yet hearing my mom answer "two" tapped something inside me and I wanted to scream, "Ask me, ask me! Mine is twelve! Twelve, you hear me? Twelve!" I now found my corporate training handy—I stuffed this emotion away, never showing my fear for what cancer could mean to Mom and me. However, my reaction to the question made a point with me—I was doing my job well for Mom, but I didn't feel as settled as I believed.

The nurse left us alone to absorb what we had heard. Soon, the surgeon joined us. She·explained Mom's diagnosis again. The nurse had spoken to our emotions, which was what Mom needed at that moment. The surgeon spoke in facts and figures, and this was the kind of discussion I needed.

The surgeon could tell I'd had previous experience with cancer, so she asked about it. After hearing my story about Dad, she assured me that breast cancer was much different from lung cancer and proceeded to dismantle many of my beliefs. I had walked in believing that Mom had two types of cancer, one in the milk ducts and one in the lobules. The surgeon made that notion less scary by saying it was one cancer that happened to spill over from one location to another. We learned the cancer was the size of a pencil eraser and the biopsy most likely had removed a significant portion of it already. We learned that the cancer was not aggressive, and in her medical opinion, it was highly unlikely that it had spread to the lymph nodes.

The surgeon left to consult with the radiology technician and returned with more news. They had compared Mom's current images with one she'd had done at the Cleveland Clinic seven years prior when she was living with us in Cleveland. The same cancer indicators were on the images in 2007, and when compared to current images, there was no obvious change. This cancer was not aggressive. For a split second, I wondered how cancer could be in Mom's body for five years without us knowing about it; I wondered how they could miss something like that, but it didn't matter. The comparison was good news. If it hadn't killed her or grown or spread in five years, it was safe to assume she could beat this. I focused on this. I eventually asked if cancer that had been left untreated increased the likelihood of this cancer spreading to the lymph nodes. The doctor confidently said no.

The surgeon described the treatment options again, repeating much of what the nurse had already said. Mom chose to do a lumpectomy with radiation to follow. I was surprised because she'd been so eager to give up not one, but two breasts. Keeping her breasts must have seemed more feasible for her once she had more information and knew that she did not have extensive cancer.

We walked out of the exam room three hours after we had entered, with a surgery date in hand. We reprocessed information and talked as we walked across the medical campus. The bleakness faded. Our hearts were lighter after speaking with the surgeon. We dared to smile and concluded that we'd gotten the best news we could after such a diagnosis.

I found *hope* once more.

First, Mom had to manage a handful of other medical issues. Then she would have surgery, then radiation, and perhaps chemotherapy. I was now contemplating how I would help her through this while holding down a job and taking care of my family. My friend Beth was there for me like she always was. This time she was on the other end of the phone and said, "Kelli, you must accept help."

The words rang in my ears. Yes, maybe I was putting too many expectations on myself. Maybe it would be okay if others helped Mom too.

Soon, Mom had her ex-sister-in-law signed up to take her to the orthopedic doctor, and another good friend agreed to take her to physical therapy appointments. Her twin sister, Kay, agreed to take her to get Mohs Surgery to remove two basal cell cancer spots on her chin, and Denny's aunt, Peg, committed to taking Mom back to the Cleveland Clinic to get pre-surgery work done. I would keep my job and save my few vacation days for surgery and any unforeseen events down the road.

With all the tactical things covered, my mind was free to observe changes that were emerging in my thinking. Just like the precious weeks after Dad got his diagnosis, I was once again aware of my limited time on this earth. I noticed that I was once again able to choose to live even as someone close to me was in a life-threatening situation. After Dad had died, I had vowed to live differently—to live more freely. As I thought about what it means to be living, I was surprised to learn I still had some limiting thoughts and beliefs. These self-limitations were unveiled to me a bit differently this time.

For one, I got a speeding ticket. Normally I'd beat myself silly for a stupid mistake and the consequences. This time, I didn't do that. Instead, I forgave myself quickly and paid the fine. When we received a bill from a contractor that was two times the expected amount, I didn't consume myself with anger or regret. Instead, I said, "We'll figure out how to pay it." When the basement filled with water two weeks before we were supposed to start a basement construction project, I didn't curse the universe for the difficulties in my life, I agreed to buy a water pump and said, "Better two weeks before than two weeks after." I simply refused to let events negatively affect my attitude and refused to let ill will hijack my actions, for that would only sabotage my ability to manifest my dreams. I remained grateful for every waking moment of life and chose to make the best of all the cards life dealt me.

The most interesting thing happened when I returned a text to a friend, and I found myself saying, "I just want to quit my job and work on my bucket list." The thought was striking; I didn't even know I had a bucket list.

Clearly, there was something behind this thought. There was something I longed to do, and I'd best get to figuring it out and doing it. We're here on this earth to live. We're not meant to bury our best dreams in our subconscious behind protective walls. We're not meant to work in jobs that pay the bills but don't feed our dreams. We're not meant to forego risks to save ourselves from unwanted pain or to accumulate riches, titles, and rewards because society has defined them as the symbols of a good person living a successful life. We are meant to be everything we want to be, to experience everything we want to experience. We are meant to live the life of our dreams.

When I looked at life this way, I realized that every action is a choice. I asked myself, what should I do with this moment, right now? What should I create today? And I realized God gives us events like Mom's cancer to remind us to live.

So, against the backdrop of cancer, life carried on. Our daughter received the Coach's Award for successfully playing on the boy's high school soccer team, overcoming the physical and emotional challenges of being a female on a male team, and playing right alongside the boys. We displayed our pride and joy! When our youngest daughter wanted to be in the Halloween parade, we got the '69 Corvette convertible out of the garage and drove it with our daughter and her three friends sitting in the back, dressed in their nerdy Halloween costumes. The sign on the side of the car didn't say "Homecoming Queen"—it said, "We're Nerdy, and We Know It." My husband and I threw our conservative spending to the wind. We took off for a weekend-long date—we indulged in a nice meal and a bottle of wine, and we did something unusual: we went to see a play in a very small theater just to experience something new. We even waltzed down the middle of a busy street just because we could.

I lived, I laughed, I loved. I appreciated it all just a little more. These moments were the way I was choosing to live my life.

In November, Mom spent a day at the Cleveland Clinic completing her pre-surgery tests. Despite the fact that her grandmother had died of breast cancer, Mom learned there was less than a 1 percent chance that she carried the breast cancer gene. That was good news for Mom, me, and my daughters. And after a twenty-four-hour stay at the Cleveland Clinic, Mom celebrated with dinner, ice cream, wine, and laughter at one of her favorite restaurants. She just seemed to go where life took her, and she found joy in who she was with, what she was doing, and where she was, even when she was dealing with cancer.

In the same way, I'd looked Corporate America in the eye and told them that they wouldn't take away the things I loved, Mom was meeting cancer, the "Emperor of all Maladies," with a positive attitude. She kept faith, trust, honesty, hard work, pure intentions, the ability to find joy, and gratitude. She was the model patient. Spiritual and medical leaders alike praised her for her approach. They said hers was the way to beat cancer.

Mom had the lumpectomy at the Cleveland Clinic main campus in early December. Before we knew it, Dr. Fanning was visiting us in the waiting room, smiling and telling us, "Your mom is a hoot." Her lighthearted opening gave promise of good news. "She is doing well. There is no cancer in the lymph nodes—I removed the sentinel node and put a drain in to be safe. You'll be able to see her shortly and be on your way home soon."

Wow. In the time it took me to pay a few bills, address, and stamp envelopes, and find a mailbox in the building, Dr. Fanning had removed Mom's cancer. And just as the doctor had predicted, there was no cancer in the lymph nodes—it had not spread!

A month after surgery, Mom began radiation, which continued for two months. A year later, doctors told her she was cancer free. Mom not only survived cancer, but she also thrived. Somehow, some way, I seemed to have come out of the experience a better person with a healthier heart—a heart that was learning what it meant to live. I had made the decision to live when I left my career, but that wasn't enough. I had to make the decision to live day-by-day, moment by moment.

It didn't take a glorious job title with a glorious paycheck. It didn't require me to wait until I had paid off all my debt or to have an abundance of savings to pay for the things I chose to do. It didn't take a wealth of intellect or a series of related feats to prove myself worthy. It is simply a choice to say yes to life. A choice to overcome the challenges I face. It is a choice to follow my heart's truest desires.

Happiness is a choice!

*Chapter 13*

# Becoming Whom I Had Always Been

"The only thing standing between you and your goal is the bullshit
story you keep telling yourself as to why you can't achieve it."
Jordan Belfort

I had walked away from the big corporate world and its big
money. We had sold our house for a sizeable loss just to walk
away from the debt. I was learning to live with less stuff. I had
moments I chose to see differently, but had I eliminated the ugly
patterns? Was I approaching life differently? Had I fully realized
the changes I wished to manifest in my life? Was I building and
living the life of my dreams? Did I love who I was? My heart
was healthier and far less cluttered. I could hear it now—and it
answered these questions with a resounding "No!"

My life was still made up of a series of unconscious and
repetitive acts formed by my past experiences. I realized I was
playing too small. I had more to offer the world, and there was so
much I wanted to experience in life.

I took a hard look at my job. I had to admit, I was uncomfortable in an industry mired in bureaucracy, and I was uncomfortable selling. While I loved the marketing work I was doing with the physical therapy company, it wasn't enough to get over my distaste for selling. Selling, in my assessment, was a process like the stack ranking process—the self-interest of the individuals in the system powered it. I no longer chose to be a part of that system. Additionally, I wanted to drive change, but I valued my relationship with my uncle more than I wanted to challenge and disrupt his company with changes I thought were needed to continue to be a viable organization in the evolving healthcare industry. I realized I was not aligned with the role. It wasn't a good fit, and I knew I'd best address it. I turned to prayer and meditation for guidance.

I had routinely been meditating since Dad passed, but only to achieve stillness and peace. It had been many months since I had received clear guidance. This night I received another rare and powerful moment with the Divine. I discovered I'd had an aversion to high paying jobs because I associated high pay with the ugly behaviors of the corporate world. It became clear that money wasn't bad—it was what I let the money do to me that was destructive. I would have to make peace with a high salary and allow myself to be open to the opportunity for a better income again. I also learned it was okay to work in information technology again. I would have to make peace with technology—I craved it. I had trained my brain for more than thirty years in math and logic, bits, and bytes, and in complex computer code. I ached to use this well-developed muscle in my head. I realized it was okay to go back into IT again if for nothing other than to give my brain something to chew on. My meditation ended with a clear lesson: "You must give up what you have to create the space for something new to come to you."

Despite this, a scary thought lingered—how could I leave a job again? Though unsatisfying, my present work was financially sustaining. When I'd left my job in Seattle without another job to go to, I took a major financial hit—a hit that I was still paying for. Why would I be guided to do this again?

I thought about this message for some time, but within a few days, I knew I had to leave my job. The next question was how. I valued my relationship with my uncle, so I knew it was best to go to him first to honor him and to preserve our relationship. I decided to talk to him after Christmas. In the meantime, while I was researching hospital staff and identifying potential sales contacts, I saw a message from a familiar recruiter. He found an IT leadership role in northwest Ohio. When I responded, he kicked himself for not remembering me from the year before. He thought I had an excellent chance and signed me up for an interview.

My first meeting with the hiring manager, the CFO, was a three-hour conversation that started in the late afternoon and extended well into the evening. Every interview I've ever had has had its surprises, and this one was no different. Here I was in Northwest Ohio where consistency and conformity are a way of life. The CFO was a white male, but everything else about him was unique. He'd been born and raised in Texas, went to a highly-acclaimed college on the west coast, lived in Cleveland, and drove one-and-a-half hours each day to get to his job. He had brass, intelligence, a metropolitan mindset, and experience with reputable firms. I found him interesting and potentially inspiring. At the same time, I sensed he would be challenging—but nothing my years of experience couldn't handle. On the way home from the interview, I called the recruiter and with brash confidence said, "The CFO is a real character. I can handle him, but not many in Northwest Ohio can. If I'm not your candidate, I don't know who in Ohio will be." It was a rare moment of confidence rather than ego, and I delivered it from the heart. I was learning to let go of the constraints that once bound me. I was learning to work and speak from my heart. It was a new way of being for me. I liked it.

I didn't hear back from the recruiter for weeks. It didn't matter. I was creating space for the new.

On the day after Christmas, after everyone had settled in for the workday, I went to my uncle's office, ensured he had time to talk, and closed the door. I didn't have a plan; I simply followed what naturally came. As soon as I started, my uncle said simply, "You're not happy here, are you? It's not a good fit?" I agreed, and with tears of relief rolling down my cheek, I thanked him for taking a risk on me, and for sustaining my family and me for the last eight months. "Let's just not tell anyone until after the holiday," he added. After New Year's, we met with the other leaders, then set January 18th as my last day.

It was as though the universe had coordinated the events in the tightest of timelines to prove to me I could and should trust the guidance I'd been given. Everything fell into place, minute by minute. On January 17th, I had a second interview for the new job. On January 18th, my current company held a gathering for me at 2:00. At 3:00, even before the crumbs from the goodbye cupcakes had been cleaned up, I had an offer. They wanted me to start Monday. There was no denying that there were greater forces at play, and I realized that if I had the courage to listen, trust, and follow them, all things would work out beautifully.

This time I approached work in a completely different and healthier way. I didn't worry about my title and power or about finding or creating places to prove my worth. I didn't follow the advice of the Harvard book, *The First 90 Days*, and deliver a strategy that would rock my boss's world. Instead, I fell into the rhythm of this privately-owned manufacturing company. I continued to learn to let go of the corporate pretenses, the dogfights, and the power plays. I trusted that I would be guided to learn what I needed to learn and do what I needed to do.

The first few months, however, did not go well from an IT operations perspective—the network crashed, we lost power and everything from phones to email to the Enterprise Requirements Planning system that ran the business crashed. Someone hacked our network, and slow response times and inexplicable outages plagued us. However, I didn't let these things bother me—I kept looking for a silver lining. I discovered that I was getting a crash course in everything I had inherited from my predecessor—I was identifying weaknesses and solving them, not through a well-tailored plan, but out of necessity. As devious and crass as it may seem, my coworkers came to believe my predecessor was hacking the network and causing many of the issues I faced. If that indeed was the case, I should thank him, for he helped me learn and gave me cause to fix the mess I inherited. The experience helped me build strength out of weakness and helped me secure myself in the role. I could have resented all of this and been angry; instead, I chose to be thankful. It was my new way of living.

I was learning to work in a new way too. The leadership liked me, and that seemed to be the most important thing. I didn't need to prove I could go toe-to-toe with them, outsmart them, or outmaneuver them. I simply needed to be a kind and caring human being and do my best to help them. I received kudos for the simple things—teaching them how to use a mobile phone, buying a printer, coming in at midnight to fix a computer that supported the 24/7 manufacturing process, all while keeping a smile on my face.

There is something beautiful about working in a small town and in a midsize company—something that's lost in big corporations. In smaller, less complex environments, you're keenly aware of the impact of your actions. Of course, everything that everyone does has an impact in this world. We're all like drops of water in a pond. Our drop, though small, ripples outward, touching everything in its path. In big corporations, the impact of the ripple is tough to see. In midsize companies, however, you see it and feel it every day. The person you cut off in the parking lot is the same person who's going to draw your blood for a health screening that day. The coworker you complain about over dinner has a daughter playing volleyball with your kid. The person you bulldozed in a meeting to get more funding sits beside you at church. And the person you cut loose from his job is now the cashier at the only grocery store in town; you'll see him every time you shop.

The fact is we're all connected. What we do and say impacts others. In a small town and a midsize company, we must act with kindness and good intents. We cannot humiliate the people we work with and expect that they'll go away as new, more likable people fill their role. We cannot accomplish our work and take the glory of the accomplishment while creating problems for others to handle. There are no others—you need to deal with the problems yourself. We couldn't downsize someone without being prepared to see that person and his kids at school functions every week. In midsize companies, the effect of our actions on coworkers, their families, and our community is clear, and we are held accountable for being our best selves. We play for a team—we play for a community. We win together, and we lose together, so we must act in a way that is best for all. That concept just gets lost in big companies, where employees can act without needing to think about the negative effects they are having on others.

Operating with the big picture in mind comes naturally to me, and I welcomed the chance to learn to do it better. I was proud to be working in an environment aligned with my natural way of being.

All the while, I managed to keep my job in perspective. It provided an income to live, but it was not my life. One way I stayed in balance was by attending my daughter's sporting events and volunteering to help the teams whenever I could. We started getting our home in order too. We worked on the house, finishing the basement, replacing the gutters and the landscaping, and building a patio out back. I planned and successfully pulled off my daughter's graduation party at our home. This time there was no meltdown—we were full of pride and had family and friends surrounding us. We traveled. We enjoyed life. I also gave myself time to enjoy the things I love—nature, music, the beach, and writing.

As if to remind me of the divine nature of life, I had another powerful experience—it came without forewarning as I walked past a colleague—a man I had not yet met. Suddenly, it seemed as if I knew him. I had a keen sense of knowing that I needed to pay attention to him and the work we would do together. As I walked on, I heard the message, "You are here to change the course of direction for him."

I had no idea what this meant, and I longed for more, but I received no clarifying information. I'd learned to trust this sense of knowing and I had faith in the message. I vowed to follow its guidance. It felt good to know that my work in this manufacturing company had more purpose than a mere income. I opened myself to whatever would come.

First, I got to know my new coworker. Our initial interaction was a disappointment. My colleague was a charmer—someone who gets work done through good looks, a pleasant disposition, and a few teasing smiles. I found it irritating, perhaps even a waste of time, to deal with charmers. I wondered why God would put a charmer in my life and direct me to "change the course of direction for him." Our first interaction made me think long and hard about my working relationship with men over the years.

My parents raised me in a culture that conditioned girls to feel secondary to men. I didn't accept that and had rebelled against the notion since birth. Still, many of my male counterparts expected me to fall in line. I'm not a flaming feminist, but their expectations and my resistance created a little friction. In college and at my first jobs, I began wondering if men enjoyed getting women to cower just for the fun of it or because putting women down made them feel bigger than they would otherwise. After a few years in the workforce, I noticed a pattern: men teased me like a sister, protected me like a daughter, tolerated me like a wife, or distanced me like a mother. Then there was the harassment. When I was in my twenties, my youthful good looks drew men to me. They joked and played with me, in the same way that cats play with mice. I often played along to keep the peace, but sometimes they went too far. Men positioned themselves behind me to watch my rear end as I walked down the hall; they stared at my chest, unable to look me in the eyes when they talked to me. I learned to dress in a way that drew less attention, but the sexual harassment continued. As the years rolled by and the pounds came on, my waning sex appeal became a reason to discount me as if my lack of youthful allure made me less intelligent or less capable. Not all men behaved like this, but I concluded that men in general just didn't know how to treat women as equals.

My "feminine" leadership style raised questions and concerns too. I was collaborative and trusting, growing people by mentoring and providing positive reinforcement through a "win-win" approach while my male coworkers were commanding and controlling. They preferred a "someone must win and someone must lose" approach. Many had no room for my style and deemed me inferior because of it. I didn't view the workplace as a competition. Nonetheless, they felt it necessary to prove themselves better than me, using verbal force and subtle intimidation and displaying their knowledge, political skill, and self-proclaimed superiority like a peacock displays its feathers. Men often cut me off and talked over me in a patronizing way, sold my ideas as their own, and told me to "calm down" or "behave" when I kept talking and represented my ideas.

I was no wallflower—I didn't abdicate to men. All too often when men couldn't command and control me, they retaliated by trying to silence me and by harshly judging my abilities.

I experienced just enough to know that workplace gender issues were real. That is why I was naturally suspicious of my new charge. I normally would have ignored a charmer like this, but I'd been called, so I embraced the challenge and risk and tried to get this relationship right. Perhaps if I wanted others to let go of their biases of me as a woman, I'd have to let go of my biases of men.

Our roles and our backgrounds were very different. It followed that our work styles were different, too. I felt I had a reason to see my coworker as a positive cause; otherwise, he might just perpetually have annoyed me. It didn't take long to see myself through his eyes, though—I was uptight and hell-bent on dollar signs. He helped me understand how I had hardened myself—a defensive shield to protect me from my male colleagues. I had long forgotten how to enjoy anything about the process of progressing towards a goal.

Ugh! I didn't like what I saw in myself, so I chose not to be that person any longer. I let my defenses down and leaned in more. I then started seeing each one of our interactions as an opportunity to overcome my old habit of being difficult and unpleasant when things didn't go my way or when others didn't match my laser-like commitment to big goals. He was having fun testing me, the new blood in the company, and in being unpredictable with each interaction. I, on the other hand, came to view each of these as an opportunity to bring forth a better version of myself.

My colleague eventually expressed some frustrations with conditions at work. I believed I had a little more experience, so I offered to help. When I couldn't help, I tried to motivate and even coach him, even though he never asked. I thought advice might be the thing I had to offer that would change his course of direction. However, as I talked to him, I realized something profound: whether my recommendation was to trust his instincts, make changes in his approach, or try something new, I realized that the advice I was giving him also applied to me. Some say that the world we experience is a reflection of ourselves, and this situation helped make that clear. What I thought *he* should do was what *I* needed to do.

When I accepted that, I started to heed my advice. It was now easy to see that if I wanted my boss to stop micromanaging me, I should stop micromanaging my direct reports or my kids. If I wanted my husband to communicate more with me, I needed to communicate more with him. If I wanted my coworkers to accept me, I just needed to accept myself. It wasn't others who had to change; it was me. The simple act of holding myself accountable to change in me the things I wished others would change in themselves began to alter my life.

I found this fascinating, plus there was more!

Over time, when he handed me comments or emails that I found awkward, annoying, trying, borderline inappropriate, or manipulative, I learned to see that these were expressions of his wit and humor and not the tools that coworkers of my past had used to belittle, criticize, minimize, and discriminate. I learned to resist the temptation to get angry (as I had in my thirties and early forties), and I never cowered to him. Instead, I learned to allow myself to see the humor in him and to my surprise, I learned I had a knack for being funny too. I laughed while we were working (how daring!). Not the sarcastic kind of laughter that teases and taunts other people for the fun of seeing them squirm, nor the insidious kind of laughter that camouflages real cuts and digs in a joke, but the easygoing, carefree kind of laughter that's integral to a lighthearted way of being. I found that laughter opened my soul so the truth could slip in seemingly unnoticed. The more we worked together, the more I lost my hard-ass attitude—and the more I became my authentic, joyful self. I re-evaluated how I was showing up at work and learned how to improve many other relationships, too.

Changing myself and learning to be less jaded by my past made huge changes in my life. I found myself less distracted and crazed by the world around me and more enchanted, for I saw almost everything as a clue to achieve desired life improvements and a roadmap full of hints that if I dared to follow, then would lead me to my goals. I wanted the world to see all the good in me, and this unsuspecting man was helping me find that good and unleash it. The more I embraced my divine appointment, the more I learned, and the more I learned, the more I improved my life.

Just as I did at Ohio State and in my work with Bringing Spirit to Leadership, I enjoyed, even thrived, on these lessons—they made me feel alive. In the years following my dad's death, I relished the feeling of being fully alive. I learned that I have a choice on the kind of impact I have on another person's life—I can be irritating, difficult, and demanding or instead, give kindness my very best shot. I learned I am not responsible for how others act or react. My responsibility is to be kind, but if they don't reciprocate my kindness, it's not my responsibility—and I don't have to alter myself to be more acceptable to them. I learned I have a choice on how I allow others to impact me. When I choose to interpret their actions as belittling, demeaning, and discriminating, that's what life gives me—more belittling, demeaning, and discriminating. On the other hand, when I choose to look at everything as an opportunity to be the very best me and trust that every situation is present in my life to create some good, life will give me exactly that—opportunity and goodness.

Eventually, our differences would stand taller than my fascination with the divine experience. Though I would have welcomed the opportunity to develop a friendship, the karmic energy between us dissipated. Once I learned the lessons, I lost the compelling force that spawned the urge. With that loss, I found one more lesson, and it was huge: the people that irritate, agitate, alarm, hurt, anger, and disappoint us are our greatest teachers. They are not inspirational role models we aspire to match, nor philosophers we follow to gain great wisdom. Rather, they are the family members that shun us, the players that play us, the co-workers that break our trust, and the friends that hurt us. They tap an emotion within us; an emotion so potent it's frightening. We can lash out and cast blame on others for these feelings, but when we have the courage to face them, we discover something true about ourselves. We can learn how to be accepting of others from the family that does not accept us; we can learn to embody a new level of honesty from those who have broken our trust, and we can learn to be kind from those that have caused us pain. In this way, I learned to stand in my truth from someone presenting me a series of games.

When I chose to see past the sense of irritation my coworker elicited, I found a wealth of opportunities to discover and step into my authentic self. I let go of the behaviors that protected me from cutthroat business environments and hurtful co-workers and grew beyond them.

I may never know if I fulfilled my divine appointment to help my co-worker change direction, but it was clear that the more I focused on following the guidance, the more I changed things for ME. It was like magic touched my life. The magic wasn't in my divine appointment or even this unsuspecting co-worker—the magic was in me! I harnessed that magic and let it go to work in other areas of my life.

At this point, I was, for the most part, comfortable in a job that met my financial obligations as well as my need to contribute and which gave my brain interesting challenges to chew on—all without stealing my personal life and without stealing my happiness. Now I could look in the mirror and get real. I recognized my physical and emotional state needed makeovers too.

On a shopping trip in search of wardrobe updates for work, I had a revelation: I was in my favorite clothing store—a store I had frequented for over twelve years because they always had stylish clothes that cleverly covered up the excess weight I had acquired. This time, though, I didn't find anything that looked nice, and their largest size was verging on tight. As I stood staring in the mirror at the half-naked body staring back at me, it hit me hard and fast: "Oh my God! I see my dad—with boobs!" On this shopping trip, I did not leave the store with clothes. Instead, I left with a harsh realization that had exposed me. I was already on medication for high cholesterol. If I didn't do something to alter my course, I was going to be in the same medical emergency-riddled path as my father's.

I'd known for years that I'd become overweight, but I just hadn't been able to lose it. I'd worked out with three different trainers, and had some modest success getting into shape, but I struggled to shed more than seven pounds. I'd tried the Atkins Diet, the South Beach Diet, protein drink meal replacements, and calorie counting, but none seriously altered my body shape. Now with my epiphany, I got more serious than I had been in the past.

Just as I was making up my mind to address my physical health, I received another signal: my employer announced a "Biggest Loser" program. I signed up with the intention to address nutrition and exercise differently than I had in the past. I knew it wasn't enough to simply commit—I had to reprogram my thoughts too. I was ready. When I reprogrammed my thoughts about my work relationships, I saw every interaction as an opportunity to be the very best "Me," and my work relationships improved—why couldn't I reprogram my thoughts about nutrition and exercise?

First, I rooted out all thoughts about failed past attempts to lose weight. I learned how our minds strive to protect us from reliving bad past experiences; in this case failing yet again. So, my brain reminded me of all the reasons why I shouldn't try to lose weight: "It's too expensive," "It's too hard," "It takes too much time," and "I have all these other things I must do." I had to replace all those thoughts. So, I started with the expense. Despite my less than stellar financial portfolio, I didn't let money rule the decision. I did what I needed to do, and I'd figure out the financials later. When I heard that voice in my head say, "It's too hard," I reminded myself of how hard it would be to deal with diabetes, the strokes, and all the other ailments my father had faced. I started to plant positive thoughts in my brain too. I told myself it would be easier to lose weight than to live day after day with the diseases associated with obesity. When I became burdened by the time commitments, I told myself I couldn't afford *not* to lose weight. When I thought that other things I had to do were more important, I re-evaluated where I spent my time. It turns out I was filling my time with a lot of things that I didn't have to do. I stopped watching TV, I limited my Internet browsing, and I lowered the priority of my creative endeavors. I put healthy food shopping and exercise in my life first, then filled the remaining time with other, less important things.

It was a good start. I'd find, though, that the thoughts about my weight and self-image ran deep, so I had to dig deeper than I had and be even more honest with myself. When I was young, thin, and shapely, I'd felt dismissed in the workplace. When I covered up that shapely body with a few pounds, I transformed to something other than "just another pretty face." In the depths of my mind, I created a thought I held on to—without the distraction of my looks, my intelligence and workplace contributions could be the focus of those around me. I had also unknowingly developed the notion that having a larger body (a more mannish one) helped my co-workers see me as an equal. Life had left my subconscious jaded. I had to let these thoughts go and replace them with healthier ones. I had to welcome a thin, shapely, beautiful Kelli back into my life. Shifting my thoughts allowed proper eating and exercise to do what they were supposed to do—help me lose weight.

The proper eating part I kept simple—I ate 1200 calories a day—an amount that was right for my body type. That's it; I would not use tricks or gimmicks. But I had to build new habits and make healthy eating a priority. No longer did I put off meals because I didn't have time to eat. I ate three meals and three snacks, evenly spaced over the day to prevent hunger pangs and to keep my metabolism burning at a steady rate. I didn't depend on convenient food and planned ahead, so I had healthful food with me at all times. I packed healthful food for work, road trips, my kids' sporting events, and everything else. I didn't fuss about spending a little more money on groceries. The perception of increased cost was a fallacy anyhow. Some of the items may have been more expensive. For example, a single serving of a Lean Cuisine macaroni and cheese meal is more expensive that a box of macaroni and cheese that feeds four, but I ate less, and I spent less on health care. I also swore off fast food. I'd eat Wendy's salad, but other fast-food choices simply blew my calorie allotment, so I stayed away. The toughest part was alcohol—something else our culture values! Though I couldn't deny that every time I had alcohol, especially beer, I gained weight, so I had to stay away from it.

When it came to exercise, I had to change my habits there, too. I'd had many stretches of good fitness levels in my life and had proven that I had the capacity to build muscle, but I wasn't doing the right kind of exercises to burn fat. I was fortunate to find a trainer that understood this—Roz. He developed a weight loss fitness routine that worked for me and adjusted that program based on my body's response. Roz kept me focused and motivated, and sometimes he was my psychologist too.

I committed to an exercise routine designed to spike my heart rate, then drop it, then spike it again, to burn fat. A typical workout consisted of jumping jacks, leg raises, kettlebell swings, triceps dips, push-ups, abdominal crunches, speed skaters, mountain climbers, burpees, deadlifts, squats, jump squats, lunges, and planks. Little to no equipment or a gym was necessary. Roz pushed me to move a little faster, to reach beyond my perceived limits, and realize more from my workouts. He also talked to me about nutrition, keeping me honest with my food choices. Working out with Roz at the local university gym with nineteen and twenty-year-olds had a wonderful impact, too. Subconsciously, I compared myself to them. At first, I was embarrassed. I couldn't move easily, and I looked bloated and old. Soon I was moving just like them, and my body started fitting in.

I continued to reprogram my thoughts as I lost weight. Self-control and discipline fueled my will to change eating habits and my commitment to exercise for a while, but they weren't enough alone. Choosing the right thoughts is what kept me going! Whenever I made a poor nutritional choice, there was the usual erroneous thinking behind it. I rooted out the misguided thoughts and traded them for new ones that supported my healthy goals. For example, for every celebration or entertainment event—every birthday, graduation, wedding, football game, concert, holiday, or cookout—my mind said I had to eat; I had to indulge! It turns out I didn't need food to celebrate—I just had to reprogram my brain to believe that I didn't have to eat to have fun. When I had a bad day at work, or I argued with my husband, my mind said, "Have a glass of wine!" or "Have some ice cream!" I reprogrammed myself to handle those challenges without food or booze.

I also learned to give up overgeneralizations. When I made a bad meal choice, that voice in my head said, "You're a failure." I had to stop that voice. After all, it was just one failure out of twenty-one successes in a week! I reprogrammed that voice to say "Great job, Kelli—twenty awesome decisions, one poor decision—now just get back on track!" It was amazing how eating healthfully was much easier when I was conscious of the thoughts driving my food choices and recognizing I could purposefully choose the right ones!

Surrounding myself with the right people was critical too. Yes, it was I who chose what to eat and powered through workout after workout, but the people around me helped me create an environment conducive to success and cheered me on. I let those closest to me know what they could do to support me. For example, I dreaded the thought of making high-calorie meals for everyone else, then eating something different to stay on plan. So, I rarely cooked—my husband and kids took over cooking. A year later, almost all of them had developed healthful eating habits too, so cooking became a nonissue. Friends and coworkers who supported my food and drink choices were helpful too, and that good feedback was often my fuel to keep going! Unfortunately, there were naysayers—people who were unsupportive and even a few who would try to sabotage my efforts. It's a shame that other people would want to see someone fail, but some folks simply wanted to see me remain my frumpy dumpy self. Perhaps it made them feel better about their lifestyle and life choices. Retraining worked for some, such as one of our suppliers at work. Before my weight loss efforts started, he showed up with doughnuts whenever he visited. After learning of my efforts, he showed up with doughnuts for my team and celery and carrots for me!

I kept observing my habits and soon discovered another interesting phenomenon. I had a pattern of taking on inhumane amounts of work, then working after hours and over the weekends to get it all done. I did the same with my personal interests too—whether it was making handmade Christmas gifts, household decorations, clever food treats for my kids' Halloween parties or hosting an elegant celebratory brunch for family and friends. Someway, somehow, I kept myself busy with big visions and extravagant standards. Now, after eating only 1200 calories for many weeks, I found I couldn't work long hours or stay up until 2:00 a.m. for my latest project. I came to realize I'd kept myself going all those years by snacking on carbohydrates like Goldfish, pretzels, and Doritos. To keep myself losing weight, I had to change this too. I pared down my commitments, stopped giving extra time to my job, and scaled back on my self-imposed grandiose standards for everything from "Feed the Team" dinners to Christmas celebrations. I had to space my home décor or craft projects out over time and reprogram my thoughts regarding the number of things I pushed myself to accomplish. I had to learn to accept that whatever I did, it was good enough.

By the end of my company's Biggest Loser program, I'd lost twenty-nine pounds, but I didn't stop. After six months, I'd lost fifty pounds and was only twenty pounds away from my goal weight. This stretch was the most difficult because the weight didn't fall off quickly. But I stayed after it. After a year, I'd lost seventy pounds. I started as a size 16W and got down to a size 6. Everything in my wardrobe changed but the socks. It was a sweet reward to get not only new clothes but beautiful ones. I no longer shopped in the store with clothes designed to cover up the bulges of middle-aged women. I shopped in stores that allowed me to express my new, fun-loving, and fit self. Most important of all, I no longer needed cholesterol medication, and my physicals delivered stellar reports.

My weight loss was symbolic too. The weight came off like unneeded baggage, as I discarded the habits and thoughts that no longer served me well.


My mental reprogramming continued into other areas of my life.

First off, farming. There was a time when I saw farming as an inferior way of life. Perhaps it had something to do with history—

the agricultural era gave way to the industrial era, which gave way to the information age. Perhaps I had inappropriately concluded that farming was inferior to industry and industry inferior to technology. Perhaps my thoughts about farming had something to do with my dad and his pushing me away from the life and on to alternative lines of work. Now I'd moved away from a community rooted in cutting edge technology and back into one based on agriculture. While there's more money in the communities tied to technology, they are not, in fact, richer. I'd learned that people live their lives similarly in both places—they all fill their lives with their kids' activities, time with family and friends, hobbies, and travel. Some people have more money, others have more time, some have less stress distracting them, and others have more exposure and confidence to try new things in life. I reframed my thoughts—farming was not inferior.

Three years after Dad died, once Denny and I had put ourselves in good financial position, we began farming the land I inherited. We had a barn, grain bins, a tractor, and a knowledge of agriculture dating back thirty years. It was a foundation to build on. We bought a planter and a second tractor and educated ourselves about fertilizers and pesticides. We arranged with other farmers to till the ground and harvest until a day we may choose to buy the equipment to do it ourselves. Also, Denny and I modified the husband-and-wife farming relationships we'd known in our past. We committed to being equal partners, jointly making decisions and as much as we could, jointly doing the work.

As I signed the checks to purchase equipment, fertilizer, and seed, I developed a newfound respect for my dad—all that he knew, all that he risked, and all that he shouldered in responsibility. Farming is a business venture like no other. Once a year, you make a large cash outlay—an outlay twice as big as most people's annual income—to purchase seed and fertilizer. You plant the seeds, fertilize them, then surrender to Mother Nature and pray for good things to happen. You marvel as seedlings turn into green stalks and wait with anticipation to see if those stalks will result in enough ears of corn and pods of soybeans to pay for the seed, fertilizer, equipment payments, diesel fuel, taxes, and other expenses. You watch the grain markets like a day trader watches the stock market, hoping you sell at the right time. It's an annual gamble, hoping you play your assets just right to cover your expenses, and make a little profit too. I had more respect for Dad. I almost gave up the opportunity to farm with Denny, because I assumed he'd be like my Dad—unable to farm in partnership with me. I was thankful Denny had the strength and grace not only to farm but be my equal.

Farming in addition to my revitalized professional life created just about the perfect balance. I still sought peace, however. I sought to be happy in every moment of every day, to live to my fullest potential, and to be content. My restlessness proved there was something yet to work on. Although I'd done a little work on my emotional health along the way, it still required some attention.

Life was increasingly amazing. It seemed that whenever I was ready to face a part of my past, the Universe would acknowledge my readiness by creating the circumstances I needed to revisit it. Each time I looked at an issue again, I had the opportunity to experience it with a different perspective. Each time I had the opportunity to understand it differently. In other words, issues repeatedly arose until I could root out the flawed thoughts and memories, heal them, then let them settle back into my memory in a healthier way.

One of the skills I'd honed while working on my weight loss was listening to my mental chatter. The more ingrained the habit, the harder I had to work to hear the mental noise that accompanied it. Now that my physical, spiritual, and career lives were in order, I began to hear a theme—my belief about success.

Now, while working or contemplating new endeavors, I could hear the voice in my head saying "You can't expect to be too successful because that's asking too much." This thought ran rampant through my subconscious. When it entered my consciousness, I explored the belief by questioning it. I asked myself, why did I believe I was only allowed a limited amount of success; who set the limits; who granted success? I wondered if it was God? That didn't make sense. I'm sure God wouldn't say I owed him a multitude of failures to have a few successes. I was sure He was willing to grant me the experience of success without suffering. The only other answer I could find was me. Was I was asking myself for permission to be successful? If that were the case, why would I not be kind to myself and simply allow it?

I suppose this was a bit like experiencing the proverbial angel on one shoulder and the devil on the other, both arguing over the correct course of action.

At this time in my life when I was financially sound enough that I could venture out to explore the world again, the mental chatter became more protective. "Most people aren't privileged to travel and experience the world—they don't like seeing you experience success. They think you're showing off and gloating. You're spoiled; you can't afford to do all these things; you can't afford success." This thought was the worst one—"You won't be accepted if you are too successful."

Acknowledging these thoughts was like acknowledging the ugliest monsters, the biggest fears, and the skeletons of painful, disappointing memories that had taken residence in my mind. It was clear now—I didn't think I deserved success! Facing these thoughts was easier than I could have ever dreamed. With a healthy body, healthy heart, and newfound strength of self, I could respond to this fear not only with reason but with humor.

I countered these ugly monsters with questions. "Being proud of success is showing off or gloating? Having multiple successes is being spoiled? What's this 'deserve' notion? What societal debts do I have to pay to earn the right to travel and experience success? Can't I travel just because I like to? As for fitting in—Geez—Really? You'd sacrifice the things you want to do in life to be more acceptable to others? C'mon, Kelli! Give yourself permission to fly, girl!"

The truth of the matter was that these were old emotional wounds—things from my childhood that were still framing current events. In fact, they might not even have been mine to own; some of them might be my parents' thoughts or my community's beliefs. Money and travel were huge issues for my parents—Mom wanted to travel; Dad didn't. He scorned Mom every time she wanted to do something he considered extravagant, especially travel. I'm sure I sensed my parent's opinions on travel expenses and had adopted them as my own. Further, most people in my community didn't spend money on anything that was "extravagant." It was a limiting belief commonly held in my hometown; perhaps a notion left over from pioneering days or the Great Depression. Or it could be a notion especially relevant to asset-rich, cash poor farmers. Whatever the origin, my community simply didn't like to spend money on things like fancy cars, expensive hobbies, or travel. It just wasn't something people there did. They lived modest lives and expected others in the community to do the same. And the notion of "showing off" came from my childhood too. When I was a teenager, it was something I often heard accusations of showing off. To some degree, that was simply a matter of circumstances—the life I was born into. Being the daughter of a man who was a successful farmer and a woman of good taste meant I had nice things in my life. What others called showing off was rooted in the fact that I was a typical teenager—acting out trying to discover who I was and who I was not. And "showing off" just may have been something I did to distance myself from the pain that existed in our family—the pain of losing Kraig and the dysfunction his death left behind.

Somehow, "showing off" and "travel" and above all "success" were thoughts living as background noise in my mind—thoughts I was not aware of. I allowed them to surface, and as I acknowledged them, I realized that I had no need for them anymore. I let go of the thoughts and the emotions they triggered. It was time to interact with everyone from strangers to co-workers to friends to family without baggage from the past. That is how I created room for new, healthier thoughts to take that space.

Just as I had with the weight loss, I reprogrammed my brain with a new mantra: "I allow success, abundance, the pride of accomplishments, and travel and adventure into my life. I give myself permission to fly, to soar, to enjoy life without shame or the need to fit in."

As if on cue, the universe gave me the experience to burn these new thoughts into my mind. Some thought I was crazy, and the truth is, I thought I was a little crazy too, but when the opportunity arose to have a foreign exchange student in our lives, I said yes.

I was in Seattle visiting my best friend, Beth when I received an email from Ohio: "Help! We have a foreign exchange student that is temporarily living in the community until a host family can be found. This student is a young man from Germany grade 11."

Till Kruger was in Ohio to begin the school year as a US student, but before he got to his host family, the arrangements fell through. Denny and I had talked about hosting a student sometime in the future, but until now it had remained just that—a goal in the future. On the surface, we were completely unprepared, but deep in our hearts, we were ready. When I got the email, I immediately thought, "if it were my son in a foreign country without a home, I'd want someone like us to step up," so I did. I called Denny. Then I called the school. Ten days later, Till moved in.

In many ways, it was perfect. Till was seventeen, right between our eighteen-year-old daughter, Michaela, and our twelve-year-old daughter, Morgan. Cody was taking the year off from college and living at home, so he'd have a chance to have a brother, our family would have a chance to connect with our German heritage, and I would have a chance to learn more about myself—to heal any additional emotional wounds buried deep inside me.

Till was timid at first, and I suppose our family was reserved as well. We soon found common ground with football. Till longed to learn the sport. Though our school district was too small to have a football team, we had a love for Ohio State football and were prepared to share it. We taught him all the OSU traditions and bonded as he became a true Buckeye. Then there was a shared passion for working out and healthy eating. It was habitual—Denny, Cody, Till, and I worked out together three or four times a week, and we frequently shopped for healthy food together—holding each other accountable for eating healthy. By the middle of winter, we were letting it all hang out. Though Denny and I were stronger than we were six months prior, we were still prone to high-energy verbal fights. Till witnessed these arguments. I wasn't proud of that, but I viewed it from a healthier perspective than I had in the past. Till experienced life with a family who lived and worked together in harmony as well as in conflict. He saw five individuals who had the freedom to follow their dreams and the tenacity to do the emotionally tough work necessary to flourish as a family. Sometimes those emotions led to quarrels. He witnessed love as a light and love as a shadow—it took both to create and maintain the strong bonds our family enjoyed.

Soon Till was feeling ready to try new things. He would learn what it meant to work hard, stay disciplined, and find the confidence required to extend himself into the American way of life. Till made friends and lost friends, went to Homecoming and Prom, threw the discus and shot put on the track team, and hung out with his American friends. Of course, we were there to support him and treated him like one of our own.

Till lived with us for nine months. He entered our home a timid, slender, seventeen-year-old German boy. Nine months later, he had transformed into a muscular young man. With a sad heart and tears running down my face, we sent him off on his travels back to Germany with a personality shining through and biceps three times as big as when he'd arrived. That was his own doing—he'd dedicated himself to eating right and working out religiously. Denny and I created an environment where the kids in our family grow confidence and were encouraged to shine. Till had the courage to do both.

Till had even wanted to stay, so we had a sense of accomplishment—that we'd been a good family for him. The letter he left us when he departed told us that he'd learned his stay was not about the American clothing, the American food, football tickets, or anything else about the American culture. What he valued were the moments we shared—the discussions we had while driving to the mall to shop for clothes, the fun we had while eating a good burger, and the laughs we had while singing songs in the car on the way to the football game. It was about being the best people we could be—in a family, in a school system, in a nation, and in the world, all connected as humankind. It made Denny and me feel proud to know he'd learned so much from his experience.

My "aha" would come weeks after Till left. Reflecting on the nine months we'd had with him; I realized this: *there wasn't anything wrong with me.*


It all had started with a simple decision to change my life. I took the big steps. I moved from Seattle to rural Ohio and traded a big income and big debt for a right-sized income and right-sized debt. I traded the stress and the pressure of an overly demanding and punishing work environment for a respectable one. I left all the big company ugliness for a company that shared my personal values. It was more than that, though. It wasn't about the expensive city, and it wasn't really about the big company.

What mattered most was changing my thoughts. And changing my thoughts changed my actions. The big steps I took were helpful, but they weren't the core components of the change. What mattered is what I did with every waking moment. We have a choice on how we spend the moments of our lives. We can allow habit to guide our choices and let flawed thoughts and memories and emotions lead us. We can see the negative in life and use that negative as a reason to believe what we believe, fear what we fear, and keep us from trying. Or, we can live in the present and approach every moment as an opportunity for some good. We can consciously choose to be our best without fear and junk from our past.

I'd rooted out my flawed thoughts, faced my fears, and made better choices. I chose to believe in my best thoughts and expect the best outcomes. I chose to be kind, healthy, and physically fit. And I chose to follow the spiritual guidance given to me. By focusing on thoughts I held in my mind, I chose to live up to my potential and change my existence in this life. Moment after moment after moment, I made a conscious decision to be the best I could be.

Now, with a different way of living, I wondered just what I could accomplish. I would surprise even myself.

*Chapter 14*

# About a Man and a Mountain

"If you always put limits on everything you do, physical or anything else, it will spread into your work and into your life. There are no limits. There are only plateaus, and you must not stay there, you must go beyond them."
Bruce Lee

In the summer of 2009, I confronted Denny about our marriage. I wasn't happy, and I wanted changes. He was unhappy too, but we were both accustomed to, and to some degree, comfortable with our charade. It may have been easier to pick up the phone to call a lawyer and plot a plan for a divorce, but we didn't. We had the hard conversations. Away from the kids, neighbors, fellow soccer parents, friends, and coworkers, we aired our difficulties in Mother Nature. We rode bikes on the Snoqualmie Valley Trail, hiked the Twin Falls trail, walked the Puget Sound shoreline on Alki Beach, and explored the Soaring Eagle Nature Preserve. We talked about things we did early in our marriage that hurt each other, vetted our financial issues, and discussed our poor communication patterns. Glimmers of the love we shared appeared in these difficult conversations, but they paled in comparison to the blaming, arguing, and yelling. We both held a lot of hurts, but we kept trying to fix it—spending weekend after weekend trying to release the hurt so we could move on. We even went to a couples retreat at a rustic mountain lodge in Oregon to learn ways to work together better. Then life grabbed me by the hand and pulled me through many challenges. We stuck together through these trying times, but we never really gave our marriage the attention it needed—we never really faced and addressed our problems.

Now, four and a half years later, as 2013 ended, we looked back to reflect on the accomplishments we made that year and looked forward to setting goals and plans for the new twelve months ahead. For me, the previous year had focused on my weight loss. I felt great, and I was in great shape—maybe the best shape of my life. I had focused on eating well, exercising, and hitting my goal weight for so long, that now that I was just a few pounds away from my target, but I found it scary to live life without a big goal. I needed a challenge beyond losing weight to keep me on a good, healthy path.

I asked for input from people around me. Some hesitated, wondering why I (or anyone for that matter) couldn't just be content with what I'd achieved. Others reluctantly offered ideas, though brainstorming potential goals for challenging oneself was a foreign process to them. A scant few found the idea exhilarating and had fun offering suggestions: body building, snowshoeing, cross-country skiing, marathon running, biking across the state, and hiking.

I ruled out body building quickly. More power to the bodybuilders, but it's just a little too showy for me. There was something about running—it probably had something to do with high school sports, where running was used as punishment for poor performance, so it wasn't right for me either. Finally, my husband weighed in with the winning idea: "Why don't you just climb Mount Rainier? That's something we'd talked about doing when we lived in Washington. Why not do it now?"

His idea felt right, and my first instinct was to say, "Yes." But my thoughts got in the way. For decades, I had just been a spectator of the things in life that required some level of physical fitness. I even thought of myself as an observer. Questions quickly arose in my mind: could I be in good enough physical shape to climb one of the tallest mountains in the lower forty-eight states? Was I courageous enough to meet such an audacious goal?

Without answering those questions, I said, "Okay! But only if you go with me!" I had learned to say yes to life, so I said yes with the confidence that I would figure everything out later, and it would all fall into place. Asking Denny to go with me was like asking him to start dating again.

On New Year's Eve, we had a nice, low-key celebration. We stayed home with our kids and their friends, ate some good food, and watched movies as the minutes ticked toward midnight. Denny and I sat in the background, using the downtime to research climbing Mount Rainier. We watched video clips, read blogs, and found a website for guide companies and read everything they offered. We became convinced it was possible; challenging, but doable. We were going to need our trainer's help to prepare us physically. We also needed an education. The equipment list referenced things we had never heard of before—what were gaiters and crampons? Plus, we were going to need a little luck—bookings were full for all the Rainier climb schedules for the 2014 season. We'd have to count on a cancellation to get on the list.

Denny and I made a pact to do more research and to seek out available climbing dates. I upheld my commitment. After three more weeks of research, I felt I had found as much as I was going to find and learned as much as I was going to learn without reserving a date. Having lived in Seattle, I knew Mount Rainier could see snowstorms as late as mid-June. Wintery conditions could return as early as September. In my mind, we had to climb in July or August. It would be perfect to climb on my fiftieth birthday, July 12!

As soon as I thought about my birthday, this climb seemed fitting. I decided my fiftieth birthday gift to myself would be climbing Rainier. I didn't need a celebration with cake, drinks, and presents—I would celebrate my redesigned life and start the second half of my life my making this climb. It would set the tone for the rest of my life.

I'd hoped Denny would take the lead and call climbing companies. After all, Rainier had been his idea. He didn't, and I was disappointed. I wondered if he was committed to this—or was I going to be on my own? The women of my parent's generation would tell me that I should be happy I had a man that is loyal and caring, that I shouldn't expect more of him. Still, in this situation, I wanted the man I share my life with to take the initiative, go after goals, and drive for success in addition to being loyal and caring. I'd spent far too many moments in my life waiting for my husband to go after new things ahead of me or in lockstep with me. Something inside me snapped. I decided I wasn't going to wait for him—I was just going to do it. I found a company, Alpine Ascents, and though their 2014 climbing schedule appeared to be full, I called. They put Denny and me on a waiting list and were optimistic they could get us on the schedule. They expected, but couldn't guarantee that they could confirm a climb date by late April. They emailed me a training guide, which I sent to our trainer, Roz. This adventure was beginning to feel real. We might just climb Mount Rainier!

In the early months of training, I'd dealt with serious bouts of light-headedness. Tests such as an EKG, electrocardiogram, blood pressure, and blood work determined that I was fine, but I needed to adjust my water and salt intake. Later I dealt with Achilles pain. These were minor; I stayed healthy. Denny did too.

I remained consistent with my eating habits. I got the right nutrition to continue toward my weight loss goal, though the last few pounds were proving to be quite stubborn. I was also consistent with my workouts, always exercising three nights a week no matter what new conflicts arose. I just made workouts a priority.

Denny, on the other hand, struggled. His job had seasonal highs and lows. The weeks leading up to the spring planting season always gave him more work than anyone could reasonably handle. He left the house at 3:00 or 4:00 a.m. and worked grueling hours to schedule corn and soybean seed shipments to warehouses and farmers throughout the Midwest. Often, he'd load those shipments early in the morning and late at night before and after the hourly workers were on the clock. He got home at 8:00 or 9:00 p.m. totally spent! He wasn't eating well, often skipping meals or eating high-calorie fast food.

While Denny struggled, I got through the workouts with some semblance of grace and felt completely energized afterward. I had more experience in the gym than Denny. I'd started working out religiously in January 2012 and had been consistent and hard at it for the weight loss effort since then. After exercising with my daughter and losing her to college, then with my son and losing him to his travels, Denny joined me. He started exercising in September 2013, but his commitment wasn't as strong as mine. I always found a way to get in three workouts a week—Denny's commitment was limited to simply supporting me. So, he'd choose to miss workouts for work or out of a belief that only he could pick up our daughter from after-school activities. Roz had, from time to time, cut back on his planned routine so Denny could complete it.

One night the previous fall, when he couldn't keep up, I blurted out, "If you're going to go down, stay down. Don't try to get back in only to drag and fall out again. When you do that, Roz worries you're going to pass out or puke, so he curtails his expectations of us, and I don't get a good workout!" Some might have seen that as harsh. I saw it as being focused on my weight loss and fitness needs.

So, Denny took to sitting out when the workout got too much. In December, I thought I might need to exercise without him so that I could keep progressing, but he got it together and made a focused effort to keep up with me. Now that we were working toward the goal of climbing Mount Rainier, Roz held his line. He kept after us to meet the goals he'd set for us. And I didn't let Denny sit out. It wasn't uncommon to hear me pushing him on in the gym: "C'mon, Miller, get your butt down." "Let's go, Miller." Somehow, calling him "Miller" took me out of the wife role and put me into a coaching role. Others in the gym were more forgiving and asked Denny if he needed to rest. But Roz told them, "Kelli is doing the right thing. Up on the mountain, he isn't going to have the option of sitting out. She'll need to encourage him on."

Over the years, I had come to believe I was a badass wife with high expectations. But Denny wasn't the type to say "yes, dear" if he didn't mean it, and Roz was offering an alternative view. I was a wife encouraging her husband to meet a goal! Why couldn't I have seen that all these years? It was good to adjust my thoughts again.

This night in February, Denny had overcome his pattern of sitting out. He stuck with it. But it hit him hard. After the workout had ended, Denny looked at me and said, "If we're going to climb Mount Rainier, something has got to change. We need to..." I stopped listening after he said "We." When he finished, I simply said, "There is no WE in this. I'm doing what I need to do. I'm doing fine. YOU need to do what YOU need to do to make this happen. But I'll support you." For the first time, I think Denny found motivation beyond supporting me. He was going to climb Mount Rainier. He had to eat better, get more sleep, make it to all the gym sessions, and find it within him to handle the whole workout from here on out.

This change was big. For the first time, I held a new line. I didn't take responsibility, mentally or spiritually, for Denny's share in this. It was a new way to approach my life and our marriage. I didn't own his boundaries as my own—I didn't have to restrain myself to the limits he put on himself. I busted free my constraints and held him accountable for doing the same. In the process, I would free him and myself from the anger and blame I would place on him when we didn't attain our goals.

I was training to climb a mountain, but I was solving marital problems too. It was something I had vowed to do before the challenge of the war room, Dad's cancer, our move, Mom's cancer, and building a new life in Ohio took over. It was something that we needed to do for both our good, and I was glad training for a mountain climb was giving us the forum to do it!


One night in March, the gym was full of family! The University was on spring break, so the gym was void of the nineteen- and twenty-year-olds that typically surrounded us. Morgan and

Michaela joined Cody, Denny, and me for a workout. It was good for me to see that one year after I'd started my weight loss journey, my whole family was routinely in the gym.

In late March, I was restless and couldn't wait until April to check in with Alpine Ascents, so I contacted them again. "Hey, just wanted you to know we've been working out for the climb since I contacted you back in January. We're still eager to get on the schedule this summer. Please let us know if you have any openings." Three and a half hours later, Alpine Ascents responded. "Good timing. We just had a couple cancel for the August 23 climb. It's not your preferred date of July 12, but it's a good time to climb. It's yours if you want it." It didn't take long for Denny and me to confer and decide. By the end of the day, I replied. "We haven't been training all this time to say no. We'll take it. We'll climb August 23."

Before we signed the paperwork, I called my godson, Zack—he was an avid rock climber and hiker and was planning to climb Rainier this summer too. He supported our decision to climb with Alpine Ascents. So, we read the paperwork, filled out the application, and made our down payment. We were a little overwhelmed with the information—but we had plenty of time to digest it. A dream was turning into reality. It felt wonderful!

April was the one-year anniversary of my weight loss efforts. I was at my lowest weight, and both my workouts and my body began to change. We started spending more time walking at a fast pace on an incline on the treadmill and climbing the steps on the Stairmaster. Soon we were carrying weights when we climbed—a lot of leg and core muscle work for strength and balance. But instead of losing weight, I began gaining as I put on muscle. I had to adjust my thinking to get good with this! By April, Denny was doing much better in his workouts too. It made me happy to know we were both on a good path to make this climb happen.

Also in April, I told my boss about our plans. I thought he'd be impressed, perhaps even excited for me. To my surprise, he was neither. He graciously agreed to the time off, but said, "That sounds dangerous. I want a succession plan for what I should do if you die on that mountain. And I advise you to get a will if you don't already have one." Needless to say, I was stunned. I hadn't thought about a succession plan or a will because I hadn't thought about dying! I wasn't even really scared about the climb until this point. Now I had a healthy dose of fear.

Maybe that is why I put off plans to tell my mother until a later date. If she became gripped with thoughts of the worst-case scenario, it was going to be a tough discussion. I decided to do trials by telling more people at work before I told Mom or anyone that might share my news with her. Handling their reactions should prepare me well for Mom.

By May, I was beginning to see just how far we had already come. The preparation was changing me. The workouts alone were lessons in discipline, consistency, and priorities. As I prepared for other aspects of the climb, I was learning to take risks and be open to new things. I was learning to believe in myself and sort through the comments others offered so I could find the gems of wisdom and dismiss comments born out of their fear and discontent. I was learning to choose the thoughts and beliefs that were supportive of my goals and to dismiss those that undermined my confidence or distracted me from my goal. I was consciously choosing how I spend each moment of my life. I routinely asked myself if I was using the present moment in a way that would move me toward my goal. Did I have the uplifting attitude I needed to get me toward it? If not, I adjusted my attitude and how I spent my time, for you never achieve big, hairy, audacious goals with one big swift action. You achieve them with a series of small wins compiled over time. I was finding great lessons on the path to being everything I could be.

Then things got ugly for a while. I had addressed my career, my physical health, and my emotional health, but my marital health was proving to be a deep challenge. It begged for healing too.

While out to dinner with the kids, Denny and I started talking about and planning for the week ahead. We had many responsibilities. For four months, his full-time job demanded working seven days a week and up to sixteen hours a day. In addition to my full-time job, I had more household chore duties because Denny couldn't share them with me at this time. Our farm demands were great too (it was a critical time—we had to get the corn and beans planted. Mother Nature doesn't wait!). Morgan had softball practices, basketball practices, and basketball tournaments in faraway places. Michaela, who was now in college, needed help moving out of one residence hall and into another. Financially, it was a stretch, and we didn't have enough time to do everything. We were overwhelmed, to say the least. In despair, Denny rebelled: "This workout schedule is demanding! It's consuming our time! Climbing Mount Rainier isn't an easy thing to do. The next time you try to talk me into doing something as big as climbing a damn mountain, I'll…" I stopped listening when Denny inferred this was all on me.

It was a pattern in our lives. We'd invest ourselves in many things and liked our kids to do the same. We'd get overwhelmed. We'd stress. We'd break down. Then we'd blame each other.

I refused to take the blame for the demands of training. The Mount Rainier climb had been Denny's idea, and we both made the commitment. We argued lightly inside the restaurant, we argued vehemently at home, and we eventually stopped talking. Two days later, we drove to the gym in separate cars, and we went through the entire workout without speaking.

I was tired of feeling overwhelmed by responsibilities and tired of feeling I didn't have enough money to do the things we loved. I was tired of taking the blame when the going got rough and of being put on the defense and forced to stand up for myself, only to be labeled as the aggressor because I didn't roll over and cower. I was simply tired of it all! I was beginning to wonder if life would be easier on my own. I was beginning to wonder if I should climb Mount Rainier on my own.

I seriously thought about both possibilities.

Ten days later, we were still arguing. The fight snowballed, gathering more and more sources of pain as it went. We weren't sleeping in the same bed, we rarely talked, and we were extremely stressed. In the heat of the battle, Denny said, "I'm covering up the fact that I really don't love you." At that, I took my wedding ring off to let him know I was serious about ending this damn blame-game and the vehement arguments by ending us!

As I pondered the idea of climbing Rainier on my own, I found a video called *Ascend Mount Rainier* and watched it on my computer at the kitchen table while Denny and the kids flitted around the room getting food. We still weren't talking. However, after watching the video and visualizing myself on the mountain alone, something moved me. I broke my silence and asked Denny to watch it too. Something drew me back to him.

Simultaneously, we put our heads into the reality of the climb. We expected many aspects that the video depicted—the rock and gravel, the long treks, the snow and ice, the gear, and camping at Camp Muir. Other things stretched our thinking. I knew the backpack would weigh up to forty pounds, but I was surprised to see its dimensions. I started wondering how that big pack would change my center of gravity and how a changed center of gravity would affect me physically as I climbed. I was also surprised to see the climbers roped together. I guessed we would get training for that! Then there were the realities of the weather. Climbing in August minimized the risk of snow, but I hadn't thought about sleet, hail, and lightning—all possibilities in August. The most frightening things in the video, however, were the glacier crevasses. I don't like heights, and some of those crevasses were very deep. The video showed climbers crossing over them on a ladder or a piece of wood. That's an awfully narrow and awkward structure for someone in hard snow boots carrying a forty-pound backpack! In some way, I had to get good with this!

A healthy conversation between Denny and me resulted from watching the video together. We were talking for the first time in days.

Soon, I reluctantly began sleeping in the same bed as Denny again. He told me that when he'd said, "I'm covering up the fact that I don't love you," he had been sarcastic, and he'd regretted saying it. I've never really liked this kind of aggressive sarcasm that is so common in my hometown. I was happy he'd admitted his own was wrong—I admitted I needed to curtail mine, too. He said he was sorry and sent flowers to the office, and I forgave him.

I do believe he loves me, though I'm a bit callous about the words "I'm sorry." "I'm sorry" is an empty sentiment if not accompanied by the intention to understand what caused the problem, take ownership of it, and prevent it from happening in the future. Denny had blamed me for things that have gone wrong in his life far too many times, which hurt beyond measure. I held out for something more meaningful than the empty words, "I'm sorry." At the same time, I was giving our relationship the best I had to try to mend it. We had far more reasons to make our relationship work than we had reasons not to make it work.


Life carried on. In the gym, I started running on the treadmill. I've never really liked to run, so I hadn't done it much in my life. But I tried it and was surprised when I went a mile without much thought. I talked to Roz, and he thought I could go longer, so I signed up for my company's 5k run and ran in it three days later. I was forty-nine years old, and I ran my first 5k on a whim. It felt odd, but it felt good. I was proud to do something I'd never done before.

Denny and I were still stressed, but he decided to go with me to the race. That gave me hope for our relationship. Instead of running, he simply went to support me. I was let down. I was hoping to go after the goal of a 5k together, not me on my own with his support, for we have a lot of practice at that! Clearly, we still had work to do in our relationship.

As we approached June, I finally found the gumption to tell Mom about our climb. I thought she'd be worried and concerned. Instead, she had the complete opposite reaction. She was thrilled! She was happy we were setting a big goal and going on a journey to meet that goal. Then she said, "I have hang gliding on my bucket list. I may not be able to do that now, so you'll have to do that too...for me!"

Wow, I earned her support and another adventurous goal in a split second!

Somehow, we got through the stress of planting crops, spring sports, and the end of the school year activities. Denny and I started finding our way again with a little less stress. It was now our twenty-seventh wedding anniversary. Six months before, I had gotten tickets for Denny to see George Strait in Boston and tickets to Fenway Park. Nothing like an adventure away from the stress sources and a twelve-hour drive in a car alone together to help us mend our differences!

During our drive, Denny and I talked to Alpine Ascents to ask about our training. We believed we needed to do something to test ourselves in the altitude. The climbing expert we talked to didn't think we needed to worry about it so much. He thought it would serve us well if we could meet all the training guidelines in the Alpine Ascents documentation. That conversation made us feel better! Worrying about wearing my contacts on the climb, I asked about them. The expert said I'd need very good glacier glasses that fit snugly to my face and would prevent wind and glare from becoming a problem.

We had a great time in Boston—we both looked and felt fabulous while we ran through the streets, danced all night long listening to George Strait and Tim McGraw, walked on the beach on the North Shore, and shopped in the quaint little New England town of Newburyport. We enjoyed ourselves in new ways now that we were physically fit!

Then on the ride home, I got an email from one of my trusted co-workers: "Did you hear? Six people died on a Mount Rainier climb last weekend." The universe was begging me to understand that this climb was dangerous, though I didn't want to focus on that. I did some research—the climbers were on the Liberty Trail, the most advanced trail for only the most experienced climbers. Denny and I discussed it as we drove from Boston to Ohio. He felt the chances of getting into a car accident were greater than a fatal accident on Mount Rainier, so he wasn't moved to change plans. I was happy he had an opinion and that his commitment held—I wanted the man in my life to be confident in the face of a challenge. After Denny had voiced his commitment to go forward, I made my decision. I felt our climb circumstances were different because we would be on a less risky trail than those who died. I wasn't moved to change plans. We both remained secure in our goal.

Recommitting to a mutual goal was good for us—good for us physically and for our relationship.

## Chapter 15

# The Rehearsal

"We cannot lower the mountain. Therefore, we must elevate ourselves."
Todd F. Skinner

For some reason, I was certain we needed a trial climb. Denny wasn't, however, though I'm sure his feelings stemmed more from our lack of money and time than from sensibility. Nonetheless, I pressed on for one—an effort to test our physical preparedness and get comfortable with equipment and concepts that were all new to us.

Something I read made me believe Pikes Peak in Colorado would be a good test. Like Mount Rainier, the Pikes Peak summit is more than 14,000 feet above sea level. Unlike Rainer, it isn't glacier-covered. Also unlike Rainier, a cog train runs to the summit. Denny and I talked about it and researched it. Our first idea was to stay in a hotel (maybe even a resort or spa hotel), make the hike up in a day's time, and take the cog train down (proof that we were rookies). Eventually, we would plan to stay at a bare-minimum camp (Barr Camp) halfway up the trail and make the hike up and down in three days. The camp's cabin was full, so we made tent camp reservations. We didn't have a tent, so we researched and bought one. We also began researching weather conditions and appropriate food. Everything was new to us.

Ten weeks before the climb, we made an expensive but fruitful trip to REI, the outdoor outfitters. We got many of the personal items we needed for the climb—things that are probably in every hiker's closet but were foreign to us. We purchased everything from synthetic underwear to long underwear, liner socks, and backpacks.

Back home, we were up to four workouts a week. Just climbing the Stairmaster at level 15 for fifteen minutes burned 300 calories, but I wasn't losing weight. I had routine hunger pangs because my workouts demanded more calorie intake, and no one could deny that I was gaining muscle. It was obvious in my legs and glutes. Denny got each of us a twenty-pound bag of corn seed, which we put in the backpacks. We did step-ups with the packs on to simulate our real climbing experience. We added more weight as the weeks rolled on. Though the workouts were more demanding than before, Denny and I were keeping up. I felt like a beast afterward!

It was interesting to watch my body change. In April, I wore size six pants and wondered if I needed to buy size four. Now in June, I was wearing size six pants, and feeling like my thighs were going to burst out of the seams, and I was wondering if my waist was crying for a size eight. As hard as I'd worked to get to that size six, I didn't care that I was blowing out of it again—I was just that focused on the climb. I was sure I would get back to that sleek, thin, hourglass figure after the climb.

At about this time, my office held a health screening. With my height and weight measures in hand, they smiled and told me I was overweight. It's a good thing I'm educated. I figured their cute little "normal, overweight, and obese" chart designed by the government was necessary and worked in many situations, but it wasn't appropriate for me. I knew enough to understand that I was better than normal, and I wasn't overweight. I rejected their label with pride.

Denny wasn't as religious about clean eating as I was. Sometimes it was hard to watch him eat Oreos and mashed potatoes while I ate salad. His body was also changing, though. He was more muscular than me. After months of listening to his admiration of my new, finely sculpted body; I came to the realization that I liked his evolving body! Plus, giving him that feedback seemed to entice him to eat better. It was hard to believe we were forty-nine and fifty-one years old, yet feeling young and admiring each other like two lusting teenagers!

At this point, we were working out three nights in a row to mimic the three-day climb. Roz had us working extra hard during our hour-long session to simulate the effort we'd put forth in four hours a day during the three-day climb. One night we did jumping jacks, 400 sit-ups, sixteen minutes on the Stairmaster, 100 lunges, 60 push-ups, mountain climbers, burpees, and balancing on the exercise ball on our knees for six minutes. The next night we'd walk at a fast pace at an 8 percent incline for forty minutes, then work out on the elliptical for twenty minutes with, of course, sit-ups at the end. The next night we would do the Stairmaster again and lift weights. I had to stay disciplined and drink adequate amounts of water every day, or my body would quickly tell me something was off by giving me bouts of light-headedness.

At about this time, Denny surpassed me in the gym. After months of wondering if he would ever be able to keep up with me in workouts, it happened—the man beat the woman! Roz exhausted our legs with leg curls, squats, calf raises, dead lifts, lunges, and leg extensions, and then at the end had us do one-legged Russian dead lifts. I couldn't stay balanced. I wobbled all over, trying to stand on one leg and touch the ground. Denny pulled it off with grace. I had conflicting feelings—I was happy he was having success, but I didn't like the feeling of being behind.

The inevitable criticism of my focus on workouts came nine weeks before the climb when I left Morgan's softball game to get to a workout on time. I had been learning to slough off unwanted remarks, but this unsolicited feedback came from someone whose opinion mattered. "If it were my daughter playing, I'd be right there at the softball field watching her no matter what."

I felt disbelief then anger. I quickly reprocessed the situation. I felt confident that I'd given my daughter the utmost of my attention throughout the year. Not only did I attend every junior high volleyball and basketball game she played this past year, but I volunteered as the scorekeeper for both teams. I also took her to every far-flung volleyball and basketball tournament while my husband worked extra-long hours. Now that we were in softball season, I worked with Roz to find a workout time that maximized our ability to attend Morgan's games. I felt confident that I was balancing all my commitments and interests well. The years before this had proved something—that when I filled my days with things that pleased others but didn't leave time to care for me, I became overweight, unhealthy, and unhappy. Surely taking thirty minutes or so away from Morgan's game would be all right. Certainly, I was setting a good example of discipline and dedication to a goal. I did my best to let my feelings of hurt, disbelief, and anger go. I worked out with a clear conscience that night.

Our fast and furious lives pressed forward while we prepared. On the rare occasions that I took a break, I could reflect on all the things we had accomplished and wonder how we got everything done.

Another Sunday found Denny and me back in the REI store. Denny got hiking boots. We got a water purification pump, and we both got a few other items for our Pikes Peak climb.

I had a magical moment at this store. While talking to one of the sales associates about our impending climb, I said, "I'll use my camera to videotape my thoughts and feelings during the climb and put them on paper at night. That's what I do, I write." Pause. The words echoed in my mind. "I write." It was magical to hear myself say that. I believed it. I owned it. I could almost hear the angels in heaven applauding my self-confession.

This is who I am. That is what I do. I write. I go on life adventures, and I write. I do not define myself as an Information Technology Geek any longer. That paid the bills, but it no longer defined me. The preparation for climbing this mountain changed me in so many ways!

That night, our workout had us cover four miles in forty-five minutes on the treadmill at a six percent incline and again on the Stairmaster, wearing our backpacks. Roz was firm and confident. "You guys are ready for your trial climb!"

I shared his confidence. I had a growing sense of pride that I was in good enough shape to climb Pikes Peak, and I was willing to put aside my preference to sleep in a comfy spa hotel and embrace camping in a rustic campsite on a mountain. I was getting excited to climb!

We celebrated the Fourth of July early, at my uncle's annual July 3rd party. The next morning, we flew to Denver, then drove to Colorado Springs. We immediately began drinking a lot of water to help us acclimate to the altitude, got a few supplies at the local REI, and loaded up on food. My friend Nina from the Denver area Influence class met us in the Barr Trail parking lot to climb the first leg of the trail with us. We strapped on our backpacks and started up the mountain together. The gentleman at the Colorado Springs REI had told us repeatedly that the first three miles were brutal and to watch out for altitude sickness. We didn't waiver though. We were confident; we were prepared for both.

Just as the man said, the first three miles were brutal. It was like doing step-ups for the entire distance. The incline was outrageous! We made our way, me with forty pounds on my back and Denny with forty-five. It was the Fourth of July holiday, so there were many people off work and on the trail, most of them coming down. We didn't know it at the time but later learned that the Manitou Incline, known by locals simply as "the Incline" was near the Barr Trail. It was nearly a mile long: a straight-up path made from railroad ties left behind when a cable car was used to take materials up the mountain to build a pipeline. It has a 68 percent incline and is used by locals for a good workout. Once at the top, people get on the Barr Trail and run down to complete the loop. We contended with a lot of traffic passing us on the narrow trail. We also encountered rain as lightning flashed nearby. Many friends and dozens of articles had warned us about lightning. Nina talked us through it as well, simply saying, "It's a real risk. Take it seriously. If you see lightning, take cover." From that moment on, I watched for rocks that could offer us shelter if needed. We got out our rain gear and kept trekking. Fortunately, the rain dissipated quickly.

Nina left us at the three-mile marker. It had been good to see my friend! And it was good to know we were past the brutal first three miles. There was a steady incline in front of us, but it was a touch easier than the three miles now behind us. I set the pace as we marched on, and Denny seemed to like it that way. He wanted to go faster, but he worried that his pace would be too fast for me and that we wouldn't make the full trek. He trusted that my pace would get us both to camp, three and a half miles ahead of us, by 6:00 p.m., which was dinnertime at Barr Camp.

I had trouble with my head pounding, an altitude sickness symptom. I stopped and drank lots of water each time I experienced it, and the pounding dissipated. Denny had a minor issue with sore feet, but he rearranged his socks, rested, and we trekked on. We got to camp at 6:30, and we were thankful that they still had dinner for us. We loaded up on spaghetti—carbs for the trail ahead. We pitched our tent and settled in for the night. We both woke up often because of the cold! Otherwise, our newly acquired tent was perfect.

We knew that getting an early start and arriving at the summit before 2:00 p.m. was in our best interest, though we failed to make that happen. We ate a hearty pancake breakfast, filtered some water, filled our water bottles, and repacked our backpacks to carry approximately twenty pounds to simulate what we would carry at the higher elevations on Rainier. We left camp at 9:00 a.m.

Denny was stronger than me the first two miles. He wanted to go faster, but again he let me set the pace. These first miles were beautiful—tall pine trees and a wide, dusty trail with a few rocks. We simply enjoyed each other's company during this stretch. We reached timberline and found the stream we'd read about. Here we filtered more water to refill our water bottles and took a moment to enjoy the beauty surrounding us. Denny would have lingered more, but I had lightning on my mind. The risk became greater with each passing hour. Beyond timberline, we had to be even more concerned. We ate and trekked on.

For the next two miles, Denny and I struck an even pace. From time to time my head continued to pound, but like the day before, I stopped and drank a lot of water, and it dissipated. Denny often got the start of a headache. I encouraged him to drink, and he did. We didn't have to reach for our medication; we kept fending off altitude sickness. Many people passed us on this stretch, but I kept telling myself it didn't matter. Getting to the top was our goal—beating a bunch of other brave souls to the top wasn't, but I could feel my competitive nature kicking in. Rain clouds loomed. We felt a few drops but nothing more. I prayed, asking God to keep the storm away. I envisioned a man with Herculean shoulders holding the rain clouds and any lightning back. I envisioned an angel keeping the skies blue over the top of Pikes Peak. We could see rain falling hard to the northeast, but fortunately, it stayed there. There was no lightning. We stayed safe.

The last two miles were brutal. On this stretch, there was no trekking—it was a constant climb through scree. I kept my head down and focused, taking one step at a time to ensure that I had good footing so I wouldn't fall or roll an ankle, and I kept up a rhythm. A good rhythm had good momentum, and good momentum would carry me to the goal. I could hear Eminem's "Lose Yourself" playing in my head—a song from my workout playlist with a rhythm appropriate to get me up the mountain. I could also hear "No Diggity," a tune with a little slower rhythm. I was amused—I had no idea I even knew that song!

I was stronger than Denny on this final two-mile stretch. We'd start out from a break, me right in front of Denny. I'd soon be ten or fifteen steps in front of him. Then Denny would call out, "I need to stop and sit for a while," and we did just that every time he asked. We didn't linger too long—I got myself up, and I got him going again, too. I didn't want to lose momentum. Just like in the gym, I'd say, "C'mon, Miller. We've got this!" Off we'd go again. At 3:30 p.m. we made the summit. When we got near the top, Denny told me, "You pulled me up the mountain the last mile!" There we found a large crowd that had taken the cog train or had driven up the mountain. Pikes Peak is one of the most accessible 14,000-foot summits in the nation. The Barr Trail took us right up to a small group of men and women in their twenties taking in the scenery. When I walked by, they asked if I had climbed the mountain. Winded and out of breath, I simply said yes, and kept walking. A minute or two later, Denny walked through. The same group of people congratulated him and asked all kinds of questions. One of the women asked to have her picture taken with him. "A real hiker!" she squealed. For a moment, Denny was a rock star! Once he joined me, I found a nice man to take some pictures of us in our state of worn-out glory. It was a beautiful moment!

After the solitude of nature, the commercialization atop the mountain struck us hard. The crowd was abuzz, people fighting to be the first to get their "six for 5 dollars" worth of the "world famous" Pikes Peak donuts or strutting by the crowd to prove they were the most fashionably dressed souls and aggressively getting in position to buy the best sweatshirt or take the next picture in front of the 14,110 feet elevation sign. Denny and I wanted nothing to do with it. We wanted three simple things: water, a bathroom, and an opportunity to catch our breath. We found the people around us unkind—we didn't enjoy the commercialization, so we got what we needed then stayed away from the crowd while waiting for the train. We'd decided to save our knees by taking the cog back down toward camp.

We rode it down to a trailhead a mile and a half from camp. When it stopped, they called for hikers to depart. Denny and I were the only two that got off. As the train began to roll away,

Denny and I put on our packs and readied our trekking poles. We wowed all the kids and some adults on the train. They shouted and waved and cheered for us. For a short moment, we were *both* rock stars! We made the relatively easy hike back to camp, arriving just in time for dinner. After eating spaghetti, all we wanted was sleep.

The next day we ate another hearty breakfast then packed up our gear and headed out. We enjoyed this hike. Some parts were hard on our knees, and it was much hotter than the previous two days, but we floated down the mountain with the personal satisfaction that we had the gall, the will, the physical ability, and the mental discipline to make the thirteen-mile trek up to the top of the mountain.

Once down, we went straight to the car, packed for the airport, got root beer floats for the ride and then stopped at our friends Marilyn and Foster's house to take a shower. I'd met Marilyn and Foster through the Wisdom Community—and I was thrilled to share this moment with them and thankful that they accepted us into their home for a shower! We had more water and a good conversation; then we drove off to the airport. There was a flight delay, so we landed in Detroit at 2:20 a.m. and got to our house at 4:30. We slept three hours, then headed back to work.

What a grand seventy-two hours!

As I look back, there were so many signs to remind me how fortunate we were. Before we even reached the one-mile marker, we passed a man in his twenties being assisted down the trail. He had blood streaming down his face and knees from multiple abrasions and was clearly dazed and confused—he probably had a concussion. We were fortunate we didn't get an injury that interfered with or prevented our climb. At the top of the mountain, there was a teenage boy throwing up. In the short time it took him to ride up the mountain and stand atop it to enjoy the view, altitude sickness struck him. We were fortunate the altitude had done nothing more than give us headaches.

The night after our climb, there was a black bear in the campgrounds. The caretakers encouraged it to leave by making loud noises with pots and pans. My lack of reaction struck me, though. I was so exhausted that I didn't care about the fact that a bear had threatened our space. Again, we had been fortunate to remain safe from wildlife. Then, after getting showers, we stood on Marilyn and Foster's deck looking toward the west and watched as a bolt of lightning struck a mountain. We were fortunate the weather had cooperated, and we stayed safe.

I walked away with a beautiful side effect too.

For three solid days, we'd lived simply. Everything we needed fit in our backpacks—the food to nourish us, the water to keep us healthy, the tent to give us shelter, the clothes to keep us cool and dry, and the sleeping bag to keep us warm at night. Our only luxury items were a camera and a soft pair of shoes to treat our feet after a day of hiking. The goal of reaching the summit was our focus. There were no unnecessary details, no distractions, and no drama. We turned off the cell phone, gave up fashion for function, traded fancy meals for trail mix, and drank water from a stream. Nature was our entertainment. We stripped away all the unnecessary factors of life for the sole purpose of accomplishing a goal. We slept to climb; we ate to climb; we collaborated to climb, and we climbed. We learned we could lose all the effects of commercialization—the things we took notice of at the top of the mountain—and we'd be just fine.

Plus, Denny and I were fine. In fact, we enjoyed each other. We worked together well, both on the trail and at camp. We cooperated, made decisions jointly, and were patient with each other. We refrained from blaming each other for problems, disappointments, and challenges. We both had the fire within us to tackle our goal—we just had to tame that flame enough to work with each other. Then we could learn to do anything together.

That was a win along the way, but it was not the end goal. There were still seven weeks to prepare for Rainier.

*Chapter 16*

# Conquering Myself, Conquering Us

"You are as amazing as you let yourself be.
Let me repeat that.
You are as amazing as you let yourself be."
Elizabeth Alraure

My friends in Colorado and Washington knew what it took to successfully climb Pikes Peak and showered us with congratulatory remarks. However, family and friends in Ohio wondered why we had wanted to climb a mountain, and they didn't say much when we returned. That's just the way it was in my hometown.

Denny and I went back to our daily living routine and our workout regimen with little ado.

Soon we heard from my godson Zack. On a Wednesday, he and his friends had received their permit for climbing Mount Rainier. They started out on a Thursday but were back in Seattle by 6:00 p.m. Friday night. They hadn't summited. He had been roped to a buddy who hadn't trained well. They didn't reach the predetermined altitude by 7:00 a.m., so they made the decision to "bail." They didn't want to get caught descending in a late afternoon rock fall caused by the sun melting the glacier. It had to be disappointing for Zack: he was in great shape and ready for the climb. They had great views and climbed all night long in the moonlight and saw an amazing sunrise. Still, they moved too slowly to summit. Zack was full of advice for us: dress for intense sun, get a lightweight neck gaiter and wear a helmet. He told us that the guided climb teams left Camp Muir (the halfway point) at 11:00 p.m. and summited around 6:00 a.m. We were sad for Zack, but thankful to learn from his experience.

Quietly, I celebrated my fiftieth birthday! There was little mention of the milestone, and I liked it that way. My focus remained on climbing Mount Rainier as my way to start the next fifty years.

The climb was now six weeks away, and somehow there was a mild loss of consistency in our routine. Many other responsibilities just required our attention, and suddenly, we'd missed several workouts in the two weeks following our Pikes Peak excursion. During the same two weeks, there was an emotional lull. Maybe it was a natural letdown following a big success like Pikes Peak. Or, maybe it was my birthday. I was very proud of who I was at fifty, but that milestone came and went, and I was left with the question, "is this all there is?" Then there was the weight. I realized I was in a phase of my Mount Rainier climb preparations where I was gaining muscle weight faster than I was losing fat weight, but I'd climbed a 14,000-foot mountain and gained two pounds. I couldn't fathom how that happened, and that led me to be disappointed. Also, I was flat-out exhausted. My job, the farm, the kids' activities, housework, workouts, and our big, hairy, audacious goals had every minute of every day packed tightly with things to do. I longed for sleep and a day to just lie in the sun and remember how to do nothing! I found it all unsettling. I had to settle back into a routine, and quickly, to make Rainier a success. When we reached the five-weeks-to-go mark, I found myself fired up, proud, and hungry—the workouts just required more calories than I was taking in. I was, interestingly, starting to wonder what was after Rainier! I had to quickly dismiss the thoughts of the next big challenge to make this one a success.

At this point, Denny and I received more information from our climbing company, Alpine Ascents. Much of it was the same as previous packets (gear list, logistics, maps, etc.), but this one included something new: the names of our eight-person climb team. Seeing the names of all eight souls working toward the same goal made the climb seem more real. I felt a natural rush of excitement.

After receiving the materials, I called Alpine Ascents to discuss some questions. I told them about our Pikes Peak performance and asked if we were on target. They said that we were for the lower half and could pick up our pace for the upper half. Wow, look at that! Just six months ago, I didn't know anything about mountain climbing. Today, I held a conversation about altitude, climb rates, and equipment with an experienced climber. Six months ago, we merely had a vision, and I had a trust that I could fulfill that vision. Today, I believed I'd be successful in climbing Mount Rainier and even had some experience to back up that belief. It made me proud to think about how far I'd come, and it boosted my confidence to know that I could pick what I wanted to experience in life and make it happen.

I shared Alpine Ascents' feedback with our trainer. Roz decided to stick to his plans but enhanced them a bit. We continued to spend a good amount of time on the treadmill, elliptical, and

Stairmaster with backpacks that now weighed thirty pounds, but we went faster with more resistance. Walking four mph at a 15 percent incline was challenging. It was the fastest I could walk without feeling like I needed to run.

Work came begging for attention at this time too. Though my boss had always been exceedingly focused on financial performance, efficient use of time, and effective strategies, he had been accepting of the traditionally casual work culture that existed in this privately-held company. He didn't ask me to optimize every aspect of my work immediately—he only asked that I do my part to continuously improve the technology and help other departments do the same. I had been doing just that, with his praise. However, four weeks before the climb, something abruptly changed. His praise evaporated, he held me to a new higher standard, and he was irritated. At the same time, a coworker dished out unkind words behind my back and later to my face—"You make the big bucks; you aren't worth my time; you should know how to fix this." And one of my direct reports delivered a sucker punch, discrediting me with key leaders and publicly opposing me on a key project after we had privately agreed on a direction. I soon discovered he was after my job.

All of this was troubling. During my climb preparations, I never failed to contribute at work sufficiently. I'd worked forty-five to fifty hours a week and continued to improve the company's technical capabilities at a faster pace than the company ever had achieved before. My team and I received routine notes of appreciation for improvements as well as an appreciation for our people-friendly approach. I never questioned my intelligence or fit for the role.

Nonetheless, pressure mounted for me to give even more time to my job, finish more, and make more highly visible contributions.

Soon it became clear the increased pressure was not about me—it was about others' attempts to tear me down. I'm not sure if my boss's demands were intended to boost my performance and dedication to prove to others what he already knew—that I was indeed a high performing employee—or if he was, in fact, reevaluating me. Whatever the case, the calculated attacks and drama reminded me of the divisive environment I thought I'd left behind. I was truly disappointed to realize that my small town and this small private company could have the same ugliness as large, Wall Street-driven corporations. It all resulted in a confrontation with my boss.

No matter how much or how little I liked a boss, I always made sure I never let anyone blindside them. I always did my best to arm a boss with information through one-on-one discussions before taking things into the public forum. In my experience, this made any boss happy. That day, it was a catalyst for a fiery explosion. When I sat down with my boss to prepare him for an upcoming meeting, he listened to just my opening two or three sentences, then started to fire verbal shots at me. He had been armed before I entered the room. I'm not sure why, but it was obvious that he felt threatened. He didn't want the information I had prepared for him—all he wanted to do was lash out and ensure I knew my place. The conversation escalated and culminated with a profound statement: "You will never be as important as me. You're just Information Technology—I am the Chief Financial Officer."

There it was—I had uncovered the quintessential learning from the last three decades of my life.

Capitalism. The pursuit of profit. Yes, it's the foundation of America, the threads of the social fabric that made the country I love, the fuel for the freedom I cherish, and funding for the way of life I enjoy and take pride in. It's a system that works when in check. But like most everything else, too much of a good thing can be bad. When people and companies pursue profit at the expense of everything else good in life, the dark side of capitalism overshadows. The kind of intellectual warfare, character assassination, and hazing of leaders who dare to climb the corporate ladder was inexcusable. Though I wanted to believe I had left all this behind when I moved home, I found it growing without restraint at my father's golf course, lurking in the quickly changing healthcare industry, and searching for fertile ground in small, privately owned companies.

Crushing another person to lift yourself up then writing it off to needs of capital is foolish. Whether you believe in God, Allah, or Buddha, I'm pretty sure the Divine Spirit is not defining our worth by the positions we hold, the money we earn, the stuff we acquire, or the intellect we enjoy. I'm certain all that will matter at the end of our lives is the love we gave and the positive impact we had on each living being we encountered. There must be room for love and positivity that go beyond financial measure in our economic system.

Regardless of my title, I'm sure I matter just as much as any chief financial officer.

So, I rejected that boss's judgment—I'm not less important than him because of my specialty or my position on the organizational chart. I didn't accept his value system. I could see capitalism for what it is—a system that finances our life, not the value system by which we measure the worth of humans.

I seriously considered walking out. I simply did not want to go through the ugliness again. Then, in a fleeting moment of friendship, the co-worker that unknowingly taught me so many lessons, taught me one more: "So you got hit with a haymaker. Get up and adjust, so you don't get hit with a haymaker again." "Haymaker"—a word that wasn't even in my vocabulary—but a haymaker it was indeed. My co-worker probably didn't know the depth of meaning his words held for me—he was more right than he would ever know. My experience in Corporate America had been an ugly series of haymakers—they knocked me off my game, and I let them. This latest blow would be a haymaker only if I let it. It was time to let the tough experience go, and it was time to let my bosses' current attack go too.

I somehow found it in me not to let unkind co-workers' stories about me become my truth. I recommitted to writing my story. I gave a few extra work hours for my good PR, stood tall without counterattacking, and focused on completing as many tasks as possible. I made a commitment to myself that these adjustments were a short-term solution and not a way of life that would steal my "happy." I let my boss's sharply spoken words go, but over time I made it clear—we would work together based on mutual respect, with a reasonable amount of time committed to work, and in support of each other, not against each other. We worked together to find a rhythm that worked for both of us. Then I got on with my life and focused on my goals.


Three weeks before the climb, Denny and I were nailing our routine at the gym and making our relationship work too. Our finances were still the same—plentiful debt, on the one hand, plentiful incomes from two good jobs on the other, with the struggle to balance both on a day-to-day basis. This climb—the gear, the travel, and the workouts—stressed our income and debt even more, but we handled it all better. We didn't let big positive numbers inappropriately lure us to big spending. We didn't let negative numbers sentence us to a life of self-punishment. We just kept plugging away, determined to make our financial state better with each move we made, while continuing to live a full life. Most importantly, we talked about our finances with cool, level heads, and we were honest. We didn't avoid difficult conversations, and we didn't hide our feelings or our wants. We didn't camouflage money issues in other issues of our lives. Denny gave me credit for living within our means and being happy about it. I gave Denny credit for freeing himself to spend on those few select things that would enhance our lives—and not blaming me when our bank account was stressed. Denny and I were nailing healthier financial habits at the same time we nailed the workouts—we improved a little more each day.

Two weeks before the climb, my nerves set in.

It was a familiar pattern. When I travel overseas, I get stressed and become highly reactive four or five days before the flight. Then as soon as I hit the seat in the plane, I relax, settle in, and enjoy the trip. I know that international travel will challenge my thoughts, feelings, and perhaps my approach to life. I welcome the growth, but the anticipation of the growth process can be rattling.

The same thing happened with the climb. Two weeks before, I became a little edgy as the enormity of it all dawned on me. Few people in the world have attempted to summit a 14,400-foot, glacier-covered mountain and fewer have achieved the feat. Glacial crevasses to cross, the possibility of melt-induced rock slides, the risk of avalanches, volcanic vents, and climbing in the dark with a headlamp were all new to me. I'd be worried if I hadn't been a bit concerned and edgy. I countered these concerns with strengths. I told myself I was in a solid rhythm in workouts—my body knew what to do and had the stamina to do it. I was physically peaking, and I was physically ready. This self-talk helped quiet the mental chatter rooted in fear and stilled my nerves. I kept focused on the vision of success.

Workouts got tougher the closer we got to the climb—Roz was quite good at his job: he was making sure that we were peaking at the right time. The closer we got to the climb, the more energy we had for workouts—we didn't mind the effort we needed to give in the gym.

Soon we were packing, which wasn't too difficult this time—we knew what was going to work and not work after our Pikes Peak experience. When we had all our gear packed and ready to go, we placed a call to Alpine Ascents to reserve the remaining equipment we'd need.

On a Thursday morning, we loaded the truck with our gear and luggage. Then Denny dropped me off at work and went on to his work. He'd be back eight-and-a-half hours later to pick me up for our flight. I'm pretty sure I walked quite tall at the plant that day, maybe even floated around with a big, pearly, confident smile—I was on a natural high. Denny picked me up as planned, and we were off to Detroit to catch our evening flight to Seattle. It was an uneventful trip and in some ways, arriving at the SeaTac airport felt like coming back home. I still loved this city.

Friday was a beautiful summer day—clear blue skies, 72 degrees, and a glorious sun beaming over the mountains, the Puget Sound, the tall, glorious evergreens, and the city void of pollution. We didn't have a rental car, so we went about all day on foot. We walked near the Space Needle to the REI to get last-minute supplies, walked around Lake Union to find the perfect place for lunch, and walked to a local grocery store to get food supplies for the climb. We had never had this much energy—walking the big hills in Seattle with ease and grace. At 2:00, we went to Alpine Ascents for the planned equipment check and met our climb team.

Denny and I must have been eager—we were the first to arrive—a rare event! When everyone was in the room, we introduced ourselves and explained why we were making the climb. First, we met Souraj, who was polite but quiet. It took us a while to get to know him. At some point in the trip, he and I would connect because we both worked in information technology. From one software developer to another, we would talk. It turned out he had recently run in the San Francisco Marathon and had climbed Kilimanjaro. Next, we met buddies Reynold and Shane. Reynold was from Washington, D.C., was in the military and had recently started running marathons. His girlfriend, who was a long-distance swimmer, recommended the climb as a fitness goal beyond his running. When his friend had backed out of the trip a few months prior, he recruited his NYC firefighting buddy, Shane, for the trip. Shane was a fitness leader for the NYFD, liked challenges of this nature, and was perpetually ready to take on something like this climb. Another husband and wife team was also on the trip—Kelly and Chris. Originally from the East Coast, they had moved to the Seattle area for the outdoor adventures. They had climbed three volcanic mountains in the months leading up to this and felt Mount Rainier was the next progressively challenging thing to do. The last person to join us was Nicole. She was on a personal mission to visit every national park in our nation—and to have one quintessential experience in each park. In Rainier National Park, she'd chosen to climb the mountain.

When it came time for Denny and me to introduce ourselves, Denny went first, but he had me explain why we were making the climb—"I'll let Kelli tell you why we're doing this." I introduced myself, then continued. "When we lived in the Seattle area a few years ago, I fell in love with Mount Rainier. It was a dream to climb the mountain, but a dream that I dismissed as soon as it had formed, for I wasn't in any mental or physical condition to make a climb. Then my dad passed away, we moved back to Ohio, and I went to work on myself. I let go of an abundance of mental baggage, lost seventy pounds, and got myself in shape. I turned fifty a few weeks ago; I'm making the climb to celebrate my first fifty years, the weight loss, and my physical condition and set the tone for the *next* fifty years. I'm making the climb to be my very best me." I was stunned when my climb team responded with spontaneous applause.

The next day, we woke at 5:00 a.m., got coffee by 5:30, and were loaded into the Alpine Ascents van with all our gear and two guides and on the road by 6:00. For any other event, I would have slept on the two-hour road trip to the park but not that day. I chatted all the way to the mountain. We picked up two more guides near the park entrance, then proceeded to the visitor center in Paradise.

I was overwhelmed in Paradise. It was a stunningly beautiful day again: clear blue sky, 72 degrees, and the majestic beauty of Rainer and the Cascade Mountains. We put on our hiking boots then stood in a circle as the guides introduced themselves. Again, I was overwhelmed. We were sharing space with some incredible people.

Our lead guide was Peter—a world-renowned climber. He had summited Mount Everest seven times (one of only four non-Sherpas to do so). Peter had led climbing expeditions on Denali and Rainier and summited Mount Rainier seventy-six times. Lhakpa, Kyle, and Travis rounded out the guide team. Lhakpa had summited Mount Everest fifteen times and held the Everest speed record, summiting in ten hours and fifty-six minutes. Kyle's background included mountain excursions for power companies and mountain climbing safety boards. Travis had graduated with a degree in physics, but his passion for extreme physical and mental challenges was the force that found him on the mountain as a guide that day. It was an honor to climb with these four men! Then the rest of us introduced ourselves to the guides in a shortened version of the day before, for we were all eager to get started.

We strapped on our forty-pound backpacks and off we went. The initial trek was on a paved path through the few trees that remained at this altitude, then into wide-open spaces devoid of trees. The wildflowers growing abundantly in the meadows made the first leg of the journey seem like a fairy-tale dream. It wasn't long before the path turned from asphalt to stones, and the green grass meadows faded to rock fields. As we climbed, fewer and fewer park visitors shared the trail with us. We passed individuals and groups descending and ascending, but for the better part of the journey, we were on our own, each one of us talking, getting to know each other and to some degree, releasing nervous energy as we took on one of the biggest challenges of our lives. Soon we were in the Muir Snowfield, which would take over three hours to climb. Once or twice we stopped just long enough to witness a rockslide off in the distance. Hearing the rockslides put me in awe of the forces of the mountain. We stopped three times to rest and refuel. This part of the climb didn't seem terribly hard, for beauty surrounded us. But it was a 4,500-foot ascent. Resting for ten or fifteen minutes and taking in enough water and the right food was essential. Denny was doing quite well. I was too, until the last leg.

After the third and final break before reaching Camp Muir, where we would spend the night, something was getting to me. I silently processed what I was experiencing, wondering if I might be short of water, low on salt, or simply struggling with the pace. I've never had a propensity for admitting I need help, so when I do, it's serious. I decided I had to say something. Still in stride, I was turning around to face Lhakpa and Peter, who were directly behind me, and I was about to say, "I need to stop for a break." As I turned, I fell backward onto my pack. I was just shy of passing out.

Lhakpa and Peter were reaching for my water bottle before I knew what had happened, both encouraging me to drink. The group took an impromptu break, while Lhakpa and Peter talked to me. To this day, Denny doesn't remember me falling over. He thought it was just another break, so he took the time to eat and drink some more. Then I realized I hadn't been drinking enough because my bladder was full. The men were peeing at will, but none of the women were relieving themselves—there were no trees or anything to squat behind. There was nothing but an open snowfield. Now I realized that staying hydrated is essential. So, I ran about fifty feet away from the group, bared my hind end to everyone on the mountain that day, and relieved my bladder, only to fill it up again so I'd stay healthy.

When we started up again, Peter asked, "How's that stride for you, Kelli?" I admitted it was a bit longer than was comfortable for me, so Peter got in front of me. He made footprints in the snow at a stride I could handle all the way to Camp Muir. I was relieved when we reached camp. Denny was reserved. He wasn't exhausted, but he was taken aback by the effort we'd put in for the day. He still had enough energy to be a wise guy, though: "That was pretty cool to see your bare hind-end on the mountain."

He still had no idea what had happened. Even after I told him, he repeatedly expressed surprise and disbelief. I gave him a hard time for being unaware, but it wasn't insensitivity that kept him from knowing what I'd experienced—he was simply wrapped up in the mental and physical focus of the climb. I was grateful our guides had the capacity to maintain that focus on themselves and the rest of us as well.

Camp Muir is in a natural rock formation between the Muir Snowfield and the glacier above it. There's a public bunkhouse, a ranger station, two shacks that serve as bunkhouses for two climbing companies, and three or four primitive outhouses. Behind the cluster of buildings and the rock that forms the camp is a tent field where climbers can pitch their tents and sleep on a glacier. Our group settled into a shack with plywood platforms that would be our bunks for the night. Here we would decompress and take in the beauty of literally being above the clouds. Our guides bunked in a weather tent that also served as a mess tent. Here they had just enough equipment and just enough supplies to cook burritos for our team for dinner.

As we relaxed, I admitted to a select few that I'd had cramps in my mid abdomen just below my rib cage before I fell over. Shane responded, "You had stitches"—a dehydration symptom. Then Reynold shared the nutritional facts and tactics he'd recently learned from running marathons. He determined I hadn't armed myself with the proper food, so he shared with me his stash of energy beans and energy goo. I shamelessly took his energy beans and stepped up my water intake too.

While eating dinner, we all learned more about each other. I enjoyed the conversation and the burrito Lhakpa had prepared, despite the fact that I had never had a burrito before in my life. I couldn't eat the whole thing, though. The guides seemed curious about how much I left on my plate, for lack of appetite is a sign of altitude sickness. I assured them I was fine. "It's not the altitude. It's the fact that I've been eating only 1200 calories a day for the last eighteen months. This burrito is huge to me." The tent went silent. In my attempt to reassure them, I caused more doubt. Not one person said anything, but I suddenly could hear what everyone was thinking: "You can't climb on 1200 calories." I was overwhelmed with the thought that I might not make it simply because I hadn't eaten enough in the days and weeks before the climb and during the climb. I would work myself through that thought and remain determined to be the best I could be.

After dinner, we sat on top of the world as we watched the sky fill with pink, purple, and orange hues. It was a long, graceful, and beautiful sunset. We went to sleep early—we needed the rest. The next two days would be big ones. I was up a record three times during the night to pee, and I kept pushing water throughout the night. I was adamant that something as preventable as dehydration would not stop me from climbing.

We were up at 6:00, packed, and full from a hearty breakfast of pancakes, eggs, and bacon. I consumed all I could, putting to rest any fears of altitude sickness lingering from the day before.

The first event of the day was climbing school. We would have to leave our trekking poles at Camp Muir and climb with an ice axe from here on up. First, we had to learn how to use an axe and how it could keep us from sliding if we fell. We also learned rope management and climbing techniques with the harness and rope for crossing glaciers and climbing rock. We learned how to put crampons on our snow boots, how to use the avalanche transponder, and how to put on the harness. Throughout the training, I had a repeated thought—"Am I really doing this?" A bolstering voice answered from within—"You can do anything you put your mind to!"

By midmorning, we were roped together in our three-man teams and crossing the Cowlitz Glacier. Denny and I, roped to Peter, had Peter leading, me in the middle, and Denny following. We crossed the glacier on a precise path that was determined by the guides and rangers as mountain conditions changed with snow melt and precipitation. Nonetheless, it was a strange phenomenon to trek near, around, and over glacial crevasses. I could let my mind wonder and worry about the safety of the path we were on, or I could trust that the guides were well-educated and made good decisions. I chose the latter. I'd been trained to question everything and to have a logical equation in my head, ensuring everything added up and logically supported all my life choices. But today I simply trusted the four guides on my team and guides and park rangers I had never met.

At the end of the glacier, we climbed loose gravel and steep piles of rock up the side of a rock formation separating the Cowlitz Glacier from the Ingraham Glacier on the other side. This formation was known as Cathedral Gap. I didn't mind the incline, and I had plenty of energy, but I was terribly unsure of my footing in the loose gravel. Peter could place his foot just about anywhere and hoist himself up step by step. I, on the other hand, slid backward no matter how I placed my foot. I kept trying, and I kept sliding—I wanted to scream out in frustration. I stood frozen for some time, afraid I would slide all the way down to the glacier below. I wasn't afraid of getting hurt; I just didn't want to go to the bottom and start over again. I wanted to avoid the punishment of climbing this rock a second time. Somehow, though, my slides were limited to short setbacks, and somehow my footing got better, and I made it up that incline. Then I learned to climb in the crampons with two-inch metal teeth on softball-size rocks, boulders, then ice-covered rocks, and ice-covered boulders.

Our path thus far had taken us due north, up the south side of the mountain and across the east side. Atop Cathedral Gap, we made a sharp left, taking a route due west, up the east side of the mountain. Paradise and Camp Muir, the only signs of civilization, were no longer in sight. We were now crossing Ingraham Glacier. Everything about it was exaggerated when compared to Cowlitz—the incline was steeper, the rock slides were closer and more frequent, and the crevasses more plentiful, wider, and deeper. The path we walked grew narrower, with the risks of an unseen crevasse or a rocky ledge just one step to the side.

I kept my head down and focused on my footing. The sun was beating down on the glacier, so there was slippery ice, slushy snow, hard ice, hard snow, rocks, gravel, ledges, boulders, and crevasses. The path crossed these, some as wide as two feet, and went around others that looked like cliffs. Almost every new step put my foot in a new circumstance. The three teams that had gone before us were out of sight now. It was just Peter, Denny, Mother Nature, and me. We talked and got to know each other a bit more, and then we talked to keep our minds from focusing on what we were enduring. We had gained only 1,500 feet in the climb that day, but I could feel the difference. The air was thinner at this altitude, and the effort we put forth was more draining. It felt like a grand accomplishment to reach High Camp.

High Camp is a unique stop for Alpine Ascents climbers. Other climb teams make the ascent from Camp Muir to the summit in one day, but Alpine Ascents makes the ascent in two legs, using High Camp as a resting point. There were six two-man tents and a food tent situated near the upper end of the Ingraham Glacier, an area known as The Flats. To the south, the enormous Gibraltar Rock jutted out of the mountainside, serving as a shield to the wind and weather that often come from that direction.

Little Tahoma Peak was to the east. The northern view was wide open—in fact, we could see Mount Baker over a hundred miles away rising above the Cascade Mountains. To the west stood the snow-covered, majestic Rainier summit. We rested while the guides discussed the possibility of climbing in the evening for a sunset summit or climbing during the wee hours of the morning for a sunrise summit.

As we settled into our tents, clouds set in. Within minutes, we experienced thunder, lightning, and snow—a very rare event. Due to our altitude, we were literally in the clouds—we weren't below the storm, we were *in* the storm—inside the thunder and near the lightning. As I thought about this, it seemed like I should be scared, but I wasn't. I threw my hands in the air and said, "If it's my time to get struck by lightning and die, I might as well die happy." So, I cuddled up with Denny and rested as the storm passed. When it was over, there were three inches of fresh snow at High Camp.

Lhapka cooked dinner again, chicken and noodles. I ate a hearty meal and continued to push water. The unexpected storm made the decision regarding our climb time. We made plans for a sunrise summit. It was difficult to sleep. Certainly, the time made it difficult, but the anticipation of what was to come was both exhilarating and frightening. I could have lain awake all night just processing my emotions.

We woke at 11:30 p.m., ate, and then got on all our gear. Apparently, Denny and I didn't gear up fast enough, and our guides were anxious to go. Lhapka watched and coached us for a short time; then he just took over. He put my crampons on my boots, untangled and secured my harness around my waist and legs, strapped on my avalanche transponder, and ensured that my headlamp was secure while Kyle helped Denny. Travis and I tore my tent apart looking for my missing glove. We never found it, so I relied on a pair of mitts instead. Our backpacks weighed less than when we started, but it didn't matter. Most of the things we'd taken out of our packs we were now wearing, so the weight was distributed all over our bodies.

We set off shortly after midnight. Just like the day before, Lhapka and his team went first, and Kyle and Travis and their teams followed. Peter, Denny, and I were the last team out. I presumed the order was purposeful because my pace could be slower than the others.

The space around us was deep black. The clouds from the day before had dissipated, but there was no moon illuminating our trek and no lights off in the distance. The stars were few. Our headlamps provided our only light—a pale, six-foot diameter circle illuminating the space directly in front of each climber. As before, I kept my head down and focused on my footing. I was climbing an unfamiliar path—all I could do was find the next spot I'd put my foot and trust the guides.

The first part of our journey was a steep incline up the remainder of the Ingraham Glacier. At the top of it, we turned north and hiked a narrow path between a cluster of long and deep crevasses to the left and more long and deep crevasses to the right. As we neared the edge of the glacier, there were three crevasses to cross to reach a rock formation known as Disappointment Cleaver. We crossed over a trio of bridges—one was a piece of wood, two were metal ladders dropped across the gap. Thankfully, all three had a guide rope, which gave me a sense of security. I have a fear of heights and easily could have become frozen with fear and unable to cross. As though sensing my apprehension, Peter simply said, "You don't have to think about it, just do it." And so, I did. Once we reached the Cleaver, we did some real climbing.

The Cleaver is nearly a 90-degree incline. We were walking up the side of a rocky mountain. Each time I ventured to look forward to find the team ahead of us, I saw their lights almost directly up above us. It was tiring to think about the effort yet ahead, so I rarely looked up. We zigzagged up the side of the mountain, taking ten or fifteen steps up and to the right, then ten or fifteen steps up and to the left. I thought it would never end. I was wearing thickly insulated snow boots with metal crampons, and my feet were awkward and heavy. Sure-footedness required keen focus and the careful placement of each boot between the rocks.

Doing this climb was mentally and physically tough in equal measure. The longer we climbed, the windier and colder it got. It never crossed my mind to stop, though—it would have been too damn cold to sit there and do nothing. Also, it never crossed my mind to turn around—the path down was just as challenging as the path up. Without a helicopter coming to save me, my only choice was to keep going. It's amazing what the body and the mind can do when the challenge is great, and the options are few. You just do what you have to do!

At some point, there was less rock and more snow, but the incline remained steep, and we kept climbing. I was hoping we'd soon catch up with the rest of our team. Then, at around 12,200 feet the thin air started to get to me, and I felt pressure on my chest. Sensing I might need some help, Peter started coaching me, telling me where to put each foot. Eventually, he'd say, "Just put your foot where I put my foot," which I did. When I started taking breaks more frequently, Peter shifted from his "follow my lead" stance back to coaching.

In his calm and confident voice, he said, "When we get to High Break, you may want to consider it your summit." When we reached the top of the Cleaver, the incline faded off from near 90 percent back to 20. We were now plugging away in the snow. It was still dark. If I could have seen my surroundings, I was certain I'd see a narrow path between two fairly flat rocks and cliffs on either side. We had been climbing two hours, and I was clearly past my physical limits. I would take two steps, stop to catch my breath, then take two more.

We finally caught up to our team. I was eager to sit down to rest, but as soon as I did, I worried I wouldn't have the gumption to get back up. Lhapka and Peter stood near me and talked in Lhapka's native language, Nepali.

I looked up to Peter and asked, "Are you telling Lhapka that I'm done?"

Denny and I talked. At 2:30 in the morning, in the pitch dark, sitting in the hostile terrain of this massive mountain, weathering the frigid wind in our face and the snow at our feet, we talked. It was a moment one can share only with someone they know almost as well as they know themselves—and only with someone they love. Despite all the yelling, blame, anger, and hurt, I loved him. He loved me too. If that hadn't always been clear in the journey to get to this place, it was loud and clear now.

Denny was not as challenged as I was, but he was feeling the altitude too. Also, he was dealing with exhausted feet. He wanted to try to go further, but he wasn't going on without me. It was difficult for me to say it, but yes, I was finished. Resting a bit would have given me more energy to go, and we were past the most difficult portion of the climb, but we had another 1,900 feet to gain in altitude, and my pace was simply too slow; I could hold the rest of the team back or put them at risk. They had to summit soon so they could descend before the sun beat down on the glacier and increased the risk of rockslides. I had to accept that 12,500 feet was my summit, but I still could be proud. Denny called it his summit too.

This climb was a metaphor for our marriage—the challenges we willingly sought, the risks we took, the conditioning we endured, the way I pushed for audacious dreams, his silent strength keeping us anchored in reality, and our way of knowing when to be satisfied with our achievements.

The rest of the team went on, while Peter, Denny, and I began our descent. It required just as much focus and precise footing as the ascent, but it didn't make me gasp for air. We were facing east as we descended. Though we hadn't made it to 14,400 feet, our reward was seeing a beautiful blue, gold, and orange ribbon of light breaking on the horizon. Soon there was enough light to see what we had climbed. We were in awe. The jagged rock, cliffs, crevasses, and the risks that were one wrong step or one slip of the foot away—we saw them all for the first time on our way down. Amazed at what we had done, we went down the mountain full of pride.

One other team member was also forced to descend before reaching the summit because of the altitude, but the rest of the team made summit that day. We all descended separately, then reconnected near the bottom of the Muir Snowfield. We reached Paradise around 5:00 p.m.

At the team dinner that followed, Shane kept the group entertained with his Irish cheer and fireman stories. After telling a good story, he asked the group, "Did you see some of the people we passed near the end of the descent?" Today was "Enjoy Your National Park Day," and the area around the visitor center was overflowing with people. Some of them were sharing the trail with those of us coming off the mountain. Shane continued, "So many people overweight and out of shape. And they do nothing about it. They were huffing and puffing just walking a half-mile from their cars."

The table fell silent when I replied. "Shane, that was me a few years ago—that was me!"

Because that was true, both literally and metaphorically, I could be nothing but proud. I had transformed myself physically and emotionally. I'd completely overhauled how I spent my time and the thoughts I kept in my head. I had a dream to change my life, and I made it happen.

When I first visited Rainier, I felt a pang—that silent inner sense that I longed to change my life, yet I clung to the familiarity of work, wealth, position, and power. Only when I lived in the shadow of death did I find the courage to heed the call of Mount Rainier—the courage to redefine my dream. I could reach new heights by facing and healing my past, being grateful for all that I had, embracing the concept of enough, carefully choosing the thoughts I kept in my head and deciding to be my very best moment by moment. Now, I dream a different dream. I dream to live in my authenticity. I dream to live in ways that emotionally and spiritually fulfill me. I dream to be physically and financially fit so I can experience the world and write about it with the hopes of inspiring others to break free, transform, and dare to dream anew. Most importantly, I dream to be kind and giving with love no matter what I do.

I overcame challenges of all kinds—most importantly, I overcame the ideas I had about myself. I got out of my own way to be the person I was born to be and the person I longed to be again. In search of that better person, I was surprised to find myself climbing a mountain.

But then, I'd been climbing mountains all along.

# Acknowledgments

Writing this book was a healing process. It helped to reveal and helped heal many wounds from my life. When I began writing, I was learning by writing about my past. As I neared the end of the book, I was learning to live what I wanted to write.

I am grateful for friends who stuck by me in my ugliest moments—sitting in kitchens, on the phone, in a group, around a conference room table, at the soccer field, or in the backyard— thank you for listening and caring. Your camaraderie carried me through my darkest times and kept the ground fertile for change.

Thank you to Tim Rouse and Carol Hunter for opening my mind and heart, helping me identify the seeds of change that I desired, and for encouraging me as I planted them.

When I found the courage and the conviction to change, help seemed to appear. The help may have been in a simple encounter, like someone saying the exact thing I needed to hear to help me take the next step. Or, the help may have been re-occurring, like friends and co-workers who routinely encouraged me to write. The help also came in the form of inspirational role models that shared their transformational stories and encouraged me. When I got stuck in the writing process, Tom Bird and his staff helped me along. To all of you, I am grateful. Never underestimate what a simple act of kindness can do!

The help of three people stood out. Each one of them had faced significant life challenges. They not only had the strength and grace to conquer their challenges but also to help me with mine. Each of them mirrored a part of me I loved, but a part I found difficult to share with the world. Thank you to Roz, my trainer. He matched my rational side. While working out, Roz willingly explored my raft of complex emotions and always encouraged me to leverage my intellect to think about life's challenges in a healthy way. Thank you to Chrystal, my stylist and skin-care specialist. Chrystal reflected my rebellious side—the part of me that resists professional and social influences that beseech us to conform for the sake of success. She helped me to express my unique self more fully while I was successful. Thank you to Jake, my manicurist. He shared my spiritual strengths. Every other week, Jake did my nails while we talked about spirituality. These three people were the pseudo-psychologists and friends who nurtured the transformational seeds I was planting—they helped those seeds take root and grow.

I reached the point I was ready to publish, and I remember saying "I wish someone would just drop out of the sky and help me." Along came Polly, and my wish was granted. Thank you to

Polly Letofsky, James Hallman, Sandy Chapman, Victoria Wolf, Vicki Tosher, and Andrea Costantine for their help and expertise to transition my manuscript into a book I am proud of. Through everything, there has been my incredible family. Thank you to my Mom, who showed me how to love unconditionally and to my children, Cody, Michaela, and Morgan, for continuously giving me a reason to transform.

Most importantly, thank you to my husband, Denny, for not settling for ordinary and not limiting my growth for the comfort and security of a more traditional union. Thank you for having the courage and strength to be my ally as I continue to live my audacious dreams.